About the Author

Walter L. Arnstein is Professor of History at the University of Illinois in Champaign. He is the author of *The Bradlaugh Case: A Study in Late Victorian Opinion and Politics* (Oxford University Press, 1965) and *Britain Yesterday and Today: 1830 to the Present* (D. C. Heath, 1966; 2d ed., 1971; 3d ed., 1976).

D0855907

Protestant versus Catholic
In Mid-Victorian England

Portrait of Charles Newdegate at forty, painted by T. Say to hang at Arbury Hall (Horace Dudley Studios, Nuneaton, Warwickshire; printed by permission of F. H. M. FitzRoy Newdegate).

Protestant versus Catholic
in Mid-Victorian England

Mr. Newdegate and the Nuns

Walter L. Arnstein

University of Missouri Press
Columbia & London
1982

Library of Congress Cataloging in Publication Data

Arnstein, Walter L.
  Protestant versus Catholic in Mid-Victorian
England.
  Bibliography: p. 253
  Includes index.
  1. Anti-Catholicism—England—History—19th
century. 2. Newdegate, Charles Newdigate, 1816–
1887. 3. England—Church history—19th century.
4. Great Britain—Politics and government—1837–
1901. I. Title. II. Title: Protestant versus
Catholic in Mid-Victorian England.
BX1493.A86   274.2′081   81–11451
ISBN 0–8262–0354–X   AACR2

Chapter 7 originally appeared in somewhat different form as "The Murphy Riots: A Victorian Dilemma" in *Victorian Studies* (September 1975). Reprinted with the permission of *Victorian Studies* and the Board of Trustees, Indiana University.

Chapter 8 originally appeared in somewhat different form as "The Great Victorian Convent Case" in *History Today* (February 1980). Reprinted with the permission of the editor.

To Sylvia

Acknowledgments

Research on this book was done over a period of more than ten years in libraries on both sides of the Atlantic: the British Library, the British Newspaper Library at Colindale, the Warwickshire and Northamptonshire Record Offices, the Institute of Historical Research and the University Library of the University of London, Chicago's Newberry Library, the University of Illinois Library, and others. Staff members at all these institutions provided assistance. Cmdr. F. H. M. FitzRoy Newdegate of Arbury Hall, Nuneaton, kindly gave me permission to use and to cite the papers of his collateral ancestor on deposit at Warwick. I am grateful to Lord Blake for the right to peruse relevant papers of the fourteenth earl of Derby in his custody and to the trustees of Hughenden Manor for access to the papers of Benjamin Disraeli while they were on deposit there.

My friend Josef L. Altholz of the University of Minnesota saved me from numerous errors of detail while reserving the right to differ with several of my conclusions, and my friend J. C. K. Cornwall of the Colchester Institute of Higher Education provided invaluable assistance with Chapters 2 and 3. My friends and colleagues at the University of Illinois Bennett D. Hill and Paul W. Schroeder were good enough to read the entire manuscript and to make a number of helpful suggestions. The work of two graduate research assistants sponsored by the University of Illinois Research Board also deserves praise—Dr. Prudence Moylan for her bibliographical research and Robert Mark Scott for double checking several hundred citations from the *Parliamentary Debates* and other publications. Mrs. Irene Blenker of the University of Illinois Department of History was good enough to type the greater portion of the manuscript. I am grateful to the reviewers of the University of Missouri Press for their several suggestions and to the Press staff for the sense of dedication that they brought to their labors. Chapter 7 first appeared, in somewhat different form, as an article in the September 1975 issue of *Victorian Studies;* a portion of Chapter 8 appeared in the February 1980 issue of *History Today.* The Southern Conference on British Studies provided an attentive and responsive audience for an early formulation of Chapter 4. A fellowship from the American Council of Learned Societies made possible much of the initial gathering of source materials. A semester as associate in the Center for Advanced Study of the

University of Illinois provided time for the initial drafting of the greater portion of the manuscript, a manuscript first read with critical acumen and then promoted with loyal devotion by my wife. The ultimate handiwork, admittedly unorthodox in its organization and in some of its interpretations, remains my own.

W. L. A.
September 1981
Champaign, Illinois

Contents

Illustrations

Protestant versus Catholic
In Mid-Victorian England

When an enlarged and complete dictionary for our times shall appear containing the word "bicycle," and all others of recent coinage you will find in its columns that a "Newdegate" is a noun substantive, meaning a Nun hater; and "Newdegatory" is an adjective, meaning preternaturally unfair and barbarous to Nuns.

Father Peter Gallwey, S.J. (1870)

I must remind you that Petition after Petition has come to the House praying for protection to the inmates of these convents. I am prepared to show that girls when they enter them do not know to what discipline they will be subjected, and that they have not the means of communicating with their friends. I am also prepared to show that English women are inveigled out of this country and placed in convents, which deserve to be termed dungeons, abroad.

Charles N. Newdegate, M.P. (1870)

1. Introduction

Despite the fact that many themes of Victorian history have been rehearsed thrice over, a sustained analytical and narrative history of the nineteenth-century "No Popery" movement has yet to be written. G. F. A. Best provided a perceptive article on the subject a decade ago,[1] and soon thereafter E.R. Norman brought out *Anti-Catholicism in Victorian England*.[2] Its comprehensive title notwithstanding, Norman's work consists primarily of a 108-page introduction to a series of reprinted documents and does not pretend to be either a comprehensive narrative or a complete analysis. Why is it that relatively little scholarly attention has been paid to what Best has called a "wide and weighty phenomenon," an attitude and a movement that was at times remarkably successful in uniting peer and peasant, Anglican and Dissenter, right-wing Tory and left-wing Liberal beneath the banner of a common cause? In an introduction to a book treating a significant facet of the encounter between Protestant and Catholic in mid-Victorian England, some tentative explanations may be appropriate for this relative neglect, for this retrospective sweeping under the carpet of Victorian propriety one of the era's major sources of domestic disunity and disorder.

One explanation may well lie in the widespread assumption that no explanation is necessary. What names and incidents, after all, does the theme "No Popery" conjure up to the student who looks back upon the centuries of British history? "Bloody Mary," Guy Fawkes, Titus Oates, the Glorious Revolution, and—as a curious eighteenth-century afterthought—the Gordon riots. The nineteenth century, in contrast, conjures up the Catholic Emancipation Act of 1829; a vision of religious toleration ever broadening precedent by precedent; of Roman Catholics as home secretary and as viceroy of India; of a Roman Catholic convert, John Henry Newman, as the "chief religious figure"[3] of the age. "In Europe," writes the chronicler of *The Expansion of Christianity*, "the nineteenth century after 1815 was one of . . . relative calm in the competition between rival religions and between the chief schools of Christianity."[4] If we use the wars of religion of the sixteenth and seventeenth centuries as our criterion, the observation is doubtless apropos, and any signs of Protestant–Catholic conflict in Victorian Britain can therefore be dismissed as the fugitive remnants of a less civilized age.

1

A collateral explanation may well lie in a lack of historical motive. The Labour party historian who seeks out and celebrates working-class consciousness among his Chartist forebears may pay greater heed to the strikes that these forebears organized in defiance of capitalist exploitation than to the stones that some of them, with equal satisfaction, hurled at the windows of Roman Catholic chapels. Twentieth-century Roman Catholic historians, in turn, although willing enough to commemorate the martyrdom of Edmund Campion and the bravery of various Elizabethan and Jacobean recusants, prefer to emphasize the role of their communion in the United Kingdom during the past century and a half as that of a legally equal (and perhaps morally superior) subdivision rather than as that of an alienated minority.

A final explanation may well lie in the contradictory manner in which we have learned to view the Victorian period. On the one hand, we look back upon it as an age of political and legal reform, as a period of increasing toleration, an age in which the Anglican monopoly was broken in Parliament and in local government, in the civil service, in elementary education, and eventually even at Oxford and Cambridge. Any incident after 1832 demonstrating religious intolerance can therefore appropriately be dismissed as a temporary aberration, as "one of those outbursts of anti-Catholic sentiment which periodically disgraced the good sense of the English people."[5] On the other hand, it has become equally fashionable, and appropriately so, to look upon the nineteenth century as an age of religious revival. George Kitson Clark has suggested that in no other century, "except the seventeenth and perhaps the twelfth, did the claims of religion occupy so large a part of the nation's life, or did men speaking in the name of religion contrive to exercise so much power."[6]

If we view the age in such a light, if we acknowledge it to have been a time when the religious conversion of a single individual might literally become a question of state, if we contrast the heroic missionary and church-building efforts of the early nineteenth century with the widespread and complacent latitudinarianism of the eighteenth century, then must we not acknowledge the logical consequences as well? That a sizable portion of the outpouring of religious energy generated in the nineteenth century might exhaust itself in interdenominational strife. That, if a strong affinity exists between religious tolerance and religious indifference and if ecumenical movements are most likely to prosper in a secular atmosphere, then may it not be equally plausible to remind ourselves that ages of faith are likely to be ages of religious discord?

It is the purpose of this study to test three hypotheses: first, that it is more fruitful to look upon the Victorian conflict between Protestantism and Catholicism as a separate chapter rather than as a mere footnote to studies of the Reformation; second, that to describe that conflict solely in negative terms—as No Popery or anti-Catholicism—is deceptive in that it ignores the manner in which Roman Catholics in Victorian Britain could be both ardent missionaries and militant claimants of legal privilege rather than the merely passive victims of discrimination or the silent recipients of whatever crumbs of toleration happened to have been tossed their way; and, third, that the liberalization of the law often unwittingly helped to inspire religious discord. Just as a decade of favorable judicial rulings and successful civil-rights acts in the United States of the 1960s did as much to breed racial militancy as to allay racial discontent, so measures of religious liberalization in the Britain of the 1820s, 1830s, and 1840s—and even in the 1860s and 1870s—did as much to rouse ultra-Protestant fears as to allay Roman Catholic dissatisfaction. Liberalization may even have helped to inspire the "aggressive" tactics associated with Archbishop (and later Cardinal) Henry Edward Manning, which contemporaries contrasted wistfully with the attitude of quietist seclusion exhibited by almost all English and Scottish Roman Catholics during the eighteenth and early nineteenth centuries.

The early nineteenth-century movement for Catholic emancipation paradoxically coincided with the high tide of a Protestant evangelical revival that was fundamentally antagonistic to the tenets of Rome. By the 1820s, John Wesley's Methodist movement had become a rapidly growing (and already splintered) separate denomination. Methodism, in turn, had helped to instill a new sense of purpose and religious inspiration within the quiescent Nonconformist denominations of seventeenth-century origin—Presbyterians, Independents, and Baptists—and within the established and numerically predominant Church of England itself. The evangelical revival had resharpened the sense of difference between Protestant and Roman Catholic beliefs. The faithful evangelical looked upon such Roman Catholic institutions as the priesthood (a celibate caste wielding miraculous powers), the mass (a reenactment of Christ's original sacrifice), and the papacy (an institution with supreme spiritual jurisdiction over all Christians) as theologically erroneous and morally repugnant. Statesmen like Spencer

Perceval, "the evangelical Prime Minister," and philosophers like Joseph Priestley were wont to interpret the prophecies of the Old Testament so as to equate the pope with the Antichrist and to identify Rome with "the scarlet woman" of the Book of Revelation.[7] In the eighteenth century, it had seemed a waste of time for students of theology to court controversy with Rome and for clergymen to preach on the dangers of Catholicism. In the early nineteenth century, this reluctance visibly diminished.[8]

Closely tied to the revived sense of repugnance toward Rome's theological tenets was a revival of the historical fears of a divided loyalty among English Roman Catholics and a renewed concern with the immoral practices that, in Protestant eyes, seemed all too likely to result from clerical celibacy, the seclusion of young women in convents, and the secrecy of the confessional. The priest was viewed as a rival father likely to disrupt the domestic unity of the patriarchal Victorian family.[9]

Like the evangelical revival, the roots of the legal emancipation of Roman Catholics may be found in the eighteenth century. An act of 1778 (18 Geo. 3, c. 60)—designed to encourage the enlistment of Roman Catholic recruits in the British army—substituted a simple oath of loyalty to the king for the denunciation of the papacy required heretofore. An act of 1791 (31 Geo. 3, c.32) remitted many of the earlier penal laws and, under strict conditions, permitted private freedom of worship.[10] Not until 1829, however, did the Catholic Emancipation Act open both Parliament and most state offices to professing Roman Catholics.

The measure was designed to avert civil war in Ireland, and it accomplished that objective. At the same time it also provided a focus for revived Protestant fears and suspicions. For a large section of the Tory party, indeed, the act implied a betrayal not merely of political principle but also of the very foundations of England's political structure. No countermeasures against a ministry that had betrayed its pledges were too extreme for ultra-Tories like the marquess of Blandford, not even "political reform"; thus anti-Catholics may well have been as influential as unenfranchised industrialists among the extraparliamentary inspirers of what became the Reform Act of 1832.[11] At Oxford, young William Ewart Gladstone found the lower classes—the college bedmakers and "the old egg-woman"—fearful of all concessions to Catholicism. "You would be beyond measure astonished," he wrote to his father, "how unanimous and how *strong* is the feeling among the freeholders . . . *against* the catholic question.''[12]

Tories like Blandford looked back upon the religious settlement of 1689 as a contract against popery, and they viewed the politically privileged established church as a permanent acknowledgment of the truth ''that the state had religious as well as secular dimensions.''[13] In the eyes of the ultra-Tories, the theory had received abundant pragmatic support in the obvious military and economic successes that Britain had attained since the establishment of the Protestant ascendancy in 1689. The act of 1829 was interpreted as an example of Catholic ''aggrandisement,''[14] and it spurred the formation of numerous pressure groups like the prestigious Protestant Association, founded in 1835, which sought to stem the Catholic torrent that was expected to innundate the land now that the constitutional floodgates had been cast open. Protestant missionaries, many of them from Ulster, began to blend edification with entertainment as they toured England and Scotland to warn their audiences of the perils in store for the now theologically defenseless kingdom. In the 1830s, as Daniel O'Connell and his Irish parliamentary adherents established a political entente with the Whig ministry of Lord Melbourne and as the tiny English Roman Catholic electorate adhered likewise to the Whigs, anti-Catholicism increasingly became at the constituency level a significant *raison d'être* for the Conservative party, whose fortunes Sir Robert Peel was industriously striving to revive. ''Conservative Associations, meeting on Monday evenings, so often reappeared as Protestant Societies on the following Thursdays.''[15]

As the duke of Wellington was to recall two decades later, the purpose of the Catholic Emancipation Act had been ''to repeal all the laws adopted against the Roman Catholics, . . . to get rid of these altogether,''[16] and more recently Best has described the measure as ''innocent of all but a few insignificant face-saving securities.''[17] A perusal of the act makes clear, however, that several complex oaths and restrictions were retained and in a few cases strengthened: priests might not wear their cassocks outside Roman Catholic chapels; all monastic orders were banned; and Jesuits found in the country were to be banished from the United Kingdom for life.[18] Neither Roman Catholic church property nor church schools were granted state recognition, nor were priests as yet given the right to cater to the needs of Roman Catholics in workhouses, in prisons, or in the armed forces. The very measure that was deplored by ultra-Protestants as a veritable Magna Carta for papists to undermine the state was seen by its beneficiaries as only one step of the many yet required before true legal equality would be achieved.

The fear of Roman Catholicism among Britain's upper classes might well have subsided during the 1830s and 1840s had it not been for the Oxford movement. The original purpose of the tractarians was to give renewed emphasis to the theological and political independence and the apostolic orthodoxy of the Church of England, but as they turned their backs deliberately upon what most Anglicans and Nonconformists had assumed to be the Protestant nature of the Anglican church, they inspired a sense of foreboding. Those Anglican clergymen who were honoring saints, proclaiming the infallibility of the church, making use of the sign of the cross, and recommending auricular confession, penance, and absolution seemed to be leading their flocks, in the words of Prime Minister Lord John Russell, "step by step to the very verge of the precipice."[19] By implication, the abyss of Rome lay immediately below.

Rome seemed to lie immediately across the Irish Sea as well, and the efforts of a Conservative ministry during the 1840s to appease Irish Catholic discontent helped to stoke the fires of English and Scottish Protestant feeling. Despite the efforts, by now several centuries old, of representatives of the Irish wing of the Church of England to convert all Irishmen to the officially established faith, contemporary observers grudgingly conceded that these efforts had largely failed and that three-quarters of all Irishmen remained in some sense Roman Catholics. Peel, the prime minister, took cognizance of this state of affairs in 1845 by proposing to triple (from nine thousand to twenty-six thousand pounds a year) and to make permanent the annual government subsidy to Maynooth, the leading Roman Catholic seminary in Ireland. The grant had been initiated by the autonomous Dublin Parliament during the 1790s as a wartime measure, but it had been continued by the Westminster Parliament after the Act of Union with Ireland in 1801. Peel's purposes were pragmatic, and his hope was henceforth to prevent the religious debate incited by each year's discussion of the Maynooth grant.

The legislation of 1845 raised a public storm, however, on the matter of principle involved: the permanent endowment (with however modest a sum) and, by implication, the official establishment of an institution that, in the minds of millions of English Protestants, epitomized superstition, idolatry, and subversion. Opposition to the measure united Anglicans who objected to state recognition of Roman Catholicism (but who wanted the Church of England to remain the established church) and Nonconformist Protestant "voluntaryists" who had come to oppose all official state support for religion. The public outcry against the Maynooth grant was sufficient to cause a majority of Peel's Conservative followers in the House of Commons to vote against their leader, thereby providing a dress rehearsal for the party split over the repeal of the Corn Laws that was to break up Peel's government and party a year later.[20]

The Maynooth grant was saved in 1845 by Russell's Whigs, who favored it by a ratio of 164 to 30, and, in the words of Benjamin Disraeli, "the middle classes of England, roused from their religious lethargy, called in vain to the rescue of a protestantism betrayed."[21] Religious discord remained very much in the air during the general election of 1847. According to *The Times* of 3 August 1847,

> The whole country has put on the appearance of a vast pro-Protestant anti-Papal league. The solicitors who manage the purchase of the borough seats are forced to cram their candidates with a sort of theological catechism, now published for the occasion . . . where they learn their attachment to religious truth as held pure and undefiled from any Romish adulteration.
>
> The newspapers teem with addresses to electors all breathing the same firm attachment to Protestant principles, all professing the most intense love for the reformed faith.

The climax of Catholic–Protestant tension in Victorian Britain was reached, it is generally agreed, during the autumn and winter of 1850–1851 when a papal bull restored the Catholic hierarchy to England. The resulting controversy over "papal aggression" (discussed in greater detail in Chapter 4) led to much popular agitation and to a parliamentary statute, the Ecclesiastical Titles Act of 1851.[22] In the aftermath of the dispute, new societies and journals, such as the Scottish Reformation Society and *The Bulwark*, were founded; dozens of pamphlets were printed; and numerous inquiries into Roman Catholic practices and institutions were projected. By 1854, however, the military threat of the Russian bear had taken precedence in the popular imagination over the spiritual threat of the papal bull, and the Crimean War contributed to a relaxation of Roman Catholic–Protestant tension.

To call the Ecclesiastical Titles Act "the last hysterical cry of 'No Popery' in England," as one modern historian has done,[23] would be a mistake, however. Religious tensions did not disappear, and a case can be made for the conclusion that in 1870 they reached a second (and only marginally secondary) climax in the movement instigated by Charles Newdigate Newdegate to investigate and inspect Roman Catholic convents and monasteries.

It is the purpose of the chapters that follow to test the hypotheses set forth earlier in the context of a largely chronological narrative of events during the 1860s and early 1870s. In order to add life and continuity to a theme that might otherwise add up to no more than a miscellany of episodes and reflections, the story will in large part be woven about Newdegate's career as a member of Parliament for North Warwickshire. Although not central to every episode to be recounted, Newdegate was both a major actor in the drama and an appropriate symbol of significant Victorian attitudes. He was one of those Victorians who, if recalled at all, is most likely to be remembered not as a hero but as a bigot or as, at best, a Don Quixote fighting windmills of his own invention. No attempt will be made in this study to cast him in the heroic mold, but in Chapters 2 and 3, enough will be said about his personal and political life before he became the prime parliamentary champion of popular Protestantism in the 1860s to make clear that he was a comprehensible human being as well as a symbol or prototype.

Chapter 4 presents the midcentury Roman Catholic church as it appeared to those who stood in awe or fear of its pretensions. Twentieth-century historians have been more conscious of its limitations in wealth and influence than of its power, but Victorian Protestants were far more likely to view it as an imposing and mysterious Wizard of Oz than as a puny Frank Morgan pulling levers behind a curtain. Chapter 5 takes up the convent issue as it emerged in the 1860s, and Chapter 6 explores other contemporary causes of religious friction. Chapter 7 reminds us that parliamentary debate provided a generally civilized veneer over the more elemental religious passions that excited English men and women in the provincial towns, and Chapter 8 provides evidence that the courtroom could easily rival Parliament as a stage for religious drama. In Chapters 9 and 10, the story reaches its climax in a transient triumph for Newdegate and in a poignant dilemma for Gladstone, the preeminent representative of Victorian liberalism. Chapters 12 and 13 are designed to remind us that the Roman Catholicism of the 1870s preoccupied not only back-benchers like Newdegate and princes like Otto von Bismarck but also prime ministers as diverse as Russell, Disraeli, and Gladstone. Chapter 14 concludes the biography of Newdegate, and Chapter 15 briefly traces the late nineteenth-

and early twentieth-century aftermath of mid-Victorian Protestant–Catholic rivalry. It also provides a number of retrospective reflections upon the subject.

The intended focus of this book is England and not the United Kingdom, though the shadow of Ireland can no more be expunged from a consideration of this aspect of Victorian history than from most others. The intended form is deliberately hybrid—part monograph, part biography. In the words of a distinguished practitioner of both arts, Robert Rhodes James: "The historian's complaint against the biographer is that, by isolating a single individual, he puts too strong a light on one tiny detail in a vast canvas and leaves the rest plunged in darkness. This is a valid criticism. It can be said in defense of the biographer that, by this isolation, he often provides the kind of illumination which is the historian's principal task."[24]

Whatever warrant may exist for a full-scale biography of Newdegate, the case for an analytical study focused on his role as parliamentary Protestant champion is yet stronger. Newdegate, it will become clear, was neither an intellectual prepared to wield the pen on behalf of subtle theological distinctions (as Gladstone could be on occasion) nor a grand master seeking to outflank the Vatican or its temporal champions on the diplomatic chessboard of Europe (as did Bismarck) nor, finally, was he a monomaniac (like William Murphy, the psychologically obsessed anti-Catholic crusader whose career is taken up in Chapter 7). Instead, Newdegate was a representative Englishman who sought to defend, in a manner sometimes foolish but not necessarily ignoble, a cherished heritage that appeared threatened by alien forces. A consideration of his limitations may advance our ability to understand this portion of the past more fully than might concentration upon a more monumental, but ultimately atypical, figure. For the past, in all its complexity, becomes real only if we view it neither as an interplay of impersonal forces nor as a morality play starring cardboard heroes and villains. A study of a significant aspect of what is usually called "Victorian anti-Catholicism" should reveal—and indeed does reveal—an abundance of conflicting attitudes and assumptions illuminated not only by Newdegate himself but also by his interactions with numerous other multidimensional personalities.

2. The Making of a Tory Stalwart

"In the Victorian mixture," George Kitson Clark has written, "in which progress and liberalism are such important elements, conservatism and the survival of habits, types of human beings and institutions from earlier, and one might have thought irrelevant, centuries remain important also."[1] An example of one such type was Charles Newdigate Newdegate of Arbury Hall, Warwickshire. Newdegates had been living at Arbury Hall since Tudor times, when the 350-year-old Augustinian monastery there was dissolved under the auspices of King Henry VIII. In Surrey, Newdegates have been traced as far back as King John's reign (1199–1216), and they had established themselves at the manor of Harefield, Middlesex—which was also to descend to Charles Newdigate Newdegate—in the mid-fourteenth century. One of his ancestors, Sir John Newdegate (1571–1610), had been knighted by King James I. His son Richard Newdigate (1602–1678) preferred to spell the family name with an *i* rather than an *e*, a practice followed by his immediate descendants. Richard Newdigate rose to the position of justice of the Upper Bench during Oliver Cromwell's protectorship and served briefly as Chief Justice (1659–1660). He resigned that position prior to the restoration of the Stuarts, however, and his subsequent demeanor toward King Charles II proved to be sufficiently diplomatic to warrant his being created a baronet a year before his death. The second baronet was also named Richard (1644–1710), and he introduced into Warwickshire the gunmaking industry that flourished there until after the Crimean War.[2]

The most famous of the Newdigates was the fifth baronet, Sir Roger Newdigate, who inherited the estate in 1734 when he was fourteen and who presided at Arbury Hall until his death seventy-two years later. During that time, he represented the county of Middlesex in the House of Commons for six years (1741–1747) and his alma mater, Oxford University, for almost thirty (1751–1780). At Oxford, he also established the Newdigate Prize for poetry, an annual award of twenty-one guineas for the best undergraduate effort. The family coal mines spurred his interest in the expansion of the canal and turnpike systems in Warwickshire, and he transformed Arbury Hall from an Elizabethan manor house into the finest surviving example of the early Gothic revival style of English architecture. George Eliot, who, as Mary Ann Evans, was born on the Arbury estate a few years after Sir Roger's death, transmuted the Newdigates into the Cheverels and Arbury Hall into Cheverel Manor in her *Scenes of Clerical Life* (1857). She credited Sir Roger with having turned "ugliness into beauty."[3]

Sir Roger had been the only surviving son among seven children and, although twice married, had no surviving children of his own. According to his will, his lands therefore descended to the sons of his first cousin Millicent Newdigate who had married William Parker of Warwickshire. Millicent Newdigate Parker had two sons: the elder Charles (who died in 1795), and the younger Francis. When Sir Roger died in 1806 and the baronetcy became extinct, his lands were divided between Charles's son (also named Charles), who received the estate at Harefield, Middlesex, and his uncle Francis, who received Arbury Hall for his lifetime. Both the younger Charles and Francis thereupon adopted the name and arms of Newdigate—though the former, in accordance with Sir Roger's will, restored the spelling of the name "as anciently written"—"Newdegate." Upon Charles Parker Newdegate's death in 1833, Harefield devolved upon his son Charles Newdigate Newdegate, whose parents had endowed him with both spellings of the name as if to make doubly sure of his inheritance. Two years later, upon the death of his grand-uncle Francis in 1835, young Charles, in accordance with Sir Roger's will, inherited Arbury Hall as well; the two family properties were thus reunited under a single ownership. Young Charles and his mother were never to forget their debt to the late Sir Roger; in 1849, when Maria Newdegate was presented with a lock of Sir Roger's hair, she promised to treasure it as yet one more memorial to "his worth and goodness."[4] Thirty years later, Charles was still identifying himself in *Dod's Parliamentary Companion* as "heir of the late Sir Roger Newdegate, bart."

We know almost nothing of Charles Newdigate Newdegate's childhood. He was born at Harefield on 14 July 1816, the only child of a doting mother, born Maria Boucherett in Lincolnshire and presumably of French Huguenot descent. Some time early in his childhood, young Charles had a Roman Catholic tutor—so all later accounts agree[5]—but it appears no longer possible to pinpoint the person, the time, or the circumstances. From 1829 until 1834 Charles attended Eton College; after a brief period at King's College of the University of London, he matriculated at Christ Church, Oxford. Although he preserved his father's parchment for moistening snuff, he seems scarcely to have recalled his father in later years. It was his mother who was the prime object of his devotion, and she, in turn, treasured his letters after he went off to school. "My darling's first letter— God bless him," she wrote on one of them. While at Oxford, young Charles remonstrated mildly with his mother for opening his mail in his absence: "I had rather you did not open my letters another time for though I have nothing to hide from you, yet my friends may have things to say to me which must not be repeated, and I only ask you to ask your own Mummy whether she would have thought it a safe thing either in herself or in any other mother to open her son's letters, however little he might wish to conceal anything from her." When his mother indicated her displeasure, nineteen-year-old Charles was immediately repentant: "My own Mummy, I am very very sorry my last letter has vexed you so much, but I must have expressed my-self very much like a fool as I am to have made you think all you have done about it, but I was worn and vexed by reading and I daresay I said enough to provoke a saint." There were days when his mother failed to write. "I should like to have heard from you today," he noted on one such occasion, "but I know I am an unreasonable rogue about such things." This letter and another were labeled "2 most precious letters from my beloved Boy" by his mother.[6]

That Newdegate had been spoiled by his doting mother seemed clear to Benjamin Disraeli. "She wanted to make a Pitt of him, not that she or anything could have done, but she, at any rate, took the wrong way to do it."[7] At Oxford Newdegate seems to have been "worn and vexed" with reading more than once. He had no opportunity there to indulge in the fox hunting he had grown to love, and he was often sick. Since he did not receive his B.A. degree from Oxford until 1849, by which time he had already been a member of Parliament for six years, it seems clear that he interrupted his studies to return to his mother and his newly inherited estates—to hunt, to entertain, and to play the numerous other roles expected of an early nineteenth-century country squire.

In Newdegate's day, Warwickshire was growing rapidly in population (from 274,000 in 1821 to 475,000 in 1851 to 737,000 in 1881) largely because of the continuing expansion of its major city, Birmingham, and the slower but still steady growth of its second largest city, Coventry. Almost a third of the county's acreage was devoted to the growing of grain and clover and almost two-thirds to permanent pasture land that supported more than one hundred thousand head of cattle and almost three times as many sheep. According to Victorian statisticians,

Arbury Hall from the south (courtesy of F. H. M. FitzRoy Newdegate).

some seventeen thousand acres of woodland could also be found in Warwickshire.[8]

Arbury Hall was located just southwest of the small town of Nuneaton, about seventeen miles east of Birmingham and six miles north of Coventry. If one required a minimum of 1,000 acres to qualify as a landed gentleman in Victorian England, then Newdegate qualified several times over. According to the famous census of landowners of 1873, his Arbury estates totaled 5,318 acres with an estimated annual rental value of £8,318. They also included a 230-acre deer park boasting a magnificent stand of ancient oaks. Arbury sufficed to make Newdegate the twelfth largest landowner in Warwickshire. His holdings in Harefield, Middlesex, added 1,491 acres valued at £2,524 per year.[9] Newdegate was to become renowned as "a kind and considerate landlord" as well as a fine horseman "and an intense lover of the chase,"[10] and a clothing list that survives from the 1870s suggests that Newdegate soon learned to dress the part. In 1875, he owned sixteen morning coats, twenty-seven pairs of trousers, seven dress coats, five pairs of dress trousers, seven shooting coats, eight shooting trousers, five scarlet hunting coats, twenty-eight pairs of cuffs, twenty-one hunting scarfs, sixty-five morning scarfs, and thirty-five pairs of boots.[11]

Like many country squires, the Newdegates of Arbury had long been involved in commercial activities. Coal mining had been carried on since the beginning of the eighteenth century, and a parliamentary report of 1843 suggests that a fourteen-hour night shift during which the coal was hauled from the shafts by boys, men, and horses and a ten-hour day shift during which it was stacked for sale constituted a tradition more than a century old.[12] In its heyday, the Newdegate colliery employed as many as two thousand men, and a few years before Newdegate sold it in 1882, he could boast that, although many nearby coal works had been afflicted with strikes, his own had remained exempt.[13]

The life of a country squire involved more than hunting, entertaining, and business management; it also involved religion, education, and local government. Between Arbury and Harefield, Newdegate was the patron of four clerical livings; that is, he had the right to nominate Church of England clergymen whenever the positions fell vacant. As his surviving letters to a neighbor demonstrate, of these, the nearby parish of Chilvers Coton troubled him most: "At this moment," wrote Newdegate in 1852, "I do not know any parish, which is so manifestly invaded by the Agents of the Church of Rome." Unfortunately, the "habits and health" of the incumbent clergyman, a Mr. Hake, precluded his making "the requisite exertions." Not only was Hake perpetually in debt, but he also held "ultra-Calvinist" theological notions and refused to prepare the parish children for confirmation by the bishop. After a seven-year campaign, Newdegate finally induced the morally and theologically delinquent clergyman to resign—and then only by personally paying off Hake's outstanding debts at a cost of seven hundred pounds—so that he might be replaced with "a good Christian, a sound Protestant, and a judicious person."[14]

Newdegate took his religious and educational responsibilities seriously. In 1851 he felt obliged to open "a new Infant school *gratis,* in order to prevent the abstraction from the Protestant Church Schools of the children of Protestant and Church of England Parents by the Roman Catholic Priests."[15] Some years later he reported to the bishop of London that he had spent six thousand pounds on the church, the churchyard, the parsonage, and the schools at Harefield and that he had recently added one thousand pounds to the endowment of each of the two clerical livings there. Harefield Parish and Parish Church, he recalled with pride, was a "Peculiar and Donative and exempt jurisdiction of very ancient date regranted to John Newdigate my ancestor by King Henry the 8th.''[16] In addition to helping to support the Church of England schools "for boys and girls of the working classes" at Harefield and Nuneaton, Newdegate in due course became a trustee of Rugby School; of Queens College, Birmingham; and of the Birmingham School of Medicine.

As early as 1838, Newdegate had been appointed a justice of the peace for the county of Middlesex. This position, which he continued to hold until shortly before his death, involved both administrative and judicial responsibilities. When a mob of six thousand men threatened "a breach of the peace," as it did during the depression year of 1842, the role of justice of the peace was endowed with danger as well as prestige. In due course, Newdegate also became an officer in the Middlesex County Militia,[17] and in Warwickshire he became both a justice of the peace and a deputy lieutenant. That office had become primarily ceremonial, but it did involve advising the lord lieutenant on the suitability of recruits to the county militia. That a young squire whose interests were being drawn in such a variety of directions should also seek a seat in Parliament was hardly surprising.

Newdegate's political convictions, like his lands, were inherited from Sir Roger Newdigate. At a time when Toryism was not in fashion, Sir Roger had been a steadfast Tory, a firm upholder of the Church of England, and a staunch opponent of any alteration in its structure, its liturgy, or its privileges. He was also profoundly suspicious of foreign princes and of alliances with foreign countries.[18] Newdegate, it is true, much preferred the label "Conservative" or even "Pittite" to "Tory." According to Thomas Babington Macaulay, the word *Tory* was of Irish origin and had been "given to Englishmen who refused to concur in excluding a Roman Catholic prince from the throne." Unlike his eighteenth-century relation, Newdegate harbored not even the vaguest of Jacobite sentiments; he was to list himself in *Dod's Parliamentary Companion* as "attached to the principles of the Constitution as established in 1688," and those principles were unmistakably Protestant.[19]

It was in 1841 that Newdegate was first considered as a possible candidate for Parliament both in Middlesex and in Warwickshire. In 1832 even Warwickshire had fallen to the "Reformers," but by 1837 a Conservative revival was in full swing. This revival would be confirmed nationally in the general election of 1841. Newdegate was fearful of the new radicalism exemplified by the Anti–Corn Law League, however, and he discouraged proposals that he become a candidate in Warwickshire. "The forthcoming Election struggle is of no ordinary character," he assured a correspondent; "it is not merely a question of Party preponderance but what is infinitely of greater consequence, one of *life or death to the Agricultural Interest.*" A split in the vote of the county agriculturists might permit an Anti–Corn Law League member to slip in. He had therefore decided "on this occasion" not to enter the field against William Stratford Dugdale and Sir Eardley Wilmot, the two Conservative members standing for reelection.[20]

Two years later, when rumors reached Warwickshire that Wilmot might resign his seat, Maria Newdegate threw her son's hat into the ring by privately alerting a number of friendly neighboring landowners. "My son has promised to come forward," she assured them, "should he receive a requisition sufficiently signed to that effect."[21] When Wilmot was appointed lieutenant governor of Van Diemen's Land (Tasmania), the seat fell vacant. After Sir Robert Peel, the prime minister and the member for the nearby borough of Tamworth, and William Dugdale, North Warwickshire's other M.P., both had given a nod toward young Newdegate and some seventeen hundred electors had signed a petition supporting his candidacy, the twenty-six-year-old squire proudly accepted. "My political principles," he declared, "are decidedly Conservative, but, I trust, neither extreme nor such as will lead me to close my eyes to any parts of those time-tested institutions of our country which the change of circumstances may have rendered inapplicable, or the lapse of years impaired." Those who did seek change, he suggested, would do well to be ever guided by the experience of the great men of the nation's past.[22]

The fact that a majority of the registered electors had signed the invitation to Newdegate discouraged local Whigs, the Anti–Corn Law League, and the Complete Suffrage Union from offering candidates of their own. Newdegate, who had observed political democracy in action (he had witnessed the election of William Henry Harrison as president during a visit to the United States in 1840), was as unsympathetic to the tenets of the last-named organization as to those of the free traders. As Newdegate was to observe a few years later, "I do not want to see the country merely cut into squares in order to form constituencies, or to Americanize our institutions."[23] The Warwickshire electorate included numerous farmers bound to local magnates by ties of loyalty, habit, or economic obligation,[24] and on election day, 10 March 1843, a cavalcade of such electors rode on horseback into the tiny market town of Coleshill, where the hustings

had been set up. Charles B. Addersley, M.P. for neighboring
Staffordshire, formally nominated Newdegate. The latter outlined his program: first, a temporary reduction in tariffs to meet
widespread economic distress but no reduction that would lead
simply to a lowering of wages and thus "seriously curtail the
home-market for our manufactured goods"; second, the continuation of the income tax, "odious impost" that it was, in
order to meet the budget deficit left by the Whigs; third, opposition to the principle of free trade since it was likely to deprive
England of commercial bargaining power abroad; fourth, pro-
motion of national education, provided it was kept in the hands
of the Church of England, "the church of the poor"; and, fifth,
opposition to the new Poor Law, which was too cumbersome in
its machinery and too harsh to the indigent.

These were his principles, Newdegate declared, but he had
no wish to "cramp his hopes of future utility by specific pledges
as to particular votes he might hereafter be called upon to
record." He would be proud to be chosen their representative,
he told the assembled electors, but he was determined "never to
seek, or accept a seat in Parliament as the mere nominee or the
fettered delegate of any man or any set of men." Their earnest,
lanky young candidate had made an excellent impression, and
when no other candidate came forward, the sheriff declared
Charles Newdigate Newdegate elected knight of the shire for
North Warwickshire. Amid great cheering, the new member
thanked his supporters, and the entire party adjourned for the
dinners that, under his sponsorship, were being provided at the
principal public houses of the community.[25]

Newdegate took the train to London, found lodgings just
off the Strand, and on 13 March 1843 swore the requisite oath of
allegiance to Queen Victoria and took his seat in the House of
Commons. He thereby entered upon a routine that for more
than four decades was to keep him in the imperial capital for the
greater part of the first six or seven months of each year. A
significant majority of his fellow parliamentarians were, like
him, large-scale landowners, and most of them also partook of
the London club life that soon became part of his weekly
schedule.[26] The Carlton Club (the social home of Conservative
politicians), the National (noted for its staunch Protestantism),
White's (whose members all boasted lengthy genealogical
pedigrees), the Traveller's, Arthur's, and Boodle's all were in
due course to claim Newdegate as a member.[27] But the youthful
M.P. did not neglect his constituents. He answered all their
letters in his own careful hand, methodically noting down the

date on which he did so, even if he did sometimes misspell their names. Nor did he hesitate long about making his own contributions to parliamentary debate. He was to do so twice in 1843, ten times in 1844, fifteen times in 1845, forty-six times in 1846, fifty-three times in 1847, and he was to remain a vocal parliamentarian for the remainder of his political career.

Although he had been elected to Parliament with Peel's special blessing, and although he acknowledged that he had been returned "with the view of generally supporting the present government," Newdegate was quite willing to oppose that government when principle intervened.[28] It did so in the case of Peel's Bank Charter Act with which the prime minister hoped to stabilize the British monetary system by concentrating the issuance of currency in the hands of that financial Rock of Gibraltar, the Bank of England. Newdegate opposed the measure because he feared that the currency was being tied too rigidly to the gold standard and that in time of financial distress the bank would be barred from granting necessary loans. Newdegate's views echoed those of his acquaintance, the banker Richard Spooner of Birmingham. In a wider sense, they reflected the views of the Birmingham school of currency reformers associated with Thomas Attwood, who anticipated in the 1820s, 1830s, and 1840s the doctrines that the Greenbackers and the free silverites were to express in the United States during the last third of the century.[29] Newdegate's views on the currency and his attitude toward the New Poor Law of 1834 were both characteristic of a type of Tory radicalism. His 1844 speech in favor of a liberalization of the Poor Law so as to aid handloom weavers impoverished by the spread of the steam-powered loom did not require him, however, again to oppose official government policy.[30]

When Newdegate did oppose the Peel ministry in 1845 on the question of the Maynooth grant he did so secure in the knowledge that not merely a majority of his fellow Conservative M.P.s but also a large body of Church of England and Protestant Nonconformist clergymen and laymen agreed with him. The government proposal to triple and make permanent an annual grant to Maynooth, the leading Irish seminary for Roman Catholic priests, might be advanced by Peel as a necessary step toward Anglo-Irish conciliation, but it angered fervent Protestants more than it pacified aggrieved Catholics.[31]

What business was it of the government to subsidize without supervision the promulgation of the doctrines "of the most rigid and the most political sect of Romanists"? Throughout

England Roman Catholics were finding it possible to build churches and schools, monasteries and convents, and even training institutions like Oscott College in Birmingham. Why should a Protestant government underwrite this type of expansion? Newdegate was fully conscious that Anglicans, who believed in an established church, and Nonconformists, who did not, were often at odds, but he welcomed the manner in which opposition to the Maynooth grant provided grounds for a bond of union. It was, moreover, a justifiable and sufficient bond of union. For what was it

> against which all sects of Protestants in common protested? What was it against which the constitution of this country protested? Nothing more nor less than the Roman Catholic doctrine. In common we deprecate that exclusive doctrine; in common we resist domestic and civil interference on the part of the clergy, as exercised by the Roman Catholic priesthood; in common we claim for all men free access to the Scriptures; in common we claim for all men perfect freedom of conscience.[32]

Newdegate's arguments did not prevail, and the House of Commons went on to pass the measure by a vote of 312 to 191. Peel's victory was dependent, however, on the votes of the Whig–Liberal opposition; his fellow Conservatives voted against him by a margin of 161 to 148.

The fissure that had been opened by the dispute over religious policy in 1845 was to widen into a chasm a year later by a conflict over economic principle. Two years earlier Newdegate had become one of the chief backers of the Central Agricultural Protection Society. This organization, headed by the duke of Richmond, was designed to counter the drive of the Anti–Corn Law League with comparable propaganda and electoral weapons. Protectionists were losing faith in the orthodoxy of their political leaders; Richard Cobden was the high priest of free trade, Newdegate declared early in 1845, but fellow worshipers who chanted the proper responses were to be found right on the treasury bench.[33] In November 1845 Peel confirmed such suspicions by using the Irish potato blight as the occasion to announce his formal conversion to the doctrine of free trade. Lord John Russell, the Whig leader, had also come out in favor of the abolition of the Corn Laws, and after a brief interval during which Russell sought but failed to form a government, Peel returned to office to give legislative force to his newly revealed convictions. Although Peel's repeal measures did not become law until July 1846, it was obvious from the beginning of the 1846 parliamentary session that he could carry with him his lieutenants but not the party rank and file. Newdegate was bitterly frustrated by the entire course of events, and he vainly urged the Central Agricultural Protection Society to keep up the battle.[34] Peel's actions appeared as a betrayal not merely of party principle and of landholder interest but also of the ultimate economic well-being of the nation. Newdegate was quite willing to acknowledge the dictum of buying in the cheapest market and selling in the dearest as "the true principle of trade," but a principle of trade was not necessarily a precept for government. A government had the task, after all, not merely to increase the nation's wealth but also "to secure the peace, happiness, and welfare of the people." A government had to anticipate the long-term danger implicit in making an island economically dependent upon foreigners. The functions of a government were not reducible to a handful of economic axioms.[35]

Newdegate saw the Protectionists within the Conservative party as being charged "with a great and patriotic cause,"[36] but in their leaderless condition, what could prevent them from becoming mere historical relics? Of the members of Peel's cabinet, only Lord Stanley had resigned, but he was a member of the House of Lords. All the commoners in Peel's ministry remained loyal to their leader, and what there was of leadership in the Protectionist ranks consisted largely of the hitherto silent Lord George Bentinck—at least he was the son of a duke and a great horseman—and his behind-the-scenes adviser, the exotic and vaguely disreputable novelist but brilliant speaker, Benjamin Disraeli. Newdegate could match neither Bentinck's aristocratic eminence nor Disraeli's eloquent invective, but his youthful ardor sufficed to make him, with Bentinck and Disraeli, one of the three Protectionists whom Peel could never forgive for their attacks on his policy and for their role in toppling his government.[37]

Peel's resignation in July 1846 resulted not from a vote on the Corn Laws but from a defeat on a measure dealing with Irish governmental administration that both Russell's Whigs and a contingent of Bentinck's Conservatives (including Newdegate) had decided to oppose. As a consequence, Russell became prime minister, and both the Whig and the Protectionist M.P.s—who disagreed on free trade—sat for the time being on the government side of the House of Commons chamber, while Peel and his cohorts—who agreed with Russell on free trade—dominated the official opposition benches. Newdegate was a logical choice to become one of two Protectionist party whips, and for the next four years he was to be more immediately involved in the day-to-day management of his party and in its relations with the press than at any time thereafter.[38] Though Newdegate served Bentinck as a "chosen confidant," it was Lord Stanley rather than Bentinck whom Newdegate looked up to as his true political leader. Stanley was, after all, not merely the heir to the ancient earldom of Derby but also the sole Protectionist leader to have held cabinet office. It was from Stanley, therefore, that Newdegate sought advice as to the party's plans for the forthcoming parliamentary session. "Are we to initiate any course of our own . . . or merely to watch the proceedings of the Government?"[39] Stanley found the second alternative the more appealing: vigilant scrutiny was preferable to vigorous assault. There was no point in reopening the question of agricultural protection at a time when high prices had blinded farmers and factory workers alike to the long-range evils likely to result from Corn Law repeal. The only exception that Stanley was willing to make to this prescription of negativism was in the area of religion: it might be desirable to propose legislation favorable to the Church of England. "It is a most powerful friend, whom we have not cultivated enough."[40]

When Newdegate first went off to Westminster in 1843, he promised his mother to report faithfully on his activities there, and her diary reflects the enormous pride that she took in the letters and the doings of "my own beloved boy Charley." From time to time, she would visit the House of Commons and watch a debate from the Ladies' Gallery. Her son's efforts generally met with her approval, but she described one speech as "rather heavy," and when she was displeased with another, he immediately apologized.[41] Necessary as she found the fledgling Protectionist party to the welfare of the nation, Maria Newdegate often found cause to reflect on the limitations of its leaders. Even Stanley, eminent as he was and as willing as he appeared to treat her son "as an old friend," seemed all too ready to compromise on religious matters. Bentinck was equally unreliable, lacked "ebullition," and remained addicted to the turf. "And Heaven defend us from such men as D'Israeli—Protectionist that he is—he calls Charley my *dear child* to keep him down." Daniel O'Connell might be an Irishman and a Roman Catholic, but "I believe O'Connell hit his true Pedigree 'descended from the wandering Jew.' "[42]

Though his mother's reflections generally echoed Newdegate's own, their expression was largely confined to the privacy of their breakfast-table conversations and to the pages of her diary. Thus, when during the hunting season of 1846, Newde-

gate was the victim of a near fatal accident, wishes for a speedy
recovery poured in from his parliamentary associates. Bentinck
was "anxious and amiable" that Mrs. Newdegate would "always love him."[43] The most solicitous note of sympathy addressed to the intrepid hunter was sent by a fellow Protectionist who
assured him that "You are greatly endeared to all your friends
but to none more than to yours most sincerely, Disraeli."[44] On
this occasion, Newdegate was highly appreciative.

> Many thanks for your kind letter; I am wonderfully recovered
> from what was really a smashing blow, but which was more
> frightful in its first effects to the beholders, than it will, thank God,
> prove eventually injurious to me.
> My horse in getting up after a fall struck or trod upon the side of
> my head, whereby he cut my ear and broke my jaw in two places,
> besides rupturing several blood vessels in the upper part of my
> throat and mouth. I was of course insensible and bled from the
> mouth profusely, which made the friends who came to my assis-
> tance think me dying, but this very bleeding turned out for the
> best by releiving [sic] my head and my injured parts, and has
> accelerated my recovery; not that I am yet anything like my own
> master, for I have my lower jaw screwed into a machine . . . with
> a horseshoe under my chin, all very appropriate, but very
> uncomfortable.[45]

At the end of the 1847 parliamentary session, Russell recommended to the queen that a new general election be held.
This election, the first since 1841, would enable the voters to be
consulted directly on the question of free trade versus protection. In North Warwickshire, William Dugdale, Newdegate's
colleague and a supporter of Peel on the Corn Law issue, preferred retirement to the prospect of electoral defeat. In his stead,
local Protectionists nominated Richard Spooner, the Birmingham banker who had represented his native city in the House of
Commons since 1844 but who had been defeated for reelection
in 1847.

Newdegate, Sir E. Hartopp assured the assembled electors,
had proved "their able and unequalled friend." It was not often
that one could find a young man willing to "sacrifice the amuse-
ments and enjoyments of youth, and give up the sports of the
field and those numerous pleasures which his position in society opened to him" in order to exert himself so assiduously on
behalf of his constituents.

He had not broken his pledges as Peel had done, Newdegate told the electors, and he could never follow Peel again. He
admired Russell's adherence to political principle, but as "an

Old Conservative" rather than a Whig or a free trader, he could not coalesce with Russell's supporters. "I hold that the condition of the subject's allegiance is, that his life, property, and interests be cared for by the state; and I cannot concur in the total abnegation of that principle." In the face of the financial crisis earlier in the year, the government had been compelled to suspend certain provisions of Peel's Bank Charter Act; the action proved, Newdegate thought, that his opposition to that measure had signified more than "the vain crotchet of a poor young man." He would continue to support the interests of the Church of England and to advocate poor-law and sanitary reform—but not if the latter meant supplanting responsible local authorities with a national bureaucracy. Spooner promised to stand with Newdegate in the House of Commons "cheek by jowl." The nomination of Lord Leigh, an independent Liberal, necessitated a poll, and on 16 August, ten polling places were set up in North Warwickshire. Newdegate and Spooner emerged triumphant: Newdegate, 2,915; Spooner, 2,451; Leigh, 2,272. The results demonstrated, Newdegate felt sure, that the interests of the nation's social classes were not antagonistic. "A great bond of union" joined the aristocrats, squires, and manufacturers of North Warwickshire to the wealth and intelligence of Birmingham.[46] The results also demonstrated, Newdegate complained privately, how expensive even a partially contested election could be; his campaign had cost four thousand pounds, "double what I thought prudent."[47]

The national electoral verdict differed from that of North Warwickshire: Whig–Liberals, 325 members; Peelites, 108; and Protectionists, 222. Free traders of all types outnumbered Protectionists by a ratio of two to one, but the participants at a public dinner in Birmingham's town hall in honor of Newdegate and Spooner were undismayed. The body of the hall and the side galleries were filled with "gentlemen of local influence. The gallery and the lower end of the hall were filled with ladies." Peel was excoriated once more, and Newdegate pledged himself anew to uphold a system of national protection for agriculture, industry, and commerce; a flexible currency; and a firm attachment to the Constitution in church and state of what remained "essentially a Protestant—essentially a Christian nation."[48]

3. Newdegate in the Age of Equipoise

Historians of the Victorian era have increasingly tended to look back upon the 1850s and 1860s as a time of relative stability, a period of temporary balance between the storms of the 1840s—induced by economic depression and manifested in ideological militancy and political agitation—and the comparable sense of uncertainty and unrest brought on by the Reform Bill struggle of 1866–1868 and the institutional changes wrought by Gladstone's first ministry (1868–1874).[1] The political fever chart of the age that a specific member of Parliament like Charles Newdegate might have drawn, however, would probably not have coincided with the subsequent verdict of historians. Until 1851 Newdegate would have seen no cause for domestic complacency, and the Crimean War of 1854–1856 and the Indian Mutiny of 1857–1858 would soon belie all notions of universal placidity. Although he might feel an increasing sense of security of tenure as a senior member of Parliament for North Warwickshire, Newdegate remained temperamentally too earnest and too conscious of the mischief likely to be plotted by political radicals at home and by enemies of the realm abroad to find any justification for relaxation. Lord John Russell, the prime minister (1846–1852), had, Newdegate feared, "an unhappy fancy about progress, and had gazed upon it until it had turned him giddy."[2] Newdegate was not similarly afflicted.

The election of 1847 had resulted in a victory for Newdegate and in a moral triumph of sorts for his party: it had survived as a viable entity, though the issue that provided its *raison d'être*—protective tariffs—seemed to relegate it to lost-cause status for the indefinite future. Even its name was in doubt: "Tory" appeared out of date; "Conservative" was too closely associated with the archrenegade himself, Sir Robert Peel; "Protectionist" implied that the group had views on no other issues; "Country" suggested that the group had no meaning within the urban areas that, as the census of 1851 was to confirm, now provided a habitat for a clear majority of Englishmen; "Constitutional" was yet another possibility, but it too lacked universal appeal.[3] All these names were used for a time, sometimes interchangeably, but by the early 1850s, "Conservative" won out once more, somehow cleansed of its Peelite associations, while the remaining Peelite M.P.s took refuge for a time in the ambivalence of "Liberal–Conservative."

The chief problem faced by the Protectionist Conservatives

24

was not the strength of Russell's government. The latter rested ultimately upon the willingness of a ramshackle collection of Whig–Liberals, Radicals, and Peelites to allow it to remain in office; they were all sufficiently agreed upon the virtues of the policy of "free trade," if on little else, to prefer Russell to any Protectionist. The advocates of protection, in turn, found it difficult to develop additional issues to serve as focuses of unity. The dissension within their own ranks was immediately exacerbated, moreover, by the dilemma posed by the newly elected M.P. for the City of London, Lionel de Rothschild. As a professing Jew, Rothschild was unwilling to swear his allegiance "on the true faith of a Christian," and his constituency and party associate, Lord John Russell, was quite willing to introduce legislation to give his new colleague the option of omitting the words that barred him from taking his seat. On grounds of religious liberalism the bill was supported by most of Russell's followers; on similar grounds it was favored by Lord George Bentinck, the Protectionist leader in the House of Commons. A majority of Protectionists could not view so lightly a measure that appeared to de-Christianize an assembly that retained the power to legislate on the structure and even on the doctrine of the Church of England. They were angered, and in a few cases horrified, by the unorthodox manner in which Benjamin Disraeli, a Jew by birth though a baptized Anglican since the age of twelve, defended the proposed alteration in the law: Disraeli defined Christianity as the logical fulfillment of Judaism. It was "as a Christian," he declared, that he would not take upon himself "the awful responsibility of excluding from the Legislature those who are of the religion in the bosom of which my Lord and Saviour was born."[4]

"Must I . . . cheer Disraeli," asked one back-bench Protectionist, "when he declares that there is no difference between those who crucified Christ and those who kneel before Christ crucified?"[5] Newdegate's approach was similar. He publicly regretted being compelled to differ with Disraeli, and he was quite willing to acknowledge the ability, intelligence, and learning of individual Jews. He could not forget, however, that the Jews were "the very people who rejected most obstinately the truths which formed the foundation of Christian belief, and upon which the British Parliament professed to found its legislation." To destroy the religious character of the legislature in order to appease a tiny minority impressed Newdegate as an unjustifiable sacrifice.[6]

The opposition of most Protectionist Conservatives did not

suffice to stop Russell's bill from winning the assent of the
House of Commons. The House of Lords, however, was to
obstruct the measure—and thus Rothschild's admission to Parliament—in 1847 and for eleven years thereafter. Newdegate
remained steadfast in his opposition. Among the Protectionists
there was much rank-and-file murmuring against Bentinck,
who quickly took the opportunity to resign the leadership of a
party that, he felt, had "degenerated into a 'No Popery,' 'No
Jew,' League."[7] Newdegate and Beresford remained as whips,
but their prime loyalty was to Lord Stanley in the House of
Lords, and during the 1848 session the party lacked any unified
leadership in the House of Commons. About fifty M.P.s continued to follow the lead of Bentinck and Disraeli; perhaps an
equal number followed that of Newdegate and Beresford. The
situation was deteriorating into one in which the party, Stanley
feared, was being "broken up into an infinite number of small
bands, acting without concert under a number of Guerrilla
Chiefs."[8]

Bentinck's unexpected death in September 1848 precipi-
tated a crisis, and Stanley and Newdegate corresponded exten-
sively on party prospects during the months that followed. That
Disraeli was the party's ablest speaker in the House of Commons was clear to everyone. Newdegate was so impressed with
Disraeli's 1848 end-of-session critique of the Russell ministry
that he felt compelled to send a flattering account of the occasion
to Mrs. Disraeli.[9] But was the ex-Bohemian and debt-ridden
novelist truly a suitable leader for a party of traditionalist English country gentlemen? "D'Israeli, with all his talent, is out of
the question," admitted Stanley as late as December 1848. Of all
possible leaders, Disraeli was the least likely to attract the alienated Peelites back into the Conservative fold.

Newdegate tried to be fair. Disraeli, he reported to Stanley
that same month, was conscientiously preparing his party colleagues for the coming session.

> I beleive [sic] D'Israeli will be supported by Ld. Henry Bentinck
> [Lord George's brother] and part of the Press on our side, but
> there is a distrust of him among members of our party, of which
> and the Jewish difficulty our adversaries will make the worst use; I
> have been warned repeatedly not to trust D'Israeli. While I see
> nothing in his public conduct to justify the want of confidence so
> many seem to feel, this I conclude is attributable to some circum-
> stances of his earlier life, with which I am not familiar.[10]

What alternatives to Disraeli were there? Lord Granby had the advantage of being the eldest son of the fifth duke of Rutland, but he was ineffectual in manner and uninterested in the position. John Charles Herries, who could claim to have worked for William Pitt as long ago as 1800, was well liked but was already over seventy. If only Disraeli would consent to remain the party's chief voice in the Commons while leaving the formal leadership in the hands of another. In January 1849 Newdegate's fellow whip, William Beresford, declared that Disraeli's appointment as leader would be fatal to the party. Newdegate, who conceded that Disraeli was "the ablest man in the House," would not go so far; his appointment might be injurious, he told Stanley, but "without him we shall be very weak. . . . Our first object should be to give him no just cause for complaint."[11]

In the hierarchically minded Conservative party, the final decision was made not by the assembled membership but by their leader. Stanley decided on a compromise: a triumvirate of Disraeli, Granby, and Herries. Disraeli soon became de facto party head in the Commons, but the fact that the leadership remained a theoretical triumvirate for several years eased the situation for party skeptics. "I suspect many would gradually acquiesce in the reign who would rebel against the coronation," one such skeptic had written in 1848.[12] There was to be no "coronation" for Disraeli, but by the summer of 1849 even the party whips had come to accept him as Stanley's chief lieutenant in the Commons. It was to Disraeli that Newdegate resigned his office as whip in March 1850.[13] Newdegate had found the position increasingly uncongenial; "Charley complains that they work him so hard as whip," his mother had noted two months earlier. A lingering distrust of Disraeli may have contributed to Newdegate's decision, but the latter's formal relations with the leader of the Conservatives in the House of Commons remained cordial. In 1851, when the French statesman Adolphe Thiers sent Disraeli several copies of a speech favorable to protection "to present to the leading members of the Protectionist Party," Disraeli immediately forwarded a copy to Newdegate. "I think," Disraeli wrote, "you have fairly won the distinction by your valuable labour." Newdegate was pleased.[14]

Protection, which in this instance brought Newdegate and Disraeli together, was soon to drive them apart once more. What for Disraeli was a policy that might have to be sacrificed if it proved politically hopeless was for Newdegate a principle for which a man might have to sacrifice all hopes of office. As Robert Blake has reminded us,[15] the arguments of the advocates of protection in the great debate of 1846 were stronger than has often been acknowledged. "Free trade" in theory meant "free imports" in practice, since foreigners, after all, were not compelled to open their harbors to British ships and goods in as unrestricted a fashion as Britain was opening its ports to their vessels and commodities. The doctrine rested, moreover, not on experience but on a set of *a priori* assumptions on which political economists were by no means all agreed. Between 1849 and 1852, Newdegate published a series of *Letters to Henry Labouchere on the Balance of Trade* in which he suggested to the then president of the Board of Trade that the actual year-to-year figures on British trade did not bear out the contentions of the free traders. They misstated the market value of many articles, omitted many imported articles, and ignored the movement of precious metals. The Conservative *Quarterly Review* found Newdegate's reasoning clear, his facts striking, and his arguments unanswerable. To Newdegate's disappointment, neither Stanley nor Disraeli appeared to take much interest.[16]

Newdegate lost no opportunity, however, to preach the same lesson in the House of Commons. It was free trade, in the form of the repeal of the Navigation Acts, that was endangering Britain's colonial empire. It was free trade that necessitated the continuance of the income tax. It was free trade, Newdegate was sure as late as March 1850, that had "tended to degrade the working classes and to impoverish the Exchequer."[17] Even Newdegate was compelled to concede, however, that the relative prosperity that followed the recession of 1848–1849 confirmed the truth of free-trade axioms in the minds of a majority of politically active Englishmen, but he remained unrepentantly insistent that *post hoc* did not necessarily mean *propter hoc*. The Protectionists, he reminded the Commons in 1852, sought justice for all the great producing interests of the state. When *The Times* asked him what he had gained from his steadfast adherence to his Protectionist beliefs, his reply was to the point: "I have gained nothing but hard labour, but I have secured my honour—I have secured the respect of honest men."[18]

For Newdegate, the word *Protectionist* retained connotations far wider than that of "advocate of protective tariffs for the nation's agriculturists." The Protectionists were as solicitous of manufacturers as of farmers, and they also sought to protect the Christian character of the state, the Protestant character of the Constitution, and the welfare of the poor. In 1847 Newdegate was a firm supporter of the Ten-Hour Act, which limited the workday of women and of children aged thirteen to eighteen to ten hours a day. Although adult males were not specifically mentioned in the act, it seems clear that most of its supporters expected them to benefit from the measure as well. As far as Newdegate was concerned in 1850, the act had established a maximum factory working week of fifty-eight hours, and he opposed any attempts to extend that period anew.[19] For similar reasons he supported a measure intended to aid framework knitters; their employers could no longer compel them to rent knitting frames at exorbitant rates.[20]

On the one hand, Newdegate was not deterred by any faith, blind or otherwise, in the axiomatic virtues of laissez faire in upholding the claims of the poor and the helpless. On the other, he was skeptical of methods of regulation that sought to supplant the local authority with the centralized bureaucrat. The proposed Board of Health, for example, impressed him as a "departure from the free principles of the British Constitution, and a gradual usurpation, behind the backs of Parliament, of the power which ought to belong to the representatives of the people."[21] Newdegate confided to Stanley his fears that the new Board of Health districts into which the country was to be divided would form the basis of new electoral boroughs in due course to be enfranchised with a government agency established in each. "The enormous patronage it will afford to the Government will not, I am sure, escape your attention."[22] The measure passed in 1848 despite Newdegate's opposition, but it proved for the moment to be the most short-lived of the various agencies that—however small and weak by twentieth-century criteria—had come to constitute the Victorian administrative state.[23] Just as bureaucratic centralization appeared to be a danger, so did the assumption that the public should be taxed for purposes that, however intrinsically worthwhile, were not of immediate necessity; the use by towns of property taxes to build libraries and museums impressed Newdegate as falling into the latter category.[24]

The Russell government tottered visibly in 1851, and Newdegate and his mother pondered from time to time how he should respond to the tender of office. Lacking followers with administrative experience, Stanley, who had succeeded his father as the earl of Derby, did not appear all that eager to form a government, unless he could forge a coalition with the Peelite "deserters." Yet, before long, an offer might well be made. Back in 1846 his mother had noted: "Everybody likes to be Prime Minister I believe—but I wonder—and the bare idea of place for Charley distracts me—I'm sure his health would never stand the attention, the hard work it would be his duty to give it." Perhaps country gentlemen ought not to accept office at all: "if they could but keep their own," Newdegate observed in 1851, "they are quite without ambition." Besides, the new earl of Derby might well think him too uncompromising or too unworthy.[25] Yet when the London *Daily News* reported early in 1851 that a possible Derby cabinet might include Newdegate as president of the Board of Trade, he quickly related the rumor to his mother.[26]

No Derby ministry materialized in 1851, but in February 1852 the Russell government, weakened by the loss of Lord Palmerston (who had been dismissed as foreign secretary two months before), lost the confidence of the House of Commons. Derby, as head of the largest identifiable party, was invited to form a government. Would Newdegate be offered an "acceptable" post like vice-president of the Board of Trade or an inappropriate one such as poor-law commissioner or none at all?[27] The uncertainty displayed in successive diary entries by Newdegate's mother ceased when Derby summoned her son to his London home and offered to name him vice-president of the Board of Control, the number-two man in the India Office. Newdegate immediately turned the post down. "Why?" asked Derby. "I know nothing of Indian affairs [n]or am I fitted for it & My Lord it can be no secret to you *I have been roughly handled*," Newdegate responded. Derby started up in his chair: "Not by me." "Perhaps not," Newdegate conceded. "You know Mr. Newdegate," the new prime minister went on, "this is a step to the Cabinet." He asked the Warwickshire squire to think the offer over and to respond by letter later that day.[28]

Under the apparent influence of his mother and some of her friends, Newdegate turned the offer down formally: "It would have given me the most sincere pleasure it always has done to serve you to the best of my ability," wrote Newdegate, "but I know little of India and you will have no difficulty in finding men of better ability, to whom the office will not be so novel."[29] The next morning, Newdegate temporarily repented of his decision, but his mother felt certain that her son was well out of a cabinet likely to be dominated by the new chancellor of the exchequer, Benjamin Disraeli.[30] Office would necessarily have curbed Newdegate's freedom of movement—it might have kept him in London even during the hunting season. Office would also have restricted his spirit of independence at a time when, to Newdegate's dismay, Disraeli was clearly seeking to detach the politically tattered banner of import-tariff restoration from the masthead of the Protectionist party and to substitute "tax reform."

The survival of the Derby ministry depended on the temporary willingness of Liberals, Radicals, and Peelites to acquiesce in its rule, and it came as no surprise when Derby sought to strengthen his ranks by calling for a new general election in midsummer. That the election might hurt the Protectionists as much as help them was confirmed by John Bright, the leader of the Anti–Corn Law League, who warned Newdegate personally that unless he changed his opinions and policies he would not long continue to represent the electors of North Warwickshire. Newdegate, in turn, taunted Bright with failing to support the cause of the laboring classes whose champion he claimed to be. "In what manner did Mr. Bright represent the labouring classes," Newdegate asked, "when he was the vigilant opponent of the Ten Hours' Bill—when he opposed every measure for moderating the severity of manufacturing labour, and every law which had for its object the fencing of the machinery, so as to shield the operatives from injury?"[31]

In the meantime, active Freehold Land Societies were enabling hundreds of residents in North Warwickshire as elsewhere to qualify for the franchise. *The Times* anticipated "a very severe contest," and the *Spectator* expected the free traders to secure at least one of the two seats.[32] Beset by similar fears, Newdegate had organized a constituency registration society the year before and had also appealed to his more affluent local friends for financial assistance so that he and his colleague Richard Spooner might counter "the organized attack of our enemies (Cobdenites, Papists, and Jews)."[33]

The town of Coleshill was the site of extraordinary excitement on nomination day as Newdegate and Spooner, the sitting members, were escorted to the hustings by a large band of mounted and unmounted supporters wearing orange colors. But then the supporters of the free-trade candidates Keppel Craven and T. G. Skipworth entered Market Square with their adherents, many of whom had come by train from Birmingham and Coventry. Dozens of fistfights broke out between followers of the two sides, and scarcely a word could be heard from the platform where Newdegate was attempting to defend his legislative record and where the son of Sir Robert Peel (who had died in 1850) was seeking to place the free-trade candidates in nomination. In near riot conditions, the supporters of Newdegate and Spooner found themselves outnumbered and driven from the field. A formal poll was called for the following week, and the legal electors had to rely on placards and newspaper reports rather than on speeches. Men were "half murdered in the streets of Nuneaton," charged Newdegate in a letter to a fellow magistrate. Perhaps Roman Catholic priests had inspired the disorders; if so, they must be taught that Nuneaton was not in Ireland. Newdegate offered the services of his colliers as special constables for the duration of the poll, but his fellow justices of the peace decided that they could restore and preserve order without them.[34]

In their published addresses, Newdegate and Spooner stressed their support of the Derby government and their continued adherence to the principle of tariff protection, especially for the local ribbon and silk-weaving industry. They also took pride in their resistance to Roman Catholic attempts "to set up their old tyranny in this Country, and to govern you *Free Born Englishmen* with a Rod of Iron." Craven and Skipworth, in turn, emphasized the manner in which free trade had eased the lot of the working classes and declared their willingness to extend the franchise and to advance civil and religious liberties. The electoral outcome was clear-cut: Newdegate, 2,950; Spooner, 2,822; Craven, 2,038; and Skipworth, 2,021. Five hundred supporters of Newdegate and Spooner were on hand "girded with swords" to celebrate the formal declaration of the poll.[35]

Although Newdegate was in "a very uncomfortable state of mind" for several weeks after the election lest unauthorized expenditures by a member of his finance committee might lead to a formal petition to unseat him and Spooner, no such petition materialized; £5,686 had been spent to secure the reelection of the two Protectionists.[36] Their triumph in North Warwickshire was not matched throughout the kingdom, however, and in the autumn of 1852 the party still could not claim a clear majority in the House of Commons. Attempts at reunion with a significant number of Peelites failed, and it was only a matter of time before the Whig–Liberals, the Radicals, and the Peelites would find an issue on which to bring down the government. They found that issue in Disraeli's budget, and in December 1852, by a vote of 305 to 286, they exiled Derby's Conservatives to another six years on the opposition benches. Newdegate had voted to uphold Disraeli, now his party's accepted leader in the House of Commons (and for a few months leader of the Commons itself), but it may well be that Newdegate found the opposition benches more congenial to his personal temperament.

As leader of the opposition in the House of Commons,

Disraeli was forced to walk a perpetual tightrope. To broaden the political appeal of the Conservative party, he found it useful to seek tactical allies among the members of the coalition who sat on the government benches and to emphasize those features of the Conservative program that would attract new voters. As one political observer phrased it in 1854, "Mr. Disraeli has, consequently, only one course to take—to wrench himself out of the reach of the Spooner and Newdegate sections, and to proclaim a principle, and lead a new party representative of a principle."[37] Yet Disraeli could hardly afford to lose the support of his own right wing, and during the 1850s he solicitously sought Newdegate's attendance at the political strategy meetings that preceded the opening of each parliamentary session. "It is not a large or formal party," Disraeli wrote in 1854, "but I shall be very much gratified if you will join it."[38] More often than not, Newdegate begged off. His ambivalence toward his party leader in the Commons is illustrated by the manner in which, in his draft reply, Newdegate first wrote, "I remain, with many thanks for your invitation, Yours sincerely, C. N. Newdegate," only, upon reconsideration, to scratch out the words "with many thanks for your invitation."[39]

In 1855 Newdegate demonstrated his continued belief in the doctrine of protection by publishing *A Collection of the Customs' Tariffs of All Nations*, a lengthy and laborious compilation based in part on a German source. Disraeli acknowledged the work at once: "I received your quarto yesterday, & am greatly obliged to you for it. It does you much honor [*sic*], & will do the country great service. I trust your health is much improved, & that you will be able, next session to assist me with all y[ou]r abilities for wh[ich] I assure you, I entertain a due, & very sincere respect."[40] A letter of appreciation from only one other Conservative ex-minister survives.[41] Newdegate remained dubious, however, about the sincerity of Disraeli's frequent expressions of concern for his health and that of his mother. Newdegate and his party leader remained distant allies at best, and when his neighbor, Lord Exeter, informed the Arbury Hall squire in the summer of 1864 that Disraeli was expected for a visit, he added, "I conclude you have no especial wish to meet him."[42]

Although Newdegate's second cousin Francis W. Newdegate (the brother of his eventual heir) fought in the Crimean War as an officer in the Coldstream Guards, Newdegate felt no great personal involvement with that conflict. His most significant parliamentary contribution was to criticize the government for

buying small arms abroad rather than relying upon the manufacturers of his native Warwickshire. In characteristic fashion,
he also reminded the house that the war had not broken out
until his hero the duke of Wellington, "the great conservator of
peace," had been buried. Yet once rumors of an armistice began
to spread early in 1856, Newdegate was equally dubious: "from
what I hear of the Russians I have little faith in Peace."[43]

Newdegate's major concern in the 1850s—and the chief
concern of the succeeding chapters of this study—came to be the
presumed menace of Roman Catholicism, and he supported
Spooner's repeated attempts to reverse Peel's endowment of
Maynooth College, the leading Roman Catholic seminary in
Ireland. Newdegate also upheld such obvious agricultural goals
as ending the malt tax (which hindered farmers who sought to
brew their own beer), and he was highly suspicious of the
decision of Gladstone, as chancellor of the exchequer in the
coalition government of 1852–1855, to double the succession
duty on landed property.[44] As an upholder of the economic
interests of his own class, the county squirearchy, Newdegate
was right to feel concerned.

By 1857 the coalition government of Lord Aberdeen had
been supplanted by the Whig–Liberal government of Lord
Palmerston, whom Newdegate acknowledged to be a "high-
minded and spirited British statesman." In March of that year,
criticism of Palmerston's China policy caused a temporary coalition of Conservatives, Radicals, and Peelites to defeat him;
Palmerston recommended a dissolution of Parliament and a
new general election, the first since 1852. How much more
placid the political atmosphere had become since the late 1840s
and the early 1850s is illustrated by the fact that Newdegate and
Spooner faced no opposition in North Warwickshire. Despite
the fact that, in the judgment of *The Times*, their joint address
studiously "refrain[ed] from alluding to any of the leading questions of the day," they were sent back to Westminster at little
expense and less labor.[45]

Less than a year later, another opportunity to defeat Palmerston arose, and on this occasion, Derby—as he had done in
1852—agreed to form a ministry of his own. Again Disraeli
became chancellor of the exchequer and leader of the House of
Commons; again the tenure of the ministry was dependent on
the willingness of its miscellaneous opponents not to overthrow
it. Again, too, the new prime minister was hard pressed to put
together a respectable cabinet when the most eminent House of
Commons men of the day—Palmerston, Russell, Gladstone,

Graham, and Cobden among them—all sat on the opposition benches. Although Newdegate had deliberately removed himself from the party's inner circle by 1858, he received a second invitation to join a Derby ministry, this time as president of the Board of Health, the very institution whose creation he had opposed back in 1847 and 1848; Newdegate politely refused the offer.[46] Another possibility for Newdegate arose a year later: "This Commissionership of Excise is really a considerable embarrassment," Derby wrote to Disraeli. "I enclose you the list of candidates among whom there is hardly a good name. . . . Would Newdegate take it? and, if so, could we keep his seat?"[47] The government might well have kept Newdegate's parliamentary seat, but the fifteen-year veteran of the parliamentary wars had no desire to vacate it.

The two major measures that Derby's Conservative government sought to forward in 1858–1859 were a bill to abolish the East India Company and to establish India as a crown colony—a consequence of the Sepoy Mutiny of 1857—and a proposal to reform the franchise. Newdegate was troubled by both. He ultimately abstained on the government of India bill because he did not believe that the East India Company deserved legislative punishment, and he was far from happy with the second measure. Although he did not feel wedded on principle to the precise franchise requirements then in force, he did tend to identify political reform proposals with Radicals rather than with Conservatives. He retained an almost romantic regard for the traditional right of certain urban freeholders in Birmingham and Coventry to vote for Warwickshire county M.P.s like him; "this capacity," he told Derby, "has tended to mitigate the asperity of class distinctions between these Boroughs and the County." The prime minister had been prepared for Newdegate's unhappiness with the government's plan to lower the county franchise requirements generally, but he was astonished by Newdegate's objection to the removal of the borough electors from the county franchise register. The proposed change would, if anything, strengthen rather than weaken the Conservative influence in Warwickshire. Derby pleaded with Newdegate not to let down his own side and reminded him that the alternative to a Conservative reform bill was likely to be a Radical reform bill.[48]

Newdegate ultimately heeded Derby's plea, but the combined opposition found it possible to utilize the Conservative reform bill to defeat the government. The consequences were a new dissolution of Parliament and the second general election in two years. In a joint statement, Newdegate and Spooner told their electors that, inasmuch as they had for so long given evidence of their political opinions in action and word and since they were so closely bound to their electors by community of interest and residence, they saw no need "to trouble them with a protracted address." Again there was no opposition.[49] The situation was otherwise elsewhere in the country, however, and the second Derby ministry was duly supplanted by the second Palmerston ministry. The miscellaneous conjunction of Whigs, Peelites, and Radicals was in the process of coalescing into the great Liberal party, and the septuagenarian Lord Palmerston seemed likely to go on living forever.

Disraeli, who sought office, was more frustrated by this state of affairs than was Newdegate, who did not and who more often than not found himself in agreement with Palmerston's policy of upholding Britain's honor abroad and letting sleeping dogs lie at home. Palmerston, moreover, shared Newdegate's private assessment that the public demand for political reform did not seem urgent, and nothing came of several Liberal reform proposals during the early 1860s.[50] Relations between Palmerston and Newdegate became sufficiently cordial to cause the prime minister to offer Newdegate a peerage. Newdegate felt a high degree of respect for the senior chamber of the legislature, and in 1861, when Gladstone as chancellor of the exchequer weakened its power over finances by incorporating all the finance bills of the session into a single measure (which the House of Lords dared not deny), Newdegate sought vainly to restore the constitutional powers of the upper house. Yet when it came to exchanging his role as elected county squire for the permanent tenure that went with a barony, the Warwickshire squire decided that he preferred the former to the latter, and Palmerston's offer was politely declined.[51] By now Newdegate had established himself in the minds of numerous observers, including Walter Bagehot, as the prototypical independent county M.P. devoted to affairs of state, whose speaking style, though not exempt from mannerisms, merited his being classed as one of the abler debaters of the day.[52] Oxford University, Newdegate's alma mater, had acknowledged his achievements by granting him an honorary doctorate of civil law. Newdegate's fellow recipients, on this occasion, included ex-President Martin Van Buren of the United States, Sir Thomas Gladstone (William's elder brother), the novelist Sir Edward Bulwer-Lytton, and the historian George Grote.[53]

In his concern with national issues, Newdegate never forgot Warwickshire for long. In 1855 he recommended that the local poor-law guardians become more charitable. "The means of the poor," he reminded his fellow justices of the peace, "are much crippled in illness by the high prices of the present time, which render the purchase of necessaries for more of the Extra Nourishment which the successful treatment of fever requires, very difficult for them."[54] He was frequently concerned with the employment problems of his district's ribbon weavers, whose plight he attributed, in part, to the 1860 Cobden ("Free Trade") Treaty with France. Poor-law relief was at best a palliative— assisted emigration to Canada, Australia, or New Zealand appeared to be the better solution—but Newdegate was anxious *"not to send away the best hands."*[55] As a deputy lieutenant of Warwickshire, Newdegate also became closely involved with the creation of a volunteer rifle corps in the Nuneaton area. Prompted in 1859 by fears of the hostile intentions of the France of Napoleon III, the volunteer movement represented at once a drive for national revival and rearmament and a reaffirmation of the traditional British belief in the role of the amateur. The movement also provided an opportunity for middle-aged shop- keepers and their clerks to play soldier on weekend afternoons.[56]

When Parliament was not in session during these years, Newdegate continued to live at Arbury Hall with his mother. Invitations to visit the Warwickshire estate were invariably ex- tended in his mother's name as well as his own, and his nonpo- litical correspondents invariably extended their regards to her. By the 1850s Newdegate had become one of the busiest and most sociable men in Warwickshire. There was scarcely a local meeting or social gathering of significance from which he was absent. The annual meeting of the Literary Institution of Nuneaton, the dinners of the Rugby and Dunchurch Conserva- tive Association, the annual gathering of members of the Col- eshill Farmers Club, the annual meeting of the Warwickshire Scripture Readers' Society all would find in attendance the squire of Arbury Hall. He presided over scores of lectures, and he danced with numerous young women at hunt balls.

> Bachelor though he was, his bearing toward the fair sex had much of that reverence so characteristic of what are termed "old- fashioned manners," and whenever it fell to his lot, at a public dinner or elsewhere, to propose the toast of "The Ladies," he discharged that duty with the very best taste, and with many fanciful and pleasing figures of speech.[57]

However courtly his bearing toward the ladies on formal occasions, Newdegate does not appear to have encountered any of them in more intimate settings. His mother's diary makes no reference to a female friend, much less to a prospective wife. He enjoyed talking to the estate tenants, however, and each Christmas he sponsored a lavish party for the household servants. He remained as devoted as ever to riding and fox hunting, activities that led to their share of accidents over the years, though none of them proved serious.

Late in 1855 such pursuits were interrupted while Newdegate stood for hours on end at the behest of a portrait painter. "I am a *victim* of my mother's long deferred determination to have a picture of one," he confided coyly to a friend; "she has laid a trap for me." The painting (the frontispiece of this book) was sponsored by forty-four of the Arbury tenants, and at a formal dinner and dance a year later, the portrait was ceremonially presented to Newdegate's mother "as a token of our regard, and in grateful acknowledgement of the uniform liberality and kindness he has shown towards us." The presentation statement praised Newdegate's friendship, his encouragement of good farming, his public service, and his efforts to advance the education of the working classes. "It is a great pride and pleasure to us," the presenters concluded, "to see the Portrait of one who has proved himself so good a son, so kind a Landlord and so firm a friend added to those of his Ancestors."[58]

In the midst of what a later generation was to look back on as a placid and even complacent era, an age of equipoise, Newdegate remained ever alert to a danger that seemed to belie all notions of placidity or complacency, that of Roman Catholicism. This chapter has in large part concentrated on Newdegate's other concerns—he was single-minded but was no monomaniac—but the papal threat never seemed far off. To battle that threat, he was prepared not merely to utilize Parliament and the public platform but also to subsidize during the 1850s two weekly journals, the *English Churchman* and the *St. James's Chronicle*.[59] For many years he devoted part of each Friday to correcting articles and checking galley proofs of the *English Churchman*. When Parliament was not in session, he would make a special journey from Arbury Hall to London for the purpose.[60] As he told a correspondent in 1864, "I believe that Protestant Christianity is the foundation of the Constitution of this country and of the blessings it has conferred upon all classes, and I know that in consequence of the perpetual bartering away of the legal safeguards of this great principle we are committed to a constant struggle with deadly adversaries."[61] To battle these adversaries more successfully, Newdegate was prepared to sacrifice both office and a peerage and even to endure what to him were the laughter of the ignorant and the jeers of the indifferent.[62]

4. The Militant Minority

To the extent that historians have alluded to Victorian anti-Catholicism at all, they have tended to characterize English Catholics as a small and weak religious minority who became the object of reawakened hatred and the victim of renewed political harassment and social discrimination. The Roman Catholic church has been viewed as playing the passive role, and evangelically Protestant England as playing the active role in this latest installment of a centuries-old drama.[1] Thus it comes as an initial surprise to discover how frequently Victorian Englishmen saw the drama with the roles reversed. The situation for most of them was not one of Protestant harassment but of "papal aggression," and when *Punch* caricatured the conflict in 1851, it depicted Cardinal Wiseman, the Roman Catholic archbishop, as the giant, and Lord John Russell, the prime minister, as tiny "Jack the Giant Killer."[2]

The proper role to be assigned to the Roman Catholic church in the Victorian world depends upon whether our context is England alone or the United Kingdom or the entire world. This chapter will provide in turn a discussion of all three. In England during the early and mid-Victorian years, the Roman Catholics admittedly remained a small minority, often far more divided among themselves than their countrymen suspected. "It is well," wrote a future archbishop in the late 1850s, "that the Protestant world does not know how our work is hindered by domestic strife."[3] Yet, during these same years, that church was transformed from a tiny, isolated, quietist vestige into a rapidly growing organization that demanded a major role in the political, social, and intellectual life of the nation and that emphasized rather than minimized the ties that bound it to the universal Catholic church centered at Rome. This transformation of a half-forgotten sect into a militant minority was the product of the efforts of a new generation of English converts (who gave the reviving church social significance and intellectual distinction); of Cardinal Wiseman, under whose direction the organization of the church in England was restructured and its Roman orientation reemphasized; and of several hundred thousand Irish immigrants who helped to provide a mass following for the rejuvenated English Roman Catholic church.

Although individual cases of conversion to Roman Catholicism were not unknown in early nineteenth-century England, it was in the 1840s that a trickle became in the minds of many

LORD JACK THE GIANT KILLER.

Lord John Russell, the prime minister, wields the Ecclesiastical Titles Act against
Cardinal Wiseman, while John Bull lends support and Mr. Punch looks on (from
Punch 20 [1851]: 46).

Englishmen a flood. The Oxford movement of the previous
decade had reminded the members of the Church of England of
the apostolic roots, the non-Protestant traditions, and the
autonomy from secular authority that constituted one facet—to
its adherents the all-important facet—of their church's complex
history. The hopes of the adherents of the movement to recon-
struct the Anglican church of their day in accordance with their

historical ecclesiastical vision were blasted by the manner in which the publication of their *Tracts for the Times* was halted in 1841, by the manner in which the finances of the church were being reordered under the auspices of a lay-appointed Ecclesiastical Commission, and by the Gorham Judgment of 1850, which reemphasized the fact that the Church of England was a state church rather than an autonomous religious entity.[4] Some, like Edward Bouverie Pusey, remained within the church, but scores of others sought spiritual refuge, at the price of at least initial material deprivation, within the bosom of Roman Catholicism.

The significance of the conversion process for Englishmen of the day lay less in the absolute number of the converts than in their intellectual distinction and their social status and in the fear they induced in Englishmen who remained faithful to the Anglican church that tens might become hundreds and hundreds thousands, and that the process would completely undermine their sense of religious and national security.[5] The converts included not merely John Henry Newman, fellow of Oriel College, Oxford, and a leading preacher and theologian at Oxford University, and Henry Edward Manning, archdeacon of Chichester and one of the most promising of Anglican church administrators, but also scores of influential Anglican clergymen, such as Frederick Faber, Wilfrid Ward, and T. W. Allies, the chaplain of the bishop of London. There were peers of the realm like Viscount Feilding, the future earl of Denbigh, who was to inscribe on his banner "First a Catholic, then an Englishman."[6] The fourth earl of Oxford, the eighth earl of Abingdon, the countess of Gainsborough, and the countess of Kenmore were also among the 27 peers and the 417 members of the nobility that one chronicler was to record as Roman Catholic converts during the Victorian era. That same chronicler also identified 205 army officers, 39 navy officers, 129 lawyers, 60 doctors, and 162 literary men and women. Gerard Manley Hopkins, the poet; Augustus Welby Pugin, the architect; and Georgiana Fullerton, the novelist, were among the best known.

Most significant nineteenth-century Englishmen had either a close friend or relative who became a convert to the Roman Catholic faith. Three sons of William Wilberforce, the great evangelical religious leader and parliamentary "slave emancipator," became converts. So did a daughter and a son-in-law of Sir Walter Scott, the novelist; a niece of James Anthony Froude, the noted historian of Tudor England; and two sons of Sir John Bowring, the colonial governor and literary executor of Jeremy

Bentham. So also did a sister of William Ewart Gladstone, the prime minister. Other converts included a sister of Sir Henry Brand, the speaker of the House of Commons; a brother of John Duke Coleridge, the Lord Chief Justice of England; and a brother-in-law of Archibald Campbell Tait, the archbishop of Canterbury.[7] No wonder that Queen Victoria's eldest daughter, the crown princess of Prussia, could write from Berlin in 1867: "People will have it here that the Catholic religion is making rapid progress in England, that the aristocracy are all going over to the Church of Rome—and that there are new conversions every day."[8]

The converts often became victims of social ostracism, and they, in turn, tended to look down upon their erstwhile associates. Frederick Faber and Lord John Manners, for example, had been close personal friends, but after Faber's decision to join the Roman Catholic church in 1845, they never saw one another again.[9] Except to the extent that they sought to convert their Anglican friends in turn, most converts tended to put such friends behind them and to look back upon their previous beliefs as a compound of muddle and error. In Newman's words, they had "left the City of Confusion for the Mother of Saints."[10] They took pride in the authority their adopted faith commanded and in the historic continuity it seemed to represent; in some cases they flaunted the very devotional practices—like the veneration of the Virgin Mary—that distinguished it most from Anglican church custom.[11] On all other subjects, the converts enjoyed the natural use of their reason—so conceded a writer in *Church Opinion*—but on the subject of religion they lived "in a medieval world of their own . . . like a man who has persuaded himself that he is a teapot, and can be moved from his delusion by nothing his friends can say and do."[12]

Sir John Acton, a Roman Catholic by birth rather than conversion, privately criticized the more zealous converts as "lovers of authority, fearing knowledge much, progress more, freedom most, and essentially unhistoric and unscientific."[13] Acton's comment throws light on the tension that existed in the 1850s between many new converts and the descendants of the old Catholic families that had survived the seventeenth- and eighteenth-century penal laws, but in at least one sense, his description is profoundly misleading. However much the converts might take pride in Roman Catholic theological and structural constancy, in Victorian England they were enterprising innovators. For the time being, they might have sacrificed their careers and many of their friends, but they did not really

wish to give up their place in the social and educational class
into which they had been born. They wanted to transform their
adopted church into a major—some genuinely hoped, *the* major—spiritual force of their native land.[14]

The individual most significantly responsible for the re-
juvenation of Roman Catholicism in England was not a convert.
Nicholas Wiseman was born in 1802 in Spain, the son of an Irish
merchant some of whose more distant ancestors were English.
From age seven to age eighteen, Wiseman attended a Catholic
school in England, Saint Cuthbert's College at Ushaw near
Durham, but for the next twenty-two years, he was associated
with the newly reopened English College in Rome. There he
became an assiduous student and in due course a doctor of
divinity, a priest, vice-rector of the college, and in 1827, on the
basis of a treatise on the history of the Syriac version of the Old
Testament, he was appointed professor of oriental languages at
the Roman university. A year later, though not yet thirty years
old, he became rector of the college and unofficial go-between
for the Roman Catholic missionaries in England and the
Vatican.[15]

During a visit to England in 1835, Wiseman gave a series of
highly successful lectures in London explaining the Catholic
faith to Protestants. Soon thereafter he was instrumental in
founding the *Dublin Review*, a literate Catholic journal of opinion
designed at once to emulate and to take issue with the Whiggish
and rationalistic *Edinburgh Review*. When Wiseman was created
a bishop in 1840 and sent back to England to become the president of Oscott College near Birmingham, he was described by a
French Catholic periodical as one of "the new Augustines
whom a new Gregory [Pope Gregory XVI] sends forth to achieve
a second time the conquest of England."[16] Wiseman, it soon
became clear, had little sympathy with the English survivors of
the anti-Catholic penal laws whose prime goal seemed to be that
of being left alone, who failed to use titles like "Father" or
"priest" or to wear clerical habits or to seek a distinctive
architecture for their churches or to practice within them the
elaborate Roman ceremonies that Wiseman had learned to love.
Such "Old Catholics" seemed unaware of the Catholic revival
taking place in Germany and France and indifferent to the
opportunities of conversion that the Oxford movement was
opening for their church. Wiseman was not indifferent: he encouraged Continental churchgoers to pray for the reconversion
of England, and, in Acton's words, he enjoyed "exhibiting the
scalps" of his converts at Oscott.[17] In the late 1840s when the

papacy decided to revamp the government of the church in England, Bishop Wiseman was prepared to play a yet more grandiose role.

The Catholic Church in England was a mission church directed not by bishops but by vicars apostolic under the immediate supervision of Rome's Sacred Congregation of Propaganda. Canon law did not operate as it did in predominantly Roman Catholic lands: the country was not divided into episcopal dioceses administered from a cathedral; the dioceses in turn were not subdivided into parishes. In 1840 the four vicars apostolic were increased to eight, and in 1849 Wiseman became vicar apostolic for the London district. Then, in September 1850, while Wiseman was in Rome, a papal bull proclaimed the restoration of the Roman Catholic hierarchy in England. The land was divided into twelve dioceses and the vicars apostolic were transformed into bishops bearing the titles of English towns like Birmingham, Hexham, and Clifton. (Since the names did not duplicate any existing Anglican episcopal titles, they did not technically seem to violate the Catholic Emancipation Act of 1829.) Wiseman was proclaimed archbishop of Westminster and the next day was created a cardinal.

While Pope Pius IX exhorted the English faithful to "pray insistently that the Lord may remove all the obstacles and bring to the new church a million, three million, indeed all your compatriots who at one time were torn from the Church,"[18] Wiseman made a triumphal progress to London via Florence, Venice, and Vienna. In the meantime *The Times* began to thunder in protest. To erect the city of Westminster as an archbishopric and to appoint Wiseman as its head impressed the editor either as "a clumsy joke" or else as "one of the grossest acts of folly and impertinence which the Court of Rome has ventured to commit since the Crown and people of England threw off its yoke." The pope and his advisers had mistaken English tolerance for indifference; they had mistaken "the renovated zeal of the Church in this country for a return to Romish bondage."[19] Scarcely had the initial excitement evoked by the papal bull begun to subside when the pastoral letter that Wiseman had euphorically penned in Rome a week earlier was read in every Catholic church of his new diocese. Entitled "Out of the Flaminian Gate of Rome," it began portentously: "Nicholas, by the Divine mercy, of the Holy Roman Church by the title of St. Pudentiana Cardinal Priest, Archbishop of Westminster, and Administrator Apostolic of the Diocese of Southwark: To our dearly beloved in Christ, the clergy secular and regular, and the

Cardinal Wiseman at the age of forty-eight; a photograph of a miniature of an oil painting by J. R. Herbert (frontispiece of Wilfrid Ward, *The Life and Times of Cardinal Wiseman* [London, 1912], vol.2).

Faithful of the said Archdiocese and Diocese: Health and benediction in the Lord!" Wiseman went on to explain that "the greatest of blessings has just been bestowed upon our country, by the restoration of its true Catholic hierarchical government, in communion with the see of Peter." Henceforth, "till such time as the Holy See shall think fit otherwise to provide, we govern, and shall continue to govern, the counties of Middlesex, Hertford, and Essex as ordinary thereof, and those of Surrey, Sussex, Kent, Berkshire, and Hampshire, with the islands annexed, as administrator with ordinary jurisdiction." ("Am I Queen of England or am I not?" asked Queen Victoria, on reading this passage.) "Catholic England," Wiseman went on, "has been restored to its orbit in the ecclesiastical firmament, from which its light had long vanished, and begins now anew its course of regularly adjusted action round the centre of unity, the source of light, and of vigour." Wiseman's exuberance was applauded by the weekly *Tablet*, which was delighted with the way in which in the papal bull "the Anglican sees, those ghosts of realities long passed away, are utterly ignored." Even Newman, who usually chose his words more carefully, applauded the manner in which "the people of England . . . are about of their own free will to be added to the Holy Church."[20]

Wiseman's suggestions that the English people had forsaken Christianity and that the Church of England was a nullity infuriated not merely the editor of *The Times* but also the prime minister; Russell agreed with the bishop of Durham that the pope's actions had been "insolent and insidious."[21] *Punch* announced bitingly that "The Hindoo Government has sent over Hoki Poki to commence the functions as Brahmin of Battersea . . . The Mirzam of Moolrah has sent over Bow Wow to commence his sittings at Marylebone as Mufti of Middlesex, and Rusti Khan goes to Westminster Hall, to take his place in the Court of Chancery, as Cadi of Chelsea."[22]

Amidst the chorus of denunciations and burnings in effigy that Wiseman had aroused, there were some voices of moderation. Benjamin Disraeli observed that the British government had in effect already recognized in Ireland the type of hierarchical structure that it was now denouncing in England. The same was true in Canada, Nova Scotia, and Australia.[23] Wiseman himself sought to calm the storm with a much more moderately phrased *Appeal to the Reason and Good Feeling of the English People on the Subject of the Catholic Hierarchy*. In this pamphlet he observed that the restoration of the hierarchy did not dispossess the Anglican establishment of a single advantage and that, if Roman Catholics did not acknowledge the queen's right to interfere in their religious concerns or to appoint ministers for them, then they were claiming nothing more than what Baptists, Methodists, Quakers, and other Nonconformists had long since claimed.[24]

> If Dr. Wiseman meant [responded *The Times*] that he merely came amongst us as a dissenting minister, the head of a voluntary association, to manage the spiritual affairs of the Catholics scattered up and down England—if it was never intended to assume any rights save those which are cheerfully conceded to a Wesleyan or a Baptist, why in the name of common sense, could he not have said so?

Was it because the Roman Catholic church had two languages, an esoteric and an exoteric, "the first that more than mortal arrogance and insolence in which HILDEBRAND and INNOCENT thundered their decrees against trembling kings and prostrate emperors, the second artful, humble, and cajoling"? *The Times* suspected the worst: that the Catholic church had in no sense given up its claim to universal dominion and still considered "toleration to others . . . a crime—toleration to herself . . . an insult."[25]

Although *The Times* doubtless exaggerated Wiseman's own Machiavellian guile, its suspicion that he did not see himself as a *mere* dissenting minister was accurate enough. As befitted a cardinal, he traveled only in his splendid official carriage, with his cardinal's coat of arms emblazoned on the sides, accompanied always by at least one servant and one chaplain or secretary. Indeed, Rome sent him an annual subsidy so that he could uphold such lofty standards of archiepiscopal dignity.[26] By the spring of 1851 he once more foresaw glorious years ahead with thousands of new converts, hundreds of new churches, and the city of London enclosed within a wall of convents.[27] The Church of England, he assured a confidant in Rome, must now "admit *two* branches of the Church side by side in England, our Hierarchy being as good as theirs and coming from the same Roman source." Symptoms of a "complete and final break-up" of the Anglican establishment were everywhere at hand.[28]

Wiseman and his associates were far from oblivious to the silver lining that surrounded both the anti-Catholic rhetoric and the hostile legislation to which it gave rise. Russell's Ecclesiastical Titles Act of 1851 imposed a fine of one hundred pounds on any person who assumed an English church title—as Wiseman and his fellow bishops had done—but, though passed by the House of Commons by a vote of 433 to 95, the act was never enforced. The Royal Proclamation of 1852 warned Roman Catholics that public processions of men wearing clerical gowns and carrying church banners and objects of worship were still illegal. The proclamation was an immediate response "to the manifest danger of the public peace" demonstrated in Stockport, a town south of Manchester, where one such procession had been attacked, several people killed, and two Catholic chapels burned.[29] Yet Wiseman and his associates could take comfort in the fact that Roman Catholicism was everywhere the issue of the hour, the chief topic of conversation, the theme of numerous pamphlets and novels. "The devil is apt to howl when he is hurt," wrote Frederick Lucas, the editor of *The Tablet*.[30] "The clamour and uproar," Manning concluded a decade later, "did no more than publish to every soul of man within the realm that the Church of God summoned them to submission."[31]

The type of "martyrdom" experienced by Wiseman and his followers sufficed to give the several factions within the English Catholic body a sense of unity against the outside world. Even those who opposed the tendencies represented by Wiseman—Romanization, clerical discipline, the subordination of religious orders to the episcopacy, strong hostility to any degree of state supervision or interference, high sensitivity to any tendency toward heresy within the fold—found it prudent to make no public criticism of the new clerical regime.[32] By 1860 Wiseman regarded his Roman Catholic flock as having sufficient political power to determine the outcome of general elections.[33] *The Times* might yet doubt whether "in England, or indeed in any free Protestant country, a true Papist can be a good subject," but it had to concede that when Wiseman died in 1865, his funeral cortege, which wound its solemn way some seven miles from Moorfields to Kensal Green, was watched with obvious signs of respect by thousands of Londoners intent upon honoring "an eminent Englishman, and one of the most learned men of his time." There had been nothing comparable since the state funeral of the duke of Wellington thirteen years before.[34] Cardinal Wiseman had clearly succeeded in putting Roman Catholicism back on the religious and political map of England.

John Bossy has recently argued that the early nineteenth-century expansion of English Catholicism was the result neither of an act of Parliament nor of an act of Rome but of the internal expansion of English Catholic congregations that bore a considerable resemblance in attitude and degree of lay participation to Dissenting Protestant bodies like the Presbyterians. Bossy rightly notes that between 1770 and 1850 the Catholic population became increasingly urban and less rural, and his estimates of 80,000 Catholics in England in 1770 and 250,000 in 1850 are persuasive. Yet even Bossy's estimates suggest that the increase in the number of native English Catholics did little more than keep pace with the general increase in England's population, which tripled during those eighty years.[35] It was the actions of pope and Parliament that made mid-Victorian Catholicism a chapter in political controversy rather than a footnote in religious history, but it was Irish immigration that made the Roman

Catholic revival seem imposing in numbers as well as in words.

Hundreds of thousands of Irish men, women, and children sought refuge in England, Wales, and Scotland during the 1830s 1840s, and 1850s from their overcrowded, famine-stricken native land. There were 400,000 Irish immigrants living in Great Britain in 1841, when the census takers first counted them. In 1846 alone, 280,000 more streamed into Liverpool; in 1847, an additional 300,000 entered the country. Many of these immigrants were to move on to the United States, Canada, and Australia, but tens of thousands either remained in Liverpool or settled elsewhere in Great Britain. Between 1847 and 1851 alone, the number of Roman Catholics in England increased from 284,000 to 758,000.[36] John MacHale, the Irish archbishop, warned the English in 1851 that they would soon hear the exiled Catholics of Ireland addressing them in the language of Tertullian: "We have filled your cities, towns, fields, armies, senate."[37]

In one obvious sense, the Irish in England were a liability to the Roman Catholic church: their political influence was at first minimal, their need for social services staggering. They worked as migrant harvesters, as railway-construction workers, as dockhands and building laborers, as domestic servants, and as street peddlers, when they could find work at all.[38] Although the *Dublin Review* might lament the problems they faced in "having to educate children in the midst of a society whose moral tone is far lower than that of the Catholic Church"—English law, unlike canon law, did, after all, recognize the legality of divorce— most Englishmen saw the matter otherwise.[39] In the words of the *London City Mission Magazine* (November 1851), "there are millions of our Popish countrymen living at our own door, who are almost as thoroughly sunk in ignorance, idolatry, and moral degradation as are the Hottentots and the negroes of Africa."[40] The Irish were seen as intemperate and improvident, as dirty and diseased, as indolent and superstitious. "The Irishman loves his pig as the Arab his horse," Friedrich Engels observed, "he eats and sleeps with it, his children play with it, ride upon it, roll in the dirt with it."[41] The Irish were looked down upon because of their poverty and their "idolatrous" religion and because of their apparent tendency toward criminal behavior. At a time that they constituted 5 percent of the population of England they occupied 20 percent of the jail cells.[42] The stereotyped Irishman admittedly was also looked upon as quick-witted and good-humored, as sociable and pious. The weekly *Saturday Review* was quite willing to pay the Irish a backhanded compliment.

> If we compare for one moment London with San Francisco, we shall find that in London the lowest kind of labour is to a great extent performed by Irishmen, while in San Francisco it is performed by Chinese. Without feeling any violent partiality for Irishmen, we shall all of us probably prefer them to Chinese.

Roman Catholicism, the journal concluded, might not be the best religion, but it was surely better than none.[43]

During the 1850s the Roman Catholic hierarchy was often more concerned with preventing Irish immigrants from straying from the faith in which they had been baptized than with using them as agents of conversion. A Special Mission to the Roman Catholics of England raised more than £10,000 from pious Anglicans like the sixth duke of Marlborough (Sir Winston Churchill's grandfather) in order to convert Irish immigrants. The hierarchy resisted by forbidding Roman Catholics from attending any religious meetings at which Protestants were present and by imposing the most rigid sanctions against intermarriage.[44] If any of his parishioners sent their children to Protestant schools, warned Frederic Oakeley, the Catholic convert who served as priest in Islington, "the curse of God shall rest upon them, *body and soul, living or dead!*"[45] The seventh earl of Shaftesbury, the era's prime representative both of social reform and of evangelical Protestantism, was the target of the worst Roman Catholic abuse: he was denounced as an ogre who devoured the souls of Irish children.[46] By the early 1860s it was clear that the hierarchy had won the battle. The Special Mission had been driven from the field, the victim of hostility and, at times, of mob violence. The handful of Protestant converts had been chased from the community. Just as it subsidized Anglican and Nonconformist schools, so did the British crown begin in 1848 to subsidize Catholic schools in England. This subsidy— £250,000 a year by 1865—did much to assure the continued allegiance of most Irish immigrants and their children to the Catholic priesthood.[47]

By 1861 there were perhaps a million Irishmen in England, if one counts the English-born children of Irish parents. They made up, it is true, no more than one-twentieth of the population, and they constituted a financial drain upon their church. Yet they were all-important in making the Roman Catholics a numerically significant as well as a disciplined and even militant minority in Victorian England. Had he not seen the Irish as an asset in numbers and in piety, Cardinal Manning would hardly have boasted in his old age that he had spent his life in working "for the Irish occupation in England."[48]

Roman Catholicism, as threat or promise, loomed larger in the minds of Victorian Englishmen than the actual number of Roman Catholics might have warranted because Englishmen were likely to view the phenomenon not in the context of England alone but in that of the entire United Kingdom (England and Wales, Scotland, and Ireland). When Russell derided the practices of High Church Anglicans and Roman Catholics as "mummeries of superstition," observed one irate Catholic, then he was insulting "the faith and religious practice of at least one-third of the loyal subjects of the British realm."[49]

The population of Scotland in 1841 was 2,620,000, only one-sixth that of England and Wales, but the proportion of Irish immigrants there was almost three times as great as it was south of the Tweed. Twenty years later, well over 10 percent of the Scottish population—if we count the immigrants' children born in Scotland—was made up of Irish Roman Catholics.[50] The relatively large number of such immigrants, especially in the Glasgow area, caused immigration to play a larger role in reawakening anti-Catholic feeling in Scotland than in England.[51] Priestly influence was great, and no portion of the United Kingdom was more prolific than Scotland during the early 1850s in spawning anti-Catholic journals like *The Bulwark* and anti-Catholic organizations like The Scottish Reformation Society and The Society for Promoting the Religious Principles of the Reformation. Both groups sponsored lectures, pamphlets, and prizes, and, wittingly or not, both may have inspired Protestant gangs to damage Roman Catholic chapels and to engage in street fights with groups of equally assertive Irish Roman Catholic immigrants.[52]

It was, to be sure, Ireland rather than Scotland that was the center of Roman Catholicism in the United Kingdom. And Ireland, we must recall, loomed far larger in 1841—when one British subject in three was an Irishman—than it did by 1911—when that distinction could be claimed by only one in ten. According to the religious census of 1834, of 7,944,000 Irishmen, some 6,428,000 (over 80 percent) were Roman Catholic.[53] As the *Edinburgh Review* observed two decades later, Great Britain might best be compared to a Protestant husband who has married a Roman Catholic wife. Having taken this irrevocable step with his eyes open, he might nonetheless wish her to change her religion to his. Yet, if she proved obstinate, he was still obliged to support her and to take her wishes into account.[54]

In terms of sheer numbers, Ireland was never to loom quite so large again in the United Kingdom as it had in the early 1840s, because between 1845 and 1848 occurred the great event of modern Irish history—the famine. The blight that ruined the all-important potato crop in 1845, 1846, and 1848 permanently changed Irish society. How many hundreds of thousands of people died from disease brought on by hunger and how many hundreds of thousands fled their homeland for England, Scotland, and transoceanic refuges have never been precisely determined.[55] What is known is that a population of 8,200,000 in 1841, which had presumably grown still further by 1845, had been reduced to 6,570,000 by 1851 and to 5,800,000 by 1861.

In the short run, the famine weakened the hold of Roman Catholicism upon Ireland. Since the more prosperous (and more Protestant) inhabitants were marginally more likely to survive the famine and less likely to emigrate, the percentage of Roman Catholics declined somewhat; in 1861 it is estimated at 78 percent. The famine also gave a temporary boost to the efforts by Protestant missionaries like Alexander R. C. Dallas, whose Irish Church Mission followed in the footsteps of the Irish Society and the Scripture Readers' Society in bringing a "Second Reformation" to Ireland. During a period of profound psychological as well as economic depression, the message of a divine judge visiting punishment upon a people sunk in Catholic idolatry won a significant number of converts to Protestantism, especially in the western counties where the evangelical efforts were often carried on in Gaelic. Yet the effect was temporary. Many of the converts were shunned by their Catholic neighbors and were encouraged to emigrate. The proselytizing efforts, moreover, won only lukewarm support from the parsons of the established Church of Ireland, who preferred to see themselves as gentlemen with latitudinarian inclinations in theology rather than as fiery preachers eager to stir up sectarian strife. One Roman Catholic peer, Lord Monteagle, concluded in 1854 that "It is just as hopeless to attempt to the proselytization of Ireland as to revive the Ptolemaic system of astronomy."[56]

In the long run the role of Roman Catholicism in Irish life was clearly enhanced rather than weakened. As Emmet Larkin has persuasively argued,[57] Ireland during the mid-Victorian years underwent a "devotional revolution." In the 1830s less than 40 percent of those people counted as Catholics had attended mass; half a century later the percentage had risen to 90 percent. In 1840 there was but one priest for every 3,000 people; by 1870 there was one priest for every 1,250. The relative number of nuns and monks had increased even more rapidly. Roman Catholics had become far more likely to know their catechism, to partake of the sacraments, and to attend mass in chapels rather than in private homes. Their priests were far less likely to be drunk or avaricious or to act independently. In 1849 Pope Pius IX appointed the rector of the Irish College in Rome, Paul Cullen, as apostolic delegate to Ireland and as archbishop of Armagh. In that role, Cullen launched the Catholic Defence Association to secure the repeal of the newly passed Ecclesiastical Titles Act, and, as archbishop of Dublin from 1852 to 1878, Cullen molded the Catholic priesthood into a disciplined force garbed in Roman habits and imbued with Roman traditions and Roman devotional practices. The religious history of nineteenth-century Ireland, Larkin concludes, involved "simply the substituting, in a piecemeal fashion, of a Catholic confessional state for a Protestant one, with all that new ascendancy implies."[58]

Of the hundred members that Irish constituencies sent to the Parliament at Westminster in the 1850s and 1860s, about a third were Roman Catholics. Most called themselves Liberals or Conservatives, but a quasi-independent Irish party of the early 1850s was taunted in England as "the Pope's Brass Band."[59] As a consequence of the political reform act of 1850, which applied only to Ireland, the number of Irish electors tripled, the likelihood of Roman Catholics being elected increased, and the political influence of the priests widened. Although on occasion they used their spiritual influence quite blatantly—by threatening to withhold the services of the church from parishioners who voted for the wrong man, generally their influence was applied more subtly. They constituted a significant proportion of the local leadership that in the first instance nominated political candidates, and they aided with the canvass during elections.[60]

In 1850 the Irish hierarchy of four archbishops and twenty-eight bishops held its first synod since the twelfth century, and from then on it became increasingly efficient in exercising its influence as, for the time being, the most powerful constitutional force in Ireland. "It might be argued," writes Donald H. Akenson, "that what cabinet members were to England, the Roman Catholic bishops were to Ireland, at least after 1850."[61]

In order to assuage Roman Catholic feeling over the fact that Ireland's single university, Trinity College, Dublin, was operated by the Church of Ireland, Sir Robert Peel had in the 1840s instituted three new nondenominational Queen's Colleges in Belfast, Galway, and Cork. To the disappointment of both Peel and Russell, the Roman Catholic church refused to

THE FIERY CROSS!

Archbishop Paul Cullen summons the Irish clans, in traditional fashion, to battle against the religious policies of the British government (from *Punch*, 30 August 1851, p. 99).

cooperate. Under the influence of Archbishop Cullen and Pope Pius IX, the precedent-breaking Synod of Thurles (1850–1851) denounced the new colleges as immoral. The statesmen who framed the plan, the synod declared, "were not acquainted with the inflexible nature of our doctrines, and with the jealousy with which we are obliged to avoid everything opposed to the purity and integrity of our faith."[62] Although the colleges were not dissolved until 1882, total student enrollment never rose above three hundred at any one time. Thus an expensive piece of social legislation designed by Peel to improve the state of Ireland was strangled at birth by an authority accountable to no other person or institution in the kingdom.[63]

The hierarchy was much happier with another of Peel's educational innovations, the permanent subsidy to the Roman Catholic seminary at Maynooth (see Chapter 2). Twenty of the twenty-eight Irish bishops in 1850 had been educated at Maynooth, and during the mid-Victorian years the vast majority of all Irish priests were trained there. The church skillfully used its influence to resist the numerous attempts in the Parliament of the early 1850s to overturn the Maynooth grant. In spite of the efforts of Richard Spooner, Newdegate's parliamentary colleague for North Warwickshire and the author of *Maynooth Morals: The Real Teaching at Maynooth College* (1852), a royal commission gave the college an essentially clean bill of health in 1855. Although English opinion was shocked by the manner in which Archbishop Cullen had the commission's proofsheets checked in Rome for doctrinal error before final printing and by the manner in which he had inserted titles declared illegal by the Ecclesiastical Titles Act of 1851, Maynooth continued to prosper.[64]

Since the 1830s the Irish Catholic hierarchy had tolerated the national school system, according to which the British crown subsidized primary education in Ireland. Children of all denominations were expected to attend school together while receiving their religious instruction separately. Archbishop Cullen's prime purpose during the 1850s and 1860s was to end such "mixed education" and to make sure that all Roman Catholic children were trained in schools operated solely by his church. By 1870 schools supervised by the Christian Brothers and by comparable clerical orders supplemented the national schools to a considerable degree, and the national schools, in turn, were becoming increasingly denominational. Cullen was opposed to any cooperation, for educational purposes or otherwise, with the established Church of Ireland, "the Protestant Church, founded as it has been on the lust of a brutal king, propagated by fire and sword, and supported by robbery and confiscation of property."[65] For Cullen, clerical rather than mixed education represented the wave of the future, and when the Palmerston ministry of 1859–1865 sought to extend the national system of mixed schools from the primary to the intermediate level, Cullen and the hierarchy successfully blocked their initiative.[66] Cardinal Wiseman, who had received a hero's welcome when he toured Ireland a few years earlier in 1858, was gratified to see new Catholic churches and institutions under construction everywhere and to find "religious progress . . . far in advance of what is called social improvement." Archbishop Cullen, though quite willing to cooperate with, and to exert his influence on, the British government, saw Ireland, in the words of one hostile critic, as "a good Catholic machine, fashioned mainly to spread the faith over the world."[67]

Central and southern Europe, rather than Ireland, constituted the center of the Roman Catholic world of the 1850s. The church also dominated South America and exerted a significant influence upon every other continent. In the United States, where a formal hierarchy had been set up much earlier than in England, Roman Catholic ambitions were also growing. In spite of occasional anti-Catholic agitation—as exemplified in street battles and occasional church burnings, on the one hand, and in political successes of the short-lived Know-Nothing party, on the other—Archbishop John Hughes and many of his followers believed that the church would soon dominate the American religious scene.[68] The pope's temporal claims had been severely shaken by the Revolution of 1848, but by 1850 he was once more the ruler of a papal state in central Italy as well as the spiritual authority over Roman Catholics everywhere. Even if he were to lose all temporal power, *The Times* conceded in 1869, the pope would still remain "in some respects the most important personage in the world."[69] His political power depended upon the support of the two most powerful Catholic states: the France of Napoleon III, whose troops were stationed in Rome, and the Austrian Empire of Francis Joseph, with whom the papacy signed a new concordat in 1855. The English *Annual Register* described the treaty as "a marvelous proof of the encroaching spirit of the Church of Rome, and of the slavish subjection in which it binds kings and people, when they have not the spirit to resist its arrogant pretensions."[70]

By 1855 Pius IX, who had ascended the papal throne in 1846 amidst dreams that he might emerge as the ceremonial head of a reunified liberal Italy, had long since turned his back on liberal nationalism. The events of 1848 had left too deep a scar, and Pio Nono had come to represent instead the enemy of Italian liberalism and the symbol of a resurgence of Roman Catholic power

and influence that would have seemed impossible fifty years
before. The papal proclamation in December 1854 of the dogma
that the Virgin Mary had been born without taint of original sin
was acclaimed by English Catholics as the greatest event in
religious history since the Council of Trent.[71] The bull formally
anathematized as rebels and heretics all those who controverted
the new dogma. The Anglican *Quarterly Review* took religious
ideas too seriously to dismiss such an "extraordinary manifestation" of revived papal power. Did the new militancy of the
church signal "the energy of health or is it the delirious strength
of fever?" The *Quarterly Review* feared the worst.[72]

The papacy, as both a temporal and spiritual power, survived the unification of the rest of Italy under the auspices of
Cavour and Garibaldi in 1859–1861, and during the 1860s it
proclaimed anew doctrines and dogmas that flew in the face of
nineteenth-century tendencies toward secular rationalism. In
January 1864 the papacy condemned a congress of Roman
Catholic theologians that had met in Munich under the pres-
idency of Prof. Ignaz von Döllinger and by implication halted all
scholarly speculation that lacked a specific mandate from the
clerical hierarchy.[73] The climax of this tendency within the Roman church came later that year in the "Syllabus Containing the
Principal Errors of Our Age," which condemned as heretical the
beliefs that Catholic countries might tolerate other religions,
that any form of Protestantism was a legitimate form of Christianity, and that freedom of opinion had a positive value. The
papacy, it declared, could not and ought not to reconcile itself
with "progress, liberalism, and modern civilization."[74] Russell's
nephew, in forwarding the papal brief to Palmerston's foreign
secretary in London, described it as "the strongest claim ever
put forward by Rome since the Reformation."[75]

English Roman Catholic schoolchildren attended not
national but religious schools, and the graded textbooks
approved by the hierarchy taught them to identify themselves
with their Roman Catholic counterparts in Europe and the
world. They were members not of a minority but of a religious
majority inasmuch as Europe was composed of 122 million
Catholics, 52 million Protestants, and 43 million Greek Ortho-
dox. Variant forms of Christianity might be found in particular
parts of Europe, but only "the Catholic Church, true also to the
name she bears, is to be found everywhere."[76] Religious
teaching was carefully intertwined with secular learning from
the first year on. Second-year students were taught to make the
sign of the cross before lessons began and each time the clock

struck as well as at prayers. They were also taught that missing Sunday mass was a great sin and that God sent bears to kill boys who said bad words.[77] The third-year reader was devoted almost entirely to religious stories, to an explication of the sacraments, and to a "dialogue on the mass" in which Kitty ("a little girl who has learned her Catechism well at school") instructs Mary, a Protestant child, in its meaning and significance.[78] Fourth-year students were reminded that people who spoke out against the church spoke out against God "and put themselves out of the way of being saved."[79]

Fourth- and fifth-year students received sizable dollops of English history. Protestantism was described as the most disastrous of all the heresies that had ever affected the church and the Reformation as "the heaviest misfortune which had ever befallen our country."[80] Elizabeth I was condemned for destroying Catholicism "by a system of hanging and quartering" and for supporting Protestants throughout Europe in rebellions against their legitimate sovereigns. Her reign may have coincided with a period of temporal prosperity, but, the children were reminded, "the prosperity of the wicked is often the greatest curse God can inflict upon them. They are spared here because they are to be punished hereafter."[81] The school readers dealt with numerous other subjects as well; for example, they buttressed Victorian notions of self-help in economic affairs. The poor man ought to blame his own imprudence for his lot, and the rich man ought to be looked upon less as a consumer of worldly goods and more as a channel through which wealth flowed to others. It was best for all, in any event, if property remained secure and if each person did the best he could in the station to which God had assigned him. The virtues of a religious vocation were extolled, however, and all children were reminded most urgently that the Catholic church claimed the exclusive right to educate its children in that it alone possessed "the infallible rule alike of faith and of morals. Hence she alone can guide aright both our intellects and our wills."[82]

The man who in the later 1850s and 1860s came to symbolize most clearly and articulately all the forces tending to make English Roman Catholics a self-assertive and militant minority that firmly upheld the spiritual pretensions of Rome was Henry Edward Manning. The erstwhile Anglican archdeacon had become a Catholic convert in 1851 and a Catholic priest only ten weeks later. In 1857 he was appointed both provost of the cathedral chapter of the Westminster archdiocese and father superior of the Oblates of Saint Charles, an order of missionary priests that he had introduced into England. Two years later he took on as well the duty of serving as Cardinal Wiseman's "procurator" in Rome, his advocate within the Roman curia.[83] In contrast to the portly and sometimes lazy Wiseman, Manning was lean, ascetic, and indefatigable in speaking and organizing on behalf of his adopted faith. From the pope alone he was willing to receive correction; he would thereby provide an "example of docility in opinion at a time when we are in great danger of the contrary spirit, and in England we have neither censorship nor even counsel."[84] The pope, for Manning, was a divine teacher, "the pillar of supernatural illumination; the immovable centre of universal tradition." The pope and the church that he headed represented, for Manning, a rock of authority, of infallible teaching, within a sea of irreligion and indifference.[85]

Although he voiced private doubts about many of his new clerical associates, in his public sermons Manning waxed confident that the reconversion of England was at hand. "It is yours, Right Reverend Fathers," he told the provincial synod of Westminster in 1855, "to subjugate and to subdue, to bend and to break the will of an imperial race. . . . You have to call the legionaries and the tribunes, the patricians, and the people of a conquering race, and to subdue, change, transform, transfigure them." England still stood at the head of Protestantism, "the master-heresy of these latter days," but once weakened, once conquered in England, that heresy would be conquered everywhere. Restored to the true faith, England would become "the evangelist of the world."[86]

Manning's religious metaphors were ever those of conflict and of war. He felt certain that his was an era of momentous events during which "great conflicts are fighting." The reentry of the Catholic church into English life made necessary a new race of church teachers and administrators prepared not merely to be tolerated but also to undertake "the contact, and sometimes conflict with English society in all its classes."[87] The chief battle of the age, he wrote in 1863, was that between the Christian and the anti-Christian societies. England, by its willingness to acquiesce in, and indeed to encourage, the downfall of the pope's temporal (and therefore, by implication, his spiritual) power, had turned itself into "the most anti-Christian power in the world."[88] As a religion, Protestantism had long ceased to be meaningful; it had given way to indifferentism, incredulity, and revolution. In the ultimate analysis, all intermediate positions had been reduced to two: the Catholic and the anti-Catholic. "It is a simple question between Rome and rationalism, between the divine certainty of faith, and the instability of human opinion, between the presence of a Divine Teacher and the solitude and darkness of the human soul."[89]

Not surprisingly, Manning tended to regard as malcontents and even as disloyally schismatic all those English Catholics who disagreed with any aspect of Wiseman's propapal policies.[90] He was closely involved in the legal procedures whereby George Errington, Wiseman's episcopal coadjutant and presumptive successor, was removed from that position. He was equally unsympathetic toward the liberal English Catholicism embodied in Sir John Acton and Richard Simpson (in their successive journals *The Rambler* and the *Home and Foreign Review*) and in John Henry Newman's efforts to educate the laity. By 1864 both the liberal journals and Newman's hopes for a Roman Catholic college at Oxford were dead. Manning's *Westminster Gazette* compared the sending of Roman Catholic sons to Oxford to "an offering of innocent children to Moloch."[91] "For a holy Priesthood must command the world," Manning had declared in 1855, and he was inclined to sympathize with the attitude toward the laity privately voiced by his English confidant at the papal court, Msgr. George Talbot: "What is the province of the laity? To hunt, to shoot, to entertain. These matters they understand, but to meddle with ecclesiastical matters they have no right at all."[92]

When Cardinal Wiseman died in 1865, Palmerston privately asked the pope to ease anti-Catholic feeling in England by not appointing a successor.[93] Pope Pius IX paid no more heed to the advice of the British prime minister than he paid to the cathedral chapter of Westminster, which, fulfilling its duty to submit three nominations, chose Bishops Clifford, Errington, and Grant. On 30 April 1865, after a month of prayer and contemplation, the pope named Henry Edward Manning as the new archbishop of Westminster.[94]

5. Raising the Convent Issue

For Charles Newdigate Newdegate, the least happy aspect of the revival of Roman Catholicism in mid-Victorian England was his belief that the agents of the pope were tempting an increasing number of innocent English maidens to chain their souls to irrevocable vows of obedience and to immure their bodies within red-brick convent walls. A chivalric desire to play the role of protector to ladies in possible distress was not only a motive congenial to Newdegate's personality,[1] but also a vocation with strong family roots. His ancestral home, Arbury Hall, had originated as the medieval priory of Erdbury; the monastery had been suppressed, not under the auspices of Thomas Cromwell, but, as Newdegate liked to remind his fellow members of Parliament in a suitably ironic tone, with papal blessing under the auspices of Cardinal Wolsey because of the immorality and other abuses to be found within its walls. Christ Church College, Oxford, the institution that had conferred the bachelor of arts and master of arts degrees upon Newdegate, had been founded with the property of monasteries closed down by Wolsey under the aegis of the same papal authority.[2]

That Newdegate should focus upon the growth of convents as the most insidious manifestation of Roman Catholic expansion is not surprising when we recall that spokesmen for that faith proudly hailed "the incredible growth and multiplication of congregations of religious women" as "the most striking feature of the religious history of the nineteenth century."[3] Ever since 1851 the specter of Protestant maidens being hidden away behind Roman Catholic convent walls had haunted Newdegate's mind. A quarter of a century later he proudly recalled having in that year saved a lady from a nunnery, and even if the lady in question was a mere student in a convent-connected boarding school, there is no need to quarrel with Newdegate's insistence that the "occurrence produced a deep impression on my mind."[4] In the early 1850s, as a by-product of the widespread excitement over "papal aggression," there had been several parliamentary attempts to check into, if not to check altogether, the establishment of Roman convents. The latter was the purpose of the anonymous pamphleteer who proclaimed in 1852 that inspection was not enough and asked that candidates for the House of Commons be required instead "to demand the *suppression* of these dens of infamy."[5]

An interested member of Parliament, Henry Charles Lacy,

would have been satisfied to begin a system of inspection akin to
that instituted a few years earlier for lunatic asylums, but the
same House of Commons that had passed the Ecclesiastical
Titles Act in 1851 declined to approve Lacy's measure. Dr.
Thomas Chambers's attempt in 1853 to institute a system of
convent inspection won one test vote but was ultimately defeated, as were separate attempts in 1853 and 1854 to establish a
parliamentary select committee to consider whether the inmates
of such institutions and their property required additional legislative protection.[6] During those years, John Henry Newman
was accused of constructing dungeons beneath the oratory that
he was building in Birmingham, and one Pierce Connally
sought, and failed, to regain by legal action the conjugal rights
that his wife denied him by becoming a nun.[7] A convent in
Norwood was accused of cruelty by a member it had expelled,
and the nuns were forced to pay £450 in court costs.[8] With the
coming of the Crimean War, however, the excitement subsided.
Lord Aberdeen's government sought national unity in support
of a war being fought with a Roman Catholic ally (the France of
Napoleon III), and, by taking with her to the Crimea ten Roman
Catholic nuns and fourteen members of an Anglican sisterhood,
Florence Nightingale accented the positive side of the convent
movement.[9] At the parliamentary level, the issue lay dormant
for almost a decade.

Newdegate's attention was drawn anew to the subject of
monasteries and convents in 1863 when a man named William
Hutchison died and left his estate of five thousand pounds to
the Roman Catholic oratory at Brompton (in London) rather
than to his sister and her husband, Alfred Smee, a medical
examiner for the Bank of England. Hutchison's testamentary
inclinations are less than surprising once one learns that he had
become a convert to Roman Catholicism at Oxford in the 1840s
and that, as Brother Anthony, he had followed Father Frederick
Faber into the Order of Saint Philip Neri, which Newman had
introduced to England. During the 1850s Hutchison had fought
all attempts by non-Catholics to educate Roman Catholic children lest "they secure their damnation,"[10] and he remained a
faithful member of his adopted church until his death. Smee
questioned, however, not only the manner of his brother-in-
law's life but also the propriety of his burial. He charged the
oratory with having obtained a cemetery license for its order in
an underhanded manner and with burying his brother-in-law as
"William Anthony Hutchison" even though "Anthony" was
not part of his baptismal name. Smee's concern with what

impressed him as nefarious Roman Catholic scheming reached its apex on 7 April 1864, when he wrote an open letter to the duchess of Norfolk warning her of the likely fate in store for her daughter in a Paris convent.

Although Newdegate deprecated the tone of that letter, he felt great sympathy for Smee's plight in all other respects. Not only did he institute inquiries on Smee's behalf at the Home Office, but he also asked the House of Commons on 8 April 1864 to create a select committee to look into the law of burials and, in the process, to investigate "the existence, increase, and nature" of monasteries and convents in England and Scotland. It seemed clear that the religious discipline to which Hutchison had been exposed had undermined his health and that the religious excitement to which he had been subjected had affected his intellect. Indeed, had he not written his will in favor of his religious superior under a vow of obedience made to that same superior and witnessed only by fellow monks? The whole question of the legal status of monasteries deserved examination, declared Newdegate, and in the process an inquiry into the status of convents appeared equally appropriate. An Italian investigation had indicated that "the dowry on the average was so large, and the lives of the nuns so short, that a very handsome profit was left from year to year to these Communities." A similar situation might well prevail in England, and "our feeling is, that a person who is consigned to one of these establishments is a dead loss to his family; is a dead loss to his country; is a dead loss to himself."[11]

Newdegate's appeal received a mixed response in the Commons. Sir George Grey, the home secretary, observed that however unfortunate it might be for upright young Englishmen to be converted to Catholicism, the answer lay rather in an education better adapted to enabling them "to resist such influence" than in parliamentary committees. As for the oratory cemetery, it met all the health regulations of the applicable Burials Act. Lord Edward Howard stoutly defended the honor of his family (that of the dukes of Norfolk) against Smee's various charges and cautioned Newdegate not to become involved with so dubious an advocate. The Catholic member of the ministry, Thomas O'Hagan, the attorney general for Ireland, suggested pointedly that the mere fact that Hutchison had in the course of his life (and in his will) contributed his estate of thirty thousand pounds to a variety of religious charities did not, as such, demonstrate a loss of mental faculties. Equally significant was the fact he had made his will three full years before his death. Inasmuch as Smee had already challenged the will in the Court of Probate and inasmuch as the case was currently *sub judice*, O'Hagan deemed it "monstrous" to debate its legality in the House of Commons. After a short debate, Newdegate's motion was defeated by a vote of 113 to 80.[12] When one considers that the leading members of the government—Palmerston, Gladstone, and Grey—voted against the motion, and that they were joined by the leader of the opposition, Benjamin Disraeli, the surprise and, in the view of *The Times*, the shame of the outcome lay not in the fact, but in the narrowness, of Newdegate's defeat. He was supported by twenty-nine Liberals as well as by fifty-one Conservatives; ninety-five Liberals and eighteen Conservatives voted against his resolution.

In the course of the winter of 1864–1865, Newdegate found occasion to refresh his memory about the Colwich Nunnery case of December 1856. At that time, as the depositions in his files testified, a thirty-seven-year-old nun, afterward identified as Catherine Selby, had left her convent, Saint Benedict's Priory near Colwich, by climbing a tree and vaulting a nine-foot wall. (The tree was later trimmed, presumably to make such "escapes" more difficult.) Wretchedly clad and in a state of great agitation and confusion, Selby had rushed to the local railway station and had purchased a second-class ticket for Stafford. According to another witness, she had left the train at Stafford displaying "an air of timidity." Without purchasing an additional ticket, she had apparently boarded a train for Birmingham.

That evening, according to a telegraph operator who was afterward dismissed from his position for illegally disclosing the contents of messages, Bishop William Ullathorne of Birmingham sent a wire to the priory: "I will arrive with Miss Selby about half past nine tonight." According to a Stafford omnibus driver, Ullathorne was indeed seen arriving by train from Birmingham and hiring a carriage at the Swan Hotel in which to transport "a female covered with a thick veil" to the convent.

Nor were these the only mysterious goings-on at Saint Benedict's, which had been founded in 1830 and which, according to the census of 1851, was occupied by thirty-three English nuns and one Irish priest, as well as by eleven female and two male servants. A local carpenter recalled having helped to build "underground apartments only dimly lighted," and, more sensationally, one Caroline Bond, who had studied at the convent school between 1849 and 1852, had confided to a local Protestant minister all manner of ominous activities there. One nun was placed on a bread-and-water diet for three days as punishment for a minor offense: "When they went to look for her, I was told, she was found dead." Other nuns had frequently cried and expressed the wish that they were home again. Another prayed that she might die. Several had entrusted letters to Caroline to be mailed secretly. Another was found crying from morning to night, and yet another had been locked in "a sort of cage" because she had failed to attend confession. Caroline Bond was now "an intelligent young woman." What a pity that she had been only fourteen when last inside the convent. What a pity that none of her fellow scholars seemed willing to give confirmatory evidence; "they seem to be entirely submissive and completely under the control and influence of the priests." The fact that the young woman had "since been seduced by a servant of the Earl of Lichfield" did not altogether argue in her favor either, but, as one deponent phrased it, "Who can entertain a doubt from what source her mind was first contaminated?"[13]

The questions raised by Alfred Smee and the suspicions aroused by Newdegate's review of the Colwich Nunnery case motivated the Warwickshire squire to reopen the question in 1865 and in the process to involve himself in a public squabble with England's leading Roman Catholics, both lay and clerical. On 3 March 1865, he introduced into the House of Commons a motion asking that a select committee be appointed "to inquire into the existence, character, and increase of Monastic or Conventual Establishments, or societies, in Great Britain." The Catholic Emancipation Act of 1829 had specifically outlawed male religious orders in England, and yet it was "notorious to everyone that of late years there has been a most enormous, and, I may say, unprecedented increase in those monastic and conventual establishments in this country." Since 1841 alone, religious houses for men had increased from 1 to 58, houses for women from 16 to 187.

In support of his motion, Newdegate cited contemporary Continental regulatory practices and medieval English precedents. Henry Hallam, the constitutional historian, had long since proved that medieval monastic orders had either served as refuges for licentiousness or, in the case of those whose members abided by their vows, had withdrawn "men of pure conduct and conscientious principles from the exercise of social duties," thus leaving "the common mass of human vice more unmixed." Monastic wealth and property had been put to better use from the time of the Reformation onward, and Newdegate found deeply disturbing the thought that comparable institutions were once again growing in power and wealth.

Newdegate went on to cite several examples of the harm

that such institutions had inflicted. There was the son of an Anglican clergyman who had been "seduced" into the Oratorian order as a minor and who, to the deep distress of his parents and "to the detriment of his prospects in life," had subsequently been persuaded to become a monk.[14] Even more outrageous was the case of Mary Ryan, an English nun who had been transferred against her will to a Belgian lunatic asylum. Such deeds by "an organisation with a foreign connection which can defy the law and set an example of lawlessness" were likely to infuriate patriotic Englishmen.[15] More harrowing still was the, to Newdegate, infamous Colwich Nunnery case, which the Warwickshire M.P. recounted to the House of Commons in detail: the underground cells, the desperate flight over the convent wall, the intervention of Ullathorne, the investigation sponsored by Newdegate and the Protestant Alliance. Newdegate conceded that, once the nun had been tracked down in another convent, she preferred to remain there. Yet, he felt sure that there was reason enough for the House of Commons to take action to protect "those who, in too many cases, are, I fear, helpless women."[16] His motion, Newdegate repeatedly assured the house, was in no sense motivated by bigotry. Nor did he act "for the mere purpose of agitation, far less for purposes of party triumph, but with an honest intention of effecting an improvement in the law and performing my duty as an independent Member."[17]

Newdegate had won the enthusiastic support of George H. Whalley, Liberal M.P. for Peterborough since 1859 and, under the pseudonym of Patrick Murphy, the author of *Popery in Ireland; or, Confessionals, Abductions, Nunneries, Fenians and Orangemen: A Narrative of Facts.*[18] The Warwickshire squire had been plotting parliamentary strategy with Whalley for several weeks. The debate that ensued was lively if not particularly fruitful. John Pope Hennessy, one of thirty-two Roman Catholic M.P.s (thirty-one from Ireland, one from England), put his finger on the key flaw in the case that Newdegate had set forth: he had proposed no remedy. The law as it stood provided ample relief for any case of illegal imprisonment. The number of convents could be determined by simple reference to the annual *Catholic Directory*. Their character could be ascertained from any person acquainted with them, and Vincent Scully, one of Hennessy's Roman Catholic colleagues, immediately offered to escort Newdegate to the convent that his sister headed or to any other. Hennessy deplored the reopening of an agitation that he associated with the early 1850s. Since then, nuns had bravely served in the Crimean War, and convent schools had been

George H. Whalley, M.P., Newdegate's Liberal ally (from a scrapbook in the University of Illinois Library).

inspected and approved by the appropriate government authorities. Newdegate's sole purpose, Hennessy concluded, was to arouse popular indignation "against those ladies who passed their lives in educating the poor, attending the sick, and performing acts of charity, who had never done the hon. Gentleman or anybody else the slightest injury."[19]

Newdegate again failed to receive any support from his own party leader, Benjamin Disraeli, who was busily wooing the Catholic vote that had been alienated from the Palmerston government by its staunch pro-Italian (and, by implication, anti-Papal State) policy.[20] Grey, the home secretary, threw the government's weight against the 1865 motion as he had thrown it against the 1864 motion. He was aware of the widespread belief among members of the Protestant Alliance that many convent members were shut up against their will, yet there was no evidence to support such a charge. If Newdegate had any evidence, let him seek a writ of habeas corpus from the appropriate magistrate. If immoral convent practices existed, Grey felt sure that they would meet with universal censure. The true evil, Grey was equally certain, arose not from physical restraint, "but from that moral restraint, from that obligation which is felt to bind the consciences of those ladies" so that even if they took vows willingly, they could not subsequently, upon repentance, revoke them. But it was chimerical to expect any of them to confess such misgivings to a visiting parliamentary committee. Previous committee proposals had come to nothing, and Newdegate had failed to provide a specific legislative proposal. "We do not appoint committees merely to gratify curiosity."[21] The house defeated Newdegate's proposal by a vote of 106 to 79. Newdegate won the support (including tellers)[22] of forty-four Conservatives and thirty-seven Liberals; sixteen Conservatives and ninety-two Liberals opposed him.

The episode evoked an immediate confession by Newman, in a letter to *The Times*, that the buildings of his Birmingham oratory included "more or less" secret underground vaults that, he added, were used as wine bins, larders, and storage cellars. He cordially invited Newdegate to inspect them.[23] A more insistent critic was the head of the Birmingham diocese, Bishop Ullathorne, among Roman Catholic clerics in England second only to Nicholas Wiseman (and, after Wiseman's death, to Manning) in prestige. Ullathorne solemnly but firmly denied every statement that Newdegate had made about the convents in his diocese. Bars had been installed in convent windows to keep burglars out rather than to keep nuns in. The clanking chains reported by Newdegate's schoolgirl informant were the large rosaries that nuns wore at their sides. Ullathorne concluded with a "straight-forward appeal" to Newdegate's honor as "an English gentleman, as a man of good descent, a magistrate, and a neighbor of the ladies in question." Let Newdegate, accompanied by Protestant noblemen of the locality and by Lord Edward Howard (the sole Roman Catholic representing an English constituency in the House of Commons), "go over the whole of the establishments as much as you like, and converse with the

members of the communities as much as you desire." Although
Ullathorne did not believe in the right of Parliament to inspect
convents, he would make an exception in this instance, subject
only to the understanding that if the Protestant noblemen were
persuaded that no grounds existed for Newdegate's assertions,
the Warwickshire M.P. would make a public apology.[24]

"No, Reverend Sir," was Newdegate's reply, "I will be no
party to any such extra-judicial inquiry as you propose. Your
letter, though bearing the semblance of fairness, is artistically
written." Newdegate had no lack of evidence to bring before the
proper parliamentary committee, and he would patiently await
its establishment. "History and the current events of the time
warn that unless the civil power has free and ready scope within
these convents, they ought not to be permitted to exist, though
some—perhaps many—if you will, most of them—are well conducted." But what of the nun who had tried to escape from
Colwich and others like her? If such ladies remained without
"legitimate means of defence and reparation," the fault lay with
those who had opposed the creation of a parliamentary
committee.[25]

Ullathorne responded with an expression of surprise. For
eight years Newdegate's private investigators had been seeking
scandalous tales about what went on behind convent walls.
Why should Newdegate now deny himself the opportunity of
being taken behind those very walls? The bishop then went on
to answer Newdegate's other charges. The notorious "escaped
nun" was a somewhat emotional lady who had asked permission to be transferred to a stricter religious order and who had
been advised by her superior to remain where she was. She had
then, without permission, come to see her bishop. Ullathorne
had returned to the convent with her, and a proper transfer had
subsequently been arranged. Newdegate's own investigators
had conceded that she was satisfied with her new convent.[26] As
for the story told by the schoolgirl who had once attended the
Colwich convent school, that was no more than a rehash of the
Tale of Maria Monk, that American best-seller of the 1830s, whose
fanciful compilation of the immoral goings-on in a Canadian
convent had long since been exposed as pure fiction by a group
of Protestant magistrates.[27]

> Let me now put the case [Ullathorne continued] as you actually
> maintain it, and I will then leave it to the common sense of the
> public. Here are some 40 English ladies, of good or noble families,
> varying in age from 70 to 21; and here is an association of men of
> fortune and others pushing the spy system and every other en-

William Bernard Ullathorne, the Roman Catholic bishop of Birmingham (courtesy of the Newberry Library, Chicago).

gine of private inquisition that money and ingenuity can command against these ladies and their residence for the space of eight years, taking plans of the ground, questioning servants and neighbors, and watching their every movement, even to the carpenter's work that goes in and out of the house; and what is the result? A poor girl is got to repeat a tale only recalling old exploded fables? Would these shrewd ladies really bring a girl from the poor-school into the interior of their convent, where by the rules of the house no such person can ever enter, and there let her witness the process of starving nuns, thrusting them into cellars, and leaving them there to die?

Despite Newdegate's faith in this wondrous legend and the twenty-eight witnesses he supposedly had ready to support it, he had failed to secure enough evidence to justify even a search warrant. "And at the same time," Ullathorne concluded, "you refuse the free offer of inquiry without the necessity of a warrant."[28]

In a new letter, Newdegate categorically denied that he was

attacking ladies of any description. If a private inquiry of any type were desirable, would not an inquiry by a public authority be even better? Newdegate's inspection of the Colwich convent as Ullathorne's guest would implicitly sanction the bishop's "assumed authority" over its inmates. Newdegate declared himself fully satisfied with the evidence that he had relating to the "underground apartments at Colwich in 1857" and with the corroborating testimony he possessed for the schoolgirl's story. As for the "escaped nun," did not her silence, when told of these alleged evils, signify assent? Newdegate described himself as fully cognizant of the wealth and the power of the religious organization against whose pretensions he had taken a stand. Ullathorne might think that by maintaining secrecy he was being faithful to the pope, but Newdegate felt certain that England would not long remain the sole major power to lack effective legal control over "the kind of authority, that you assume to exercise over English women."[29]

When the London *Standard* of 14 March 1865 printed, presumably with Newdegate's cooperation, some of the evidence in his Colwich Nunnery file, a new Roman Catholic champion entered the fray in the person of the aging Charles Langdale (1787–1868), a pioneer Roman Catholic M.P. in the 1830s and since then the recognized leader of the Catholic laity in England.[30] For the previous twenty years, he observed, his sister had been a nun at Colwich. She must therefore have been either cognizant of or victimized by the atrocities to which Newdegate had alluded; "I hardly know which alternative is the more painful." If Newdegate truly had witnesses to support his stories, ought he not to speak without the cloak of parliamentary immunity so that the targets of his accusations might test the truth of his case in the law courts?

Newdegate immediately responded that he was only too anxious to place all the affidavits in his possession before a parliamentary committee. If Langdale felt aggrieved that this evidence could not be tested, then the fault lay with those M.P.s, including a number of Roman Catholics, who had failed to approve the inquiry he sought. Newdegate could not consent to having the matter investigated elsewhere, but, if his motion had influenced Roman Catholic gentlemen to devote more attention to the state of English convents, "it will in my opinion, have been productive of at least one beneficial result."[31]

Langdale was not so easily put off. "You, a gentleman and a magistrate for two counties," he told Newdegate, "charge a community of ladies living in your district with practices not merely wicked but felonious. You say you can support this charge by twenty-seven witnesses. You are asked to come into court and have the case fully investigated, and you decline to do so." Langdale had taken the trouble to investigate the charges of the Protestant schoolgirl whom the nuns out of kindness had allowed to attend their day school and had found them to be "a tissue of falsehoods."

Unwilling to leave well enough alone, Newdegate insisted in a new letter that his evidence, admittedly now eight years old, was to have been admitted to the Court of the Queen's Bench to be tested on cross-examination. Only the fact that the nun on behalf of whose liberation that evidence had been gathered declined to leave her new convent prevented that evidence from being heard in court. Newdegate had felt compelled by a sense of courtesy to reply to Ullathorne, who claimed jurisdiction at Colwich, and to Langdale, whose sister resided there, but it was his intention "no further [to] waive the privilege which guards freedom of debate in the House of Commons."[32]

Such epistolary pugilistics continued for one round more, however, with the intervention of Sir Charles Clifford, another leading Catholic layman. Sir Charles's sister, now mother superior at Atherstone, had also been a nun at Colwich, and he assured Newdegate that the latter had been grossly deceived by his informants. Now that the matter had been corrected, Newdegate owed his sister and her fellow convent members an apology for the slurs and innuendos that he had scattered upon them. When Newdegate refused, Clifford accused him of compounding the felony. In the words of the Roman Catholic priest with whom Newdegate came into collision later in 1865, if Newdegate was going to charge Catholics with calumnies, he must expect Catholics "both to think and speak of you with profound indignation."[33]

Apparently convinced that Newdegate had emerged triumphant in his encounters with his papist antagonists, the Scottish Reformation Society—the publisher, since 1851, of the monthly *Bulwark: or Reformation Journal* and Newdegate's most devoted supporter—reprinted his parliamentary speech and the ensuing correspondence and circulated the resultant pamphlet throughout the British Isles and overseas.[34] Since Parliament had proved heedless, there seemed all the more reason to alert the kingdom and the empire.

6. Defending the Ramparts

Although the more charitable of his critics—Liberal and Conservative alike—might visualize Newdegate as a misguided knight-errant charging (for the moment, vainly) against convent walls, Newdegate saw his own role not as an attacker but as a defender. And it is significant though usually forgotten that the strongest examples of anti-Catholic rhetoric to be uttered in the palace of Westminster during the 1860s were almost always evoked by a legal proposal or an administrative action designed to give a greater degree of religious equality to Roman Catholics. In 1858 it was the decision, inspired personally by Queen Victoria, to end the official Church of England service each 5 November celebrating both the foiling of the Gunpowder Plot in 1605 and the safe arrival on English shores of William III in 1688.[1] In 1863 it was the parliamentary decision to permit local magistrates to appoint paid Roman Catholic prison chaplains as they had long appointed paid Anglican chaplains. In 1864 the Middlesex magistrates, of whom Newdegate was one, voted overwhelmingly not to avail themselves of this right. If any prisoner specifically requested a visit by a Roman Catholic priest, they observed, then such a priest would be permitted to enter the jail at his own expense; they could see no reason, however, to afford additional privileges to Roman Catholics. *The Times*, lamenting that hundreds of Roman Catholic prisoners were thus being deprived of any moral guidance, went on to wonder "what horrible schemes, what new GUY FAWKES plots for the blowing up of the QUEEN, the Archbishop of CANTERBURY, and Mr. NEWDEGATE, might not be hatched if two such persons as Father NEWMAN and an Irish convict got together in a prison cell?"[2]

A major theme in many popular religious novels of the era was the Church of England clergyman who either resists the temptations of Rome or vigorously denounces its sins.[3] James Anthony Froude, the author of a multivolume history of Tudor England, was strongly commended for the manner in which he could show sympathy to Thomas More and Bishop Fisher as individuals while at the same time "he proves clearly their delusions, and the lamentable consequence to England, had their opinions prevailed."[4] When the bishops of the Anglican communion from all over the world assembled in the first Lambeth Conference in 1867, they concluded that one of their prime tasks was to warn their parishioners "to guard yourselves and yours against the growing superstitions and additions with which in these latter days the truth of God hath been overlaid; . . . especially by the pretension to universal sovereignty over God's heritage asserted for the See of Rome; and by the practical exaltation of the blessed Virgin Mary as mediator in the place of her Divine Son, and by the addressing of prayers to her as intercessor between God and man. Of such beware, we beseech you, knowing that the jealous God giveth not His honour to another."[5]

That in the face of such warnings misguided M.P.s should be perpetually at work chipping away at the oaths and legal safeguards that, in Newdegate's eyes, had long protected England's Protestant Constitution caused the Warwickshire M.P. to see himself not as a crazed knight assaulting imaginary dragons but as the defender of an ancient fortress beset by attackers from without and undermined by foolhardy idealists from within. "Any person who has ever read history," Newdegate had declared in 1858, "will agree with me when I say, that from the Revolution of 1688 is dated the commencement of that era of temperate freedom, under which England has advanced to the high position she now holds among the nations of the earth." A decade later Newdegate lamented the manner in which "step by step the House was being persuaded to disregard the restrictions which, at the time of the Revolution of 1688 and subsequently, were found necessary to guard the freedom of the country against the despotism of Rome." The trouble with too many of his fellow members, Newdegate warned, was that they treated history "like an old almanack, and assumed that our ancestors were not persons of common sense." If legal safeguards were necessary in the age of James II, why had they become superfluous in the 1860s?[6]

One such safeguard was the special parliamentary oath that Roman Catholic M.P.s, and no others, had been compelled to take since their "emancipation" in 1829; in this oath, they specifically repudiated the doctrine that the pope had any kind of temporal jurisdiction over English affairs. To abolish this oath and to break "the compact of 1829" when the pope was attacking all of modern civilization in his "Syllabus of Errors" and when a belief in his temporal authority remained widespread throughout Europe impressed Newdegate therefore as sheer folly. With so many old restrictions on Roman Catholics discarded, the oath remained "the only valid security still existing for the Constitution of this country." It also served to protect English Roman Catholics themselves, Newdegate observed, from the more repressive members of their faith. Those Protestant Dissenters who supported repeal of the oath were making the same mistake that their predecessors had made when they had hailed King James II as a religious liberator in 1687 only to feel compelled to support his deposition as a tyrant in 1688. Conservative efforts to amend the measure were narrowly defeated in the House of Commons (166 to 147), but the House of Lords came to the rescue and vetoed the bill.[7] The parliamentary session of 1865, the last before a new general election, thus provided Newdegate with a few crumbs of comfort to alleviate a nagging sense of frustration with the blindness of so many of his countrymen.

In North Warwickshire, the election of 1865 evoked more excitement than had those of 1857 and 1859. Newdegate stood for reelection once more, but his running mate was no longer Richard Spooner, who had died the year before, but William Davenport Bromley, the son of an Anglican clergyman, first elected to Parliament at a by-election in December 1864. Earlier that year Newdegate had diplomatically fended off a claim by a son of Sir Robert Peel to the second North Warwickshire seat.[8] Although Bromley preferred to label himself a "Liberal–Conservative," Newdegate found him a highly congenial colleague in other respects. He was, after all, "a supporter of Lord Derby" who at the same time would "offer no factious opposition to Lord Palmerston." He was also a convinced opponent of the "unconditional abolition of Church-rates" and a fellow graduate of Christ Church, Oxford, to boot.[9]

Although in 1865 the local Liberals conceded the first seat to Newdegate, they did have hopes of winning the second in the person of George Frederick Muntz, a Nonconformist Birmingham merchant whose father had served as M.P. for Birmingham from 1840 to 1857 and whose uncle had served for two years as mayor of Birmingham.[10] Enough Birmingham Liberals were on hand on nomination day to cause Newdegate's and Bromley's names to be received "amidst groans and hisses." Newdegate addressed the crowd in an accommodating spirit. It was true that he was a Conservative, he told them, but he was also a friend of the poor. He had pushed for the Ten-Hour Act in 1847, and he had been pleased to see the provisions of that act extended to lace factories and potteries. Nor was he oblivious to the fact that Liberals as well as Conservatives could be found in Warwickshire. Therefore, he had frequently supported Lord Palmerston during the previous Parliament. "I approved the foreign policy of Lord Palmerston which helped the Italians gain their freedom from Papal tyranny." He had discouraged Palm-erston from intervening in the American Civil War or the Polish insurrection, but he had supported the Liberal chieftain's stand on behalf of Denmark: "Alas both parties ran away. I won't run away lads."[11]

There was nothing in his record, Newdegate insisted, that should cause Liberals to feel ashamed that he was their repre-sentative. "I am no bigot, but I value the constitution of this country," and he much preferred it to that of France, which had supplanted a republic with a despotism, and to that of the United States, which, with its universal suffrage, had just sacri-ficed six hundred thousand men in fratricidal struggle. "I will resist all attempts at foreign interference in this country." Why was he resisting the Roman Catholics in the House of Com-mons? "Because their priesthood has attempted to bring a for-eign jurisdiction into England, and we will have no foreign power here."[12]

Amid great commotion, a poll was demanded and set for a week hence. In the meantime, Newdegate made appearances in several communities in the county. A meeting at Rugby was disturbed by loud heckling, and as Newdegate strode from the town hall to the George Hotel, a man wearing a cassock emerged from the crowd to denounce Newdegate for having told "a lie" about the Colwich Nunnery. He turned out to be the Reverend Joseph Akroyd, a Roman Catholic priest. A day later Akroyd sent Newdegate a letter in which he apologized for having been personally offensive but went on to add: "At the same time I may be allowed to say, that on all subjects relating to the Catholic religion, and which appear to have for you a pecu-liar attraction, and which are spoken of and brought forward by you in language and manner most strongly calculated to rouse the passions of the calumniated and their friends, you must expect Catholics both to think and speak of you with profound indignation."[13]

Newdegate in turn formally accepted Akroyd's apology, adding, "You must, however, excuse my remarking that the expressions you used in addressing me on the 18th, in the midst of an excited crowd, were not calculated to preserve the peace of the town of Rugby." In a second letter, Akroyd conceded that Newdegate would not publicly make a statement he believed to be untrue. "Your character as a gentleman in this county stands sufficiently high to forbid such a supposition." The assertions of the Birmingham *Gazette* notwithstanding, Akroyd denied that he or any other local Roman Catholics had sought to break up

the Rugby meeting; he had merely sought to challenge Newdegate to produce evidence or witnesses in support of his statements about the Colwich convent. The exchange of correspondence ended with Newdegate's refusal: although he had himself
been subjected to "systematic annoyance," he had no desire to
subject witnesses "unprotected by the Privileges of Parliament"
to the same annoyance.[14]

The electoral poll on 24 July provided a clear-cut outcome:
Newdegate, 3,159; Bromley, 2,873; and Muntz, 2,408. Newdegate congratulated the electors on the triumph of the good old
cause, "the cause of English freedom," "freedom" being "the
old Saxon expression to signify the people's rights." He might
no longer have the energy, but he possessed still the determination, of youth and he would continue to serve them as an
independent but true Conservative and Pittite.[15]

Newdegate was not the only parliamentary candidate in
1865 who stood on a program hostile to Catholicism. Charles B.
Addersley, the M.P. who had placed Newdegate's name in
nomination at Coleshill back in 1843, was also "opposed to all
concessions to the Roman Catholics." William Hodgson Bar-
row, M.P. for Nottingham, was equally "opposed to concessions to the Roman Catholic Church." Sir John Somerset (Mon-
mouthshire) was prepared to "uphold with a firm hand the
Protestant Church," and Joseph Warner Henley (Oxfordshire)
promised to "uphold and defend our reformed Protestant institutions in Church and State from all attacks, either at home or
abroad."[16] In contrast, Jonathan Pim, a Dublin Liberal, pledged
himself to oppose the inspection of nunneries, and Charles
Howard, a Liberal who represented Cumberland, declared himself "willing to endow the Roman Catholic Church."[17] The convent issue impinged even upon the campaign being waged by
John Stuart Mill at Westminster. "Will Mr. Mill support through
thick and thin the inspection of convents?" asked one elector.
Mill's reply is unfortunately not recorded.[18]

The Roman Catholic hierarchy found it difficult to give its
allegiance to either of the major political parties. The traditional
tendency to adhere to the Whigs had been broken by the "papal
aggression" crisis of 1850–1851, and during the later 1850s the
church had flirted with the Conservatives. During the early
1860s, indeed, Disraeli had diplomatically wooed the Catholic
vote, but a campaign speech by Lord Derby in which the Conservative party leader compared Roman Catholics to dogs that
required muzzling all but destroyed Disraeli's efforts; Roman
Catholic opinion drifted toward the Liberals once more.[19] "Free

trade and the hostility to Rome are the two ruling political feelings at the moment," Manning had written privately in 1861, and the choice lay between Palmerston and opposition to the temporal power of the pope, on the one hand, and Derby, Orangeism, and antipopery at home, on the other. "I dislike both and trust neither."[20]

Ultimately, it was not so much the religious crosscurrents nor the issue of political reform at home or military intervention abroad that determined the outcome of the election of 1865. Rather was it the question of whether the electorate wanted the continuation of the benign government of Lord Palmerston. The outcome: 367 Liberals, 290 Conservatives. When one considers that many a Conservative, like Newdegate, felt at least as much affection for Palmerston as he did for Disraeli, the Palmerstonian triumph was even greater than the story told by the statistics.

By the time the new Parliament assembled, however, the octogenarian prime minister was dead, and his successors, Earl Russell (as prime minister and as Liberal leader of the House of Lords) and William Ewart Gladstone (as leader of the House of Commons), held less appeal for Conservatives. A sharpening of party rivalry was underway, and Newdegate soon found it necessary to mount the parliamentary battlements anew in his campaign against concessions to Roman Catholics. Sir George Grey, the home secretary, decided to meet in a different manner the problem posed by the refusal of the House of Lords during the previous session to approve an amended oath for Roman Catholics. The separate oaths previously prescribed for Protestants, Catholics, and Jews were all to be supplanted by a simple and uniform oath of loyalty: "I, A. B., do swear that I will be faithful to Her Majesty Queen Victoria, her heirs and successors according to law, so help me God."

Newdegate resisted the bill every step of the way. As he saw the matter, no longer was the crown to be specifically recognized as Protestant in the oath. No longer were M.P.s publicly to declare their religion. No longer were Roman Catholics to be obliged to acknowledge limits to papal power. "We live in a constitutional monarchy," Newdegate observed, "in which the political power of the Crown has been almost entirely transferred to the representatives of the Crown in Parliament. The power of the Crown is not destroyed, it is only transferred." The implication of Grey's proposal was that the prerogative of the crown, still avowedly Protestant, would be transferred to a body not distinctively Protestant. Most members, lamented Newdegate, "scarcely appreciate the gravity of this change."[21]

Newdegate received only limited sympathy from his parliamentary leader. Disraeli agreed that oaths did not constitute a practical grievance and that it was unwise to disturb them. "You cannot act on mere theoretical principles in a complex society, and in an ancient country famous for its history like England."[22] Hoping to amend the bill in committee, Disraeli and most Conservatives acquiesced in giving the bill a second reading. The government dismissed Newdegate's arguments by observing that the religion of the crown was determined by the Act of Settlement of 1701 and not by the parliamentary oath.[23] It defeated Disraeli's amendment in committee. In April 1866, to Newdegate's distress, Grey's measure became law.

The concerns of the Warwickshire M.P. extended not only to the expansion of the pope's spiritual and material claims upon his English followers but also to the possibility of his physical presence. In March 1865 Newdegate had asked Palmerston whether there was any basis to the rumors that the political situation in Italy would cause the pope to move to England. The then prime minister replied guardedly that he could not anticipate all contingencies, but that, if forced to flee Rome, the pope would be welcome on the island of Malta. Any move to England, Palmerston agreed, would raise numerous objections and would, at the very least, constitute "a political anachronism."[24]

Though the pope remained far away, Henry Edward Manning, the new archbishop of Westminster, was very much part of the English scene. Newdegate lost few opportunities to call attention to the Roman Catholic leader's more extravagant pronouncements. He was especially rankled by a sermon of 1855, recently reprinted, in which the convert had called on his priestly colleagues "to subjugate and to subdue, to bend and to break the will of an imperial race." Nor was Newdegate any happier with Manning's sermon in praise of Thomas Becket, the very man who had "lost his life in consequence of his rebelling against the constitution of Clarendon . . . passed 700 years ago by our Roman Catholic ancestors, to guard the freedom and independence of this country against the intrusion of a foreign jurisdiction—that of the Papacy." Equally unsettling was Manning's campaign of parliamentary lobbying to ensure that Catholic children in workhouses would be brought up as Catholics and that all Catholic inmates had the opportunity to attend mass and to be visited by priests. Manning proved anew to Newdegate that recent converts to the Roman faith were "of all her sons the most zealous and the most extravagant in the opinions they profess."[25]

The absorption of the 1866 and 1867 sessions of the House of Commons with political reform deprived Newdegate of the opportunity to revive his agitation in favor of an investigation of convents, and he had to content himself with valiant and sometimes successful rearguard actions against what he considered still further examples of papal aggression, for were not the Roman Catholic members of Parliament "representatives of a foreign power?"[26] Newdegate was unable to stop the passage of a measure that dispensed with the offensively anti-Catholic oaths that the Protestant lords lieutenant and lords chancellor of Ireland were still required to take on assuming office. Newdegate was willing to make the oaths less odious, but he saw no harm in retaining denunciations of specific Roman Catholic doctrines such as purgatory. Sir John Gray, an Irish M.P., responded that there was an old saying in Ireland that applied readily to Newdegate: "if he did not like purgatory, he might go further and fare worse."[27]

Newdegate had greater success in halting a private member's proposal, Sir Colman O'Loghlen's Offices and Oaths Bill. It was designed to rid the statute book of yet other outmoded oaths and to make Roman Catholics eligible to hold the posts of lord lieutenant and lord chancellor of Ireland. In introducing the measure, O'Loghlen observed that, although a similar bill had won Palmerston's approval in 1859, Newdegate had successfully blocked it. Newdegate acknowledged that in such matters "too much has been left to me." O'Loghlen seemed to imagine "that the liberality of the House ought to have no bounds, for year after year these demands were increased." He would feel less fearful of the papacy and its agents had it not inspired revolution in Switzerland in 1847, in Poland in 1863, and yet more recently in Ireland. Even in the United States, "the great Republic we are so often called to admire," the pope had played a subversive role. Had not Mrs. Jefferson Davis, the wife of the president of the defeated Confederacy, described the pope as "the only Prince in the world that really wished well to our cause and sent us his blessing"? Additional concessions to Roman Catholicism would merely "encourage a deep and wide-spread conspiracy."[28] Partly because it attempted to deal in one measure with a number of disparate issues, the bill failed to receive a third reading.

Newdegate also found satisfaction in helping to prevent the passage of a bill to repeal the Ecclesiastical Titles Act of 1851, the measure that had forbidden Roman Catholic clerics to assume British territorial titles. The measure had been ignored for all practical purposes, and a parliamentary select committee had recommended its repeal, but the Conservative minority government (which had been brought to power in 1866 by the vicissitudes undergone by Russell and Gladstone's franchise-reform bill) was hesitant to act. For one thing, Queen Victoria preferred, however theoretically, to keep in her own hands the right to designate all who claimed episcopal rank in Great Britain, whether they be Anglican, Roman Catholic, or members of the Scottish church.[29] Newdegate similarly declared his unflinching opposition to attempts to permit non-Anglicans to teach at Oxford and Cambridge. For the time being, the statutes remained unaltered.

In February 1867 Newdegate was very much upset to learn that at the inaugural banquet for the lord mayor of Dublin, Cardinal Cullen had been awarded protocol precedence in his capacity as cardinal legate from the court of Rome, a state not "regularly accredited" to the court of England. Disraeli assured the squire of Arbury Hall that Cullen had been invited solely in his capacity as Roman Catholic Archbishop of Dublin and that the president of the Presbyterian Assembly and the head of the Dublin Wesleyans had been invited as well. Disraeli found comfort in the fact that Cullen was thus mixing in society.[30]

During these same years, Newdegate helped the anti-Catholic cause by contributing a lengthy and officially anonymous introduction to an English translation of a "Report on the Constitution of the Jesuits Delivered to the Parlement of Britanny" in 1761. It was only too obvious to Newdegate that the "great conspiracy against truth and human freedom" that the Society of Jesus represented had, in spite of the temporary abolition of the order between 1773 and 1814, remained fundamentally unchanged. Wherever they were not supreme, the Jesuits were revolutionaries, yet once in power, they established "a retrograde and debasing tyranny." England had thus far emerged victorious in her three-centuries-old contest with the society, but evidence of new intrigues was at hand. "Danger will come, if we are careless; if either from ignorance, or from a mistaken feeling of charity, or from cowardice, we indulge in false confidence."[31]

Newdegate was not alone in his vigilance. The Britain of the 1860s could boast a host of overlapping lay-sponsored organizations working for a kingdom and a national church free from both the taint of ritualism and the threat of Rome. The Evangelical Alliance, founded in 1846, prided itself on opposing "vigorously and actively . . . the progress of Popery, Rationalism, Infidelity, and the Desecration of the Lord's Day."[32] The Church Association was primarily concerned with the continuing growth of High Church symbolism and ceremony within the Church of England, and a typical lecture (one of a series sponsored in London's St. James's Hall in 1869) was entitled "Ritualism, the Enemy of Domestic Peace, Doctrinal Purity, Social Progress, and National Independence."[33] Even closer to Newdegate's heart was the Protestant Alliance (founded in 1835), whose annual breakfasts he faithfully attended and whose work of sermons, lectures, and tracts he strongly supported. For such organizations, the late 1860s marked the most successful period, in terms of money and membership, since the early 1850s.[34] Most important for Newdegate was the Scottish Reformation Society, which published *The Bulwark* and which sponsored a full-time parliamentary lobbyist to alert sympathetic M.P.s to the latest Roman Catholic maneuvers.[35] During the mid-1860s that organization established in London an English branch and a Protestant Educational Institute to give courses and to gather statistical information on Roman Catholic doings. "By the skilful handling of the priests," the institute observed, "the apparently insignificant minority of Roman Catholics is made a powerful force in the empire, and dictates parliamentary and municipal measures almost at its pleasure, and rules the public press."[36]

In Newdegate's eyes, the threat of political reform at home never loomed so large as did the specter of an ideology imported from abroad. This is not to suggest that Newdegate looked with undisguised favor upon the Reform Bill of 1867, a measure that, as a consequence both of chance and of Disraeli's desperate desire to reach an electoral settlement under the auspices of a Conservative government, almost doubled the electorate of England, Scotland, and Wales at a single stroke.[37] Newdegate did not desert his party, however, as is evidenced by an undated note that Disraeli sent to the Warwickshire M.P. in either 1867 or 1868.

> My dear Newdigate [*sic*]
> I find I made a great mistake in supposing that you were not wanted on Monday. The government is in danger, & without the constant presence of our friends during this crisis, we must be shipwrecked.
>
> Yrs. sincerely,
> Dis [*sic*]

Newdegate found solace in the thought that since the Commoners elected under the rules of 1832 had sanctioned such unfortunate departures from good sense as the repeal of the Corn
Laws, the subsidy to Maynooth Seminary, and the admission of
Jews to Parliament, a house elected under new rules could
hardly do worse. "I have no want of confidence in my countrymen," declared the Warwickshire squire, "and I therefore trust
that the result will be advantageous."[39]

A majority of the newly enfranchised voters were urban,
but even in Newdegate's own predominantly rural constituency, the registered electorate increased by 44 percent, from 7,107
to 10,251. Almost half of these voters were residents of either
metropolitan Birmingham or Coventry. A boundary commission had determined that the suburb of Aston should be made
part of the enlarged three-member borough of Birmingham, but
Parliament had overruled the commission at the behest of
Aston's residents, who feared that they would be subjected to
Birmingham's municipal taxes. The restoration of Aston's 2,439
voters—many of them newly enfranchised—to the county electoral list was generally regarded as auguring badly for Newdegate's reelection chances.[40]

That the Reform Act of 1867 would be followed by a new
general election was widely regarded as a foregone conclusion,
but neither the issue on which the campaign would be fought
nor the chieftains under whom the rival parties would be led
into electoral battle became clear until the spring of 1868. By
then Disraeli had replaced the ailing Derby as prime minister,
and Gladstone, for all practical purposes, had supplanted the
ailing Earl Russell as Liberal leader. It was Gladstone who threw
down the gauntlet in the form of three resolutions asking that
the Irish branch of the Anglican church, the church of less than
one-eighth of the Irish people, be disestablished and disen-
dowed and that, for the time being, all further appointments to
the Irish church be suspended. The three resolutions passed the
House of Commons, thereby demonstrating that the Conservative ministry in office since 1866 remained a minority government. To Newdegate's temporary relief, the measure suspend-
ing appointments to the Irish church was turned down by the
House of Lords. As soon as the new electoral registers could be
compiled in the autumn of 1868, Disraeli's ministry appealed to
the electorate in a new general election. The issue of the hour
was, in Gladstone's words, "the great question of the Irish
Church—which, as you know, absorbs at this time, far beyond
every other single topic, the general interest of the country."[41]

This interest was certainly high in North Warwickshire where Newdegate and his associate, William Bromley-Davenport (he had legally changed his name from William Davenport Bromley in 1865), stood as staunch champions of the Irish church, and their two Liberal opponents, George Frederick Muntz and E. F. Flower, stood as equally convinced opponents. The campaign was, by English standards, unusually lengthy and hard-fought. At several meetings, the commotion was so great that the speakers could scarcely make themselves heard, and at Atherstone on 10 November, windows were broken and the police had to be called to separate the Liberal and Conservative partisans. At a meeting in Rugby on 26 October, Newdegate criticized the prodisestablishment stand of Dr. Temple, headmaster of Rugby, who had enthusiastically pledged support to the Liberal nominees even though Newdegate was one of Rugby's trustees. Although Newdegate was quite prepared to give Dr. Temple a chance to speak, the more zealous partisans hustled the headmaster out of the meeting, which they charged him with disrupting.[42]

The disestablishment of the Anglican church in Ireland, a step that Dr. Temple hailed as "a great act of justice" to a people burdened with the support of an alien church, was to Newdegate anathema. He declared himself far from certain, first of all, that a majority of the Irish people truly sought disestablishment. Even if they did, he found it unreasonable that mere numbers in Ireland alone should determine the issue. If the union with Ireland was to be maintained, then, inasmuch as a majority of the people of the United Kingdom were Protestants, "it appears to me that justice, not less than sound policy, require [sic] that the Established Church should be maintained in Ireland as part of the constitutional organisation of the United Kingdom." The nation's Constitution was no mere mechanism "but an organism" to be conveyed by one generation to the next with all its features intact. The firm sense of duty to country that Palmerston had so often displayed was, however, a virtue "in which our modern leaders are deficient." The disestablishment of the Irish church, Newdegate concluded, would play into the hands of the Roman Catholic priests; it would subject both England and Ireland to "a foreign Power, of which the Pope may be the representative, the agent, or the stimulant."[43]

When John Bright accused him of always being in the wrong, Newdegate responded that, like Bright, he too was a reformer. "No reformer . . . shall have occasion to say that Charles Newdegate is prejudiced without reason." At least he was not so foolish as Bright who sought reduction in military expenditures while encouraging the ever greater import of food from abroad. "If the Navy were reduced, and England no longer had an adequate command of the sea, who was to convey the [tax-] free breakfast over the sea home?"

The continued establishment of the Protestant church remained for Newdegate the issue of the hour, and in his speeches he appealed far more to the English nationalism of his hearers than to their political partisanship. He recalled that he had long felt as concerned with the affairs of Birmingham and Coventry as with those of rural Warwickshire. On one occasion, he apologized for the length of his election address, but he could not simply pledge his support to a party program because "I am an independent member and have been for years." "Too independent!" shouted a voice from the crowd. Newdegate was quick to agree that he had indeed been too independent, "too independent for my own personal ambition and objects. Had I not been an independent member I might have had office and perhaps a title by this time." Yet it was precisely as an independent member that he could best resist that party of thirty or forty Roman Catholic members in the House of Commons who "made the advancement of their Church their first object and [who] would vote for any side, or any Minister, or any measure, provided they could advance their object."[44]

In the nation as a whole, Gladstone and the Liberals returned triumphant, by a margin of 112 seats, but in North Warwickshire, Newdegate and Bromley-Davenport survived the effects of the Reform Act of 1867 with flying colors, their victory margin exceeding the most sanguine expectation of their supporters: Newdegate, 4,547; Bromley-Davenport, 4,377; Muntz, 3,411; and Flower, 3,323. Newdegate had lost the Birmingham and Aston portions of his constituency by three-to-two margins but had swept every other district. After the result had been declared and the victors duly girt with their swords as knights of the shire, Newdegate proclaimed his triumph as a victory for independence, "the independence of England and the rejection of all foreign influence in the government, whether political, ecclesiastical or religious." It was Newdegate's confirmed belief that "as one of yourselves, I represent the independent will of the majority of the population of North Warwickshire." Flower, his defeated opponent, conceded that Newdegate did indeed represent the feelings of his native county, but North Warwickshire, he reminded the electors, "is not all England."[45]

The outcome spelled doom for the established Church of Ireland, but, for Newdegate, the Parliament and the election had brought satisfactions as well as frustrations. "Say what you will," declared Newdegate in 1867, "you cannot change the nature of a religion. The Protestant religion tends to freedom—the Roman Catholic religion tends to absolute government." What was maddening was the thought that at a time when the House of Commons had been subject "month after month, week after week, night after night" to "a constant system of aggression" by Roman Catholics, some people still thought of Newdegate as "an aggressor" when he was seeking to do no more than preserve the established institutions of his ideologically besieged homeland.[46]

7. Upholding Mr. Murphy

The average Englishman of the later 1860s, especially if he lived in Staffordshire or Lancashire, was more likely to have the presumed evils of Roman Catholicism called to his attention by the voice of "Mr. Murphy, the anti-Popery Lecturer," than by a newspaper report recounting Charles Newdegate's most recent parliamentary inquiry or protest. The origins of the William Murphy who became the apostle of popular anti-Catholicism in the England of the 1860s are obscure, but according to Murphy's own account he was born and baptized a Roman Catholic in the year 1834, the eldest son of Michael Murphy, master of the national school at Castletown-Conyers in the Irish county of Limerick. As a youth he was an altar boy and in due course a pupil-teacher in the national school. The influence of a friend and careful Bible reading converted the elder Murphy into a secret Protestant, and his wife and seven children followed suit. Their apostasy revealed, the Murphys moved to county Mayo, where the father was named head of a Protestant school. After a year of "scripture training" at a college in Banisloe, William Murphy at the age of eighteen became a scripture reader for the Irish Society, an evangelical Protestant organization. Two years later he transferred his allegiance to the comparable Dublin-based Society for Irish Church Missions. In 1859 he was married, and his wife temporarily persuaded him to give up "missionary" work in favor of running a boot-and-shoe shop in Dublin. The shop was not a success, however, and in 1862 he sailed to Liverpool and made his way by foot to London to offer his services as an evangelist there. The more respectable evangelical organizations were put off by Murphy, but Robert Steele, secretary of the tiny Protestant Electoral Union welcomed him. Steele persuaded Lt. Col. H. J. Brockman, the organization's president, to transform the group into the Protestant Evangelical Mission and Electoral Union and, in due course, to launch Murphy on his English career as an antipopery lecturer. "I see now," Murphy told Steele, "that God is for me after all, and by His grace I'll blaze England yet."[1]

Brockman believed that his military career in India had been thwarted by Roman Catholic pressure, and the professed object of his organization was "To maintain the Protestantism of the Bible and the LIBERTY OF BRITAIN." It sought to uphold civil and religious freedom, "to defend ourselves and others from the yoke of the Romish Priesthood and its abettors," to expose unscriptural doctrines and practices, and to promote "without reference to Sect or Party" the return to Parliament "of Christian and Patriotic men." Its methods included lectures, sermons, public meetings, and the encouragement of judicial and parliamentary investigations. Donations to enable the group to "expose the intrigues of the Jesuits" were earnestly invited, and an array of pamphlets, leaflets, tracts, and placards "specially adapted to the present requirements of the country" was promised in return. Typical titles included *Irish Priests and the Confessional, Fenianism—The Priest, the Real Fenian, Sister Lucy's Disclosures of New Hall Convent, Nunneries and the Confessional, Christian and Patriotic Songs for English Youths,* and two-penny and one-shilling editions of Foxe's *Book of Martyrs.* By 1869 the society was sponsoring some 350 lectures and 150 sermons a year and claimed to have sold several million leaflets and tracts.[2]

The Protestant Evangelical Mission and Electoral Union began to intensify its propaganda efforts in 1865 by sending to every member of both houses of Parliament a copy of *The Confessional Unmasked,* a publication exhibiting "the ATROCITY and ABOMINATIONS OF THE TEACHING OF THE GOVERNMENT COLLEGE OF MAYNOOTH." Some of the more sordid details, the introduction assured the prospective reader, were being kept in the relative obscurity of the Latin tongue, "but the time may come when it will become our bounden though painful duty to rouse the indignation of Englishmen at the expense of their modesty" lest Roman Catholic priests "convert an Eden into a Sodom."[3]

Although Murphy was to be widely connected with *The Confessional Unmasked,* he was in no sense the compiler, editor, and translator, a role that the British Library tentatively assigns to David Bryce (?–1875), an obscure London book publisher. The seventy-six-page pamphlet provides, in parallel columns of Latin and English, excerpts from the *Theologia Moralis* of Saint Alfonso Maria de Liguori (1696–1787), *The Moral and Dogmatic Theology* of Dr. Peter Dens (1690–1775), and works by other eighteenth- and early nineteenth-century Roman Catholic authorities. The subjects taken up include the acceptability of equivocation and oath breaking on given occasions,[4] the implications of the confessional seal, and the inquisitorial responsibilities of the confessor: if a female penitent appeared modest then, according to one excerpt, "that modesty must be overcome, or else he is authorized to deny her absolution." Another section deals with the temptations that might beset a confessor and with the manner in which accusations against confessors by female penitents should be handled: their complaints were not to be given credit too readily. The second half of the volume describes in graphic detail the variety of sexual practices that Catholic theologians had defined as mortal sins or as venial sins or (in a few cases) as "normal" and acceptable. Though first published in 1836 and republished in 1852, *The Confessional Unmasked* did not receive wide publicity or distribution until 1865 when the Protestant Evangelical Mission and Electoral Union printed an edition of twenty-five thousand copies; another fifteen thousand copies were printed two years later.

The details of Murphy's peregrinations between 1863 and 1867 remain partially obscure, but it is known that he lectured in Bristol and Cardiff as well as in London, where he offered a "White Blackbird" to any opponent who could successfully refute his anti-Catholic arguments. He was arrested for obstructing a Roman Catholic procession in Bath, and he was involved in a riot in Plymouth. He escaped from one unruly mob in a policeman's uniform and from another wearing a woman's dress.[5] Murphy did not gain the attention of the Home Office and of the national press until 1867. Early in February the walls of buildings in Wolverhampton were covered with posters: "ROMANISM AND PUSEYISM UNMASKED." The posters "affectionately invited" the Roman Catholic priests and laity of the city, whose population included some twelve thousand Irishmen, to attend a series of five lectures by Murphy:

    1. Purgatory, the Scriptures, and the Blessed Virgin Mary Coming down from Heaven to Release Souls out of Purgatory.
    2. Transubstantiation and the Sacrifice of the Mass.
    3. The Glories of Mary and the Glories of Jesus.
    4. The Seven Pretended Sacraments of the Church of Rome Unscriptural.
    5. Maynooth and Its Teaching and *The Confessional Unmasked*, Shewing the Depravity of the PRIESTHOOD and the Immorality of the CONFESSIONAL.

The Wolverhampton Agricultural Hall had been hired to house the lectures, and a charge of two pence per reserved seat and one penny per unreserved seat was asked for each lecture "to defray expenses." The fee for the final lecture was set at six pence, but admission was barred to all gentlemen under twenty-one and to all ladies except those accustomed to going to confession. Those admitted were promised both a revelation— the questions that priests were taught to ask both the married and the unmarried at confession—and an opportunity to purchase, for but one shilling more, the tract *The Confessional Unmasked*.[6]

The placards did their work, and by the evening of the first lecture, the agricultural hall was packed. The mayor, several justices of the peace, and a chief constable, visibly worried about the preservation of public order, were also on hand. So was a "large body of Irish," fully prepared to let the renegade Murphy know how they felt about him. William Ullathorne, the Roman Catholic bishop of Birmingham, estimated their number at ten thousand. When the lecturer appeared, part of the audience began to shout and groan. The chairman, the Reverend J. E. Armstrong, a Church of England clergyman, appealed to the assembly to grant Murphy a hearing, but the uproar was too great. Fighting broke out in the hall, several chairs were broken, and four men were taken into custody. Murphy and Armstrong reluctantly departed.

While the mayor asked the Home Office in London for protection and advice, Armstrong distributed new placards about Wolverhampton announcing that the justices of the peace had refused Murphy protection and that his life was in danger. In a letter to the home secretary, the mayor insisted that his role was to protect "all persons equally." Even special constables proved insufficient to quell a tumultuous crowd "armed with sticks and stones" that gathered outside the lecture hall the following night. Murphy indignantly refused to cancel the remaining lectures, and it was only after a large force of county police had been summoned and thirty cavalrymen had been called in from Birmingham and another troop of horsemen from Coventry that the lectures could take place. The mayor of Wolverhampton deplored the "offensive character" of the placards, but he conceded that "large bodies of respectable and well behaved persons have attended these Lectures regularly since the first night." All others were asked to stay off the streets, a request made of his fellow religionists independently by Bishop Ullathorne.[7]

With an obvious sigh of relief, the mayor was able to report to the home secretary a few days later that the final lecture, "The Confessional," had gone off without a breach of the peace. Two months later it had yet to be determined who was to pay for the men and the horses that had been called in from Birmingham and Coventry; the War Office ultimately agreed to do so. "Mr. Murphy is a perfect nuisance," mused the home secretary of Lord Derby's Conservative ministry, Spencer H. Walpole. That sentiment was to be echoed by the man who succeeded Walpole as Conservative home secretary in May 1867, Gathorne Hardy, and in turn by Hardy's Liberal successor, Henry Austin Bruce.[8]

During the late winter and spring of 1867, Murphy lectured at a number of smaller communities such as Walsall, Staffordshire. There the police chief, fearing "tumult, Riot, and Felony," called upon the 130-man county constabulary, supplemented by 160 additional citizens sworn in as special constables, to keep the peace.[9] It was at Birmingham, however, in June of 1867 that William Murphy became an English household word as "the lecturer against Romanism." He had requested the use of Birmingham Town Hall for his course of lectures on "The Errors of Roman Catholicism," but the Liberal mayor of Birmingham, aware of the troubles at Wolverhampton and elsewhere, refused. Murphy's supporters thereupon erected a wooden "tabernacle," with room for 3,000 people, on an empty lot in the center of the city.

There, on Sunday afternoon, 16 June 1867, with the arena almost filled with enthusiastic ticket holders, Murphy began his first lecture. He offered to take on "any Popish priest, from Bishop Ullathorne to the biggest ragamuffin in the lot; and if ever there was a rag and bone gatherer in the universe it was the Pope himself." In order not to add to the potential excitement, only six policemen had been assigned to the tabernacle area, but in the course of the afternoon, the edifice was engulfed by a tumultuous sea of Irish laborers, their wives, and children, many of them attempting to tear down Murphy's makeshift assembly hall. Stones began to fly in all directions, and the nearby house of the father of the secretary of the local Protestant Association was attacked. Its windows were smashed and its furniture broken. Other houses were also damaged, and only after the policemen had been greatly reinforced and had begun to use their cutlasses did they gain the upper hand against the mob. Twenty-five people were arrested.[10]

Monday, 17 June, was a day of intense excitement in Birmingham. The crowd in the streets, both the mischiefmakers and the merely curious, was estimated by the mayor as between 50,000 and 100,000. One group of Irishmen toured the city with an immense wooden cross decorated with green ribbons, while others kept up a hail of stones, bricks, tiles, and similar missiles in the tabernacle area. Roofs were climbed; doors, shutters, and signposts were dislodged. A pawnshop was invaded, a confectionery shop sacked, and a public house stormed. "The object of these outrages—unless it was robbery—is difficult to divine," commented the reporter for the *Birmingham Daily Post*. During the afternoon and evening, the mayor toured the city and read the Riot Act; at the same time, he appealed for more police and military assistance. Between Sunday and Tuesday, his police force of 580 men was supplemented by 400 soldiers, almost 100 of them calvarymen; and by some 600 special constables. It was the most serious breach of the peace in Birmingham since the Priestly riots of 1792.[11]

Birmingham's harassed mayor became the chief object of Murphy's verbal assault during his Monday night lecture. If the mayor had given Murphy the right to use the town hall, as he had previously done for Archbishop Manning and the sponsors of a Roman Catholic bazaar, then, Murphy insisted, he would not have invited such attacks by a Roman Catholic crowd. Murphy declared that he was ready to risk his life at the hands of that mob in the interest of Protestant liberty. His tabernacle stood as "a witness for the right of speech and liberty of conscience." Stones had been thrown at the mayor that day; perhaps a few more "Popish stones would let him see what Popery was." In the meantime, Protestants were fully justified in defending themselves against Catholic attack. During the Monday evening meeting, which began with a hymn, Murphy was supported by Armstrong, who counseled all denominations of Protestants "to sink their differences and unite against the common enemy." Murphy was given additional backing by George H. Whalley, the Liberal M.P. for Peterborough, who likewise defended Murphy's right to be heard.[12]

Before Monday night was over, a band of Murphy's supporters, armed with staves, had marched to the Irish district of Birmingham. They broke into the houses on two streets and sacked them and damaged a Roman Catholic chapel while singing "Glory, Glory, Hallelujah" and "John Brown's Body." "It is said," wrote *The Times* correspondent, "that the Irish were the great culprits on Sunday and Monday. Even if that was so, the retribution is fearful." It was after midnight before the police and the soldiers could restore order of a sort to Birmingham. By then, some seventy additional persons, most of them Irish, had been placed under arrest. The leaders were committed for trial at Quarter Sessions; the others were given summary sentences of two to six weeks' imprisonment. Dozens of casualties were treated at local hospitals.[13]

The crowd was as large as ever on Tuesday, 18 June, amidst rumors of a proposed attack on the Catholic cathedral and on the armories located in Birmingham's gunmaking district. There

The Murphy riots in Birmingham in 1867: "The Scene in Park Street" (from the *Illustrated Times*, 29 June 1867, p. 401; by permission of the British Newspaper Library).

were also rumors of a projected demonstration against a High Church Anglican house of worship and against the local synagogue. But policemen and soldiers now seemed to be stationed on every corner. In the presumably civilized 1860s, declared *The Times*, it was "a sad and even portentous sight" to see such a force arrayed to protect against "a desperate mob" not in strife-ridden Belfast but in Birmingham, "one of the most flourishing and not the least enlightened of English manufacturing towns."[14]

During the remainder of the week, Murphy lectured in relative peace on the asserted iniquities of Roman Catholicism. In one lecture he sought to prove "that every Popish priest was a murderer, a cannibal, a liar, and a pickpocket." In another he suggested that "If the Catholic priests have the power to make God Almighty out of a bit of bread, they must be the greatest imposters in the world to ask money from the people, for they have only to say 'hocus pocus' over six-pences and they will become sovereigns." In yet another lecture he endeavored to show that "the Virgin Mary was a Protestant, and no Roman Catholic." The Virgin Mary, Murphy felt sure, did not believe in nunneries and other such "societies of misery," which deserved government inspection just as much as did hospitals, prisons, workhouses, and asylums. Murphy went on to warn his listeners against the impudent demands of the "Pope's Brigade" in Parliament; England had not been so threatened by alien religious forces since the era of James II.[15]

The final lecture on the confessional attracted, as it had in Wolverhampton, the largest audience. According to *The Times*, some six thousand tickets had been sold for a hall holding only three thousand people. Birmingham's mayor suspected that some thirty thousand copies of *The Confessional Unmasked* were sold during that week. Although that compilation of "the most obscene passages" culled from supposed textbooks for Roman Catholic priests was professedly not sold to women or minors, *The Times* feared that young people had managed to gain access to copies and were clearly "corrupted in mind and morals" as a consequence.

Murphy's anti-Catholic lectures and writings doubtless served, in the words of Richard Hofstadter—as "the pornography of the Puritan."[16] They also confirmed in the minds of many a Victorian paterfamilias a very genuine fear that the Roman Catholic "father" would serve as a rival household head and assert an alternate authority over his wife and daughters. "Well knowing the influence which the female sex possess," Roman Catholic priests were suspected of deliberately seeking to undermine "their simple and susceptible natures" rather than "those of the sterner and more unyielding sex." As one contemporary novel warned its readers, "it would be a fatal day for England if ever England's wives and daughters were led to deem the confessional a more sacred place than the home."[17]

The next year provided new opportunities for William Murphy and his associates to travel and to speak. In March 1868, when two fellow lecturers found a Rochdale hall that they had hired closed against them, they attempted to speak from their carriage. When that maneuver failed, they appealed to the home secretary for aid—"surely the authority will not allow a Popish Mob to deprive a man of liberty of speech"—but Hardy replied that the preservation of the peace was a local concern. The announcement that the lectures would take place the next day caused a large crowd to assemble, with the Irish arrayed on one side of the street and the English on the other. In the ensuing scuffle, one of the Protestant lecturers, George Mackey, shot a policeman and was placed under arrest, while the other, James Houston, sought vainly to address the crowd from outside the town limits.[18]

Rochdale became an instant magnet for Murphy. After calling attention to the problems encountered by Houston and Mackey—"a loyal Man has now to stand in a fellons [sic] dock instead of the guilty party"—Murphy appealed to the Home Office for protection against "Mob Law and Fenian Asassination [sic]." As a faithful subject of Queen Victoria, Murphy was "entitled to all the protection the State can give me"; otherwise, "I shall then be obliged to protect myself as best I can." The home secretary referred Murphy to the town authorities who would doubtless "take proper steps to prevent any breach of the peace." Murphy reported the next day that he had applied for protection at Rochdale, but that the mayor had indicated "he would rather imprison than protect me." The home secretary responded that he presumed that the local authorities "know and will do their duty."[19]

Despite these unpromising beginnings, Murphy managed to hire the Rochdale Temperance Hall for a 3 April debate between Edward Mooney and himself on "The Depravity of the Priesthood and the Immorality of the Confessional." The sponsor was "The United Committees of Protestants and Catholics." Each speaker was to have half an hour to state his case and a quarter of an hour for rebuttal. Tickets were six pence apiece. The Roman Catholics were to sit on one side of the chamber, the Protestants on the other, but neither group was to display any sign of either approval or disapproval. In his half of the debate, Murphy set forth anew his contention that in the very process of asking women about their sexual practices—of whether they had been guilty of incest, adultery, sodomy, masturbation, contraception, abortion, or any other action "contrary to the order of nature"—priests put ideas into women's heads that would not otherwise have occurred to them. The confessional placed the priests themselves into "the midst of temptation and wickedness" and thus corrupted priest and penitent alike. As for Murphy, he placed his hope in God and the Bible rather than in priests.

Mooney apologized for his inexperience in public speaking and disclaimed responsibility "for any evil that may accrue from the foul, filthy language that has come from the lips of Mr. Murphy during the last half hour." He then went on to call attention to two Latin passages that Murphy (presumably) had mistranslated in *The Confessional Unmasked* and asked Murphy for the one hundred pounds that he had promised anyone who could prove that the book contained a misstatement. Murphy ignored the challenge and reiterated that the filth Mooney alluded to was not Murphy's but "the filth of Rome" as found in the textbooks read at Maynooth; he implored his audience "not to dabble in the filth and depravity of the confessional." Mooney reiterated in turn that Murphy had failed to admit his errors—his "lies." Murphy was "a man of inconsistency, and ignorance, and impudence, and filth, and foulness." As for the Roman Catholic church, "you may as well try to stem the ocean as try to stay the progress of the Catholic Church." At the conclusion of the debate, the moderator ignored the participants but congratulated the audience on remaining calm. Three days later, the mayor of Rochdale was able to report to the home secretary that all soldiers had been sent home and all special constables dismissed. The town was "settling down to its usual peace and quietness."[20]

Matters were less quiet at Stalybridge, Bacup, and Ashton-under-Lyme. A group of men who had been attending an anti-Catholic lecture at Ashton were ambushed on their return to Stalybridge late at night by a group of Irishmen who had extinguished all street lamps and placed ropes across the road. The men returned to their homes battered and bleeding; at their workshop the next day, they plotted revenge. "To the chapel" was the cry, but the Roman Catholic chapel was guarded by hundreds of stone-throwing protectors and one rifle-wielding priest. It took two days more before the police and the army were able to halt the disorder. Lord Denbigh, the Roman Catholic peer who called Hardy's attention to this flare-up, put all the blame on Murphy. "That rascally firebrand Murphy ought to be stopped somehow. He is demoralizing the whole of the lower classes and bringing all religion into discredit." Hardy replied that the Home Office could act only when the local authorities requested aid and that those authorities appeared to have done their best to quell the storm.[21]

At nearby Bacup, Murphy again appealed to the home secretary for protection from "Popish Mob Law." As things turned out, the week's lectures went off with no more than a series of demonstrations and counterdemonstrations. A few of Murphy's supporters were knocked down in the street, and a few windows were broken in the Irish section of town. "Take the priest away from Ireland and her people would be noble and free," Murphy had declared. In the meantime, the editor of the *Bacup Times* had fired a Roman Catholic reporter for providing an erroneous and "petti-fogging" report on Murphy's lectures and published a letter from "A Protestant" who had expected to find Murphy "a rough, and . . . uncivilised Irishman" but found him instead to be intelligent, earnest, and good-looking. Many who had been Murphy's critics before his arrival, reported the anonymous letter writer, had now become his enthusiastic supporters.[22] Although *The Times* took for granted that Murphy's audience was confined to "the lower portions of our populations," the Protestant Evangelical Mission and Electoral Union took pride in the fact that justices of the peace, military officers, Anglican and Dissenting ministers, respectable tradesmen, and ladies were often to be found among Murphy's listeners.[23]

The May 1868 riot at Ashton-under-Lyme began with an attack by a group of over two hundred Irishmen on a large gathering of "Murphyites and Orangemen" wearing ribbons and rosettes. "Come on boys," shouted John Flynn, "we will drive the ———— English out of the town." The Irish attack was followed by an English counterattack that severely damaged a Roman Catholic chapel and left twenty houses in the community's "Little Ireland" without a vestige of furniture or clothing; one Irishman died.[24] Although the riot did not involve Murphy directly, he had lectured at Ashton earlier in the year, and a published transcript of his debate with Mooney had received wide circulation. Wherever Murphy lectured, John Francis Maguire observed to the House of Commons, the result was riot, destruction of property, and even loss of life. Might not the home secretary assure the house "that the delivery of such addresses could be prevented for the future"? The M.P. for Cork, who was also the editor of the *Cork Examiner*, conceded that the Irish "were parties to the riot" in Ashton and elsewhere. No doubt it would be better if they ignored Murphy, "but that was asking more than human nature was capable of." The fact remained that Murphy had excited evil passions and had sowed dissension wherever he traveled; he ought to be stopped. There was, after all, "a great difference between free discussion and a license to abuse and outrage the religion of others."[25]

Gathorne Hardy replied that he was not aware of any law "by which a person can be prevented from delivering controversial lectures either in a room which he takes or a structure which he carries about for the purpose. No person is compelled to attend those lectures." If such a person used language calculated to lead to a breach of the peace, the local authorities could swear information to that effect before the magistrates and obtain a restraining order. This was not, in the first instance, however, a matter for the Home Office.[26] The home secretary was equally reluctant to entertain the suggestion of another Roman Catholic M.P. that he introduce a bill to forbid all lectures reflecting on the religious faith of any of Her Majesty's subjects that had not first received Home Office clearance.[27]

Whalley, the M.P. who had accompanied Murphy to Birmingham the year before, defended him as an honest and truthful man and suggested that Maguire's parliamentary intervention was part of a "deliberate organisation on the part of the Romish priesthood for putting down freedom of speech." Charles Newdegate was not willing to go as far as that. He did not know Murphy personally nor was he connected with the Protestant Evangelical Mission and Electoral Union, but he had been sufficiently disturbed by the Birmingham riots of the year before to send his personal observer to the scene. That person had learned that the attacks on Murphy's tabernacle and on people seeking to attend his lectures had begun before Murphy had even begun to speak. "The people of England," Newdegate observed, "were not accustomed to have free, if lawful, discussions put down by violence." Neither in Birmingham nor in Ashton had the Protestants been the first aggressors, Newdegate pointed out. Maguire should persuade his fellow religionists "to abstain from outrage." The Warwickshire M.P. was equally disturbed by the recent decision of the Court of the Queen's Bench to condemn *The Confessional Unmasked* as "obscene" and, under Lord Campbell's act of 1858 (20 and 21 Vict., c. 83), to ban its publication and distribution. That the book might be objectionable per se, Newdegate conceded; the judges had, however, reached their "extraordinary" decision on the basis of a false premise, namely, that the doctrines that the book sought to expose and condemn were no longer current. Newdegate feared that they remained all too current.[28]

The Ashton riot was followed in late May by disturbances in Oldham where a Protestant mob attacked a Roman Catholic chapel and an Irish Catholic mob broke windows in the Anglican parish church and in several Dissenting chapels. There also was fighting in Bolton where Murphy, finding it impossible to hire a hall, threatened to lecture from a balloon.[29]

The Murphy lectures played a distinct role in the general election of 1868. In September, Murphy, upon arrival in Manchester, was immediately lodged in Belle Vue prison and released only after he had provided financial sureties for his good behavior. While in jail, Murphy offered himself to the citizens of

Manchester as a "Protestant candidate" prepared to oppose "the tools of Rome" in the interest of "liberty of speech" and "freedom of thought." As an enemy of popery, he declared himself to be as genuine a Radical as John Bright, whom he dubbed "John Dark" for his willingness to disestablish the Protestant Church of Ireland. Murphy conducted several indoor and outdoor election rallies, and the police were called out to control a group of Irishmen who sought to break up one of the latter. By nomination day, 16 November, Murphy was no longer in the vicinity, however, and his name was not formally presented to the electorate. Manchester chose two Liberals and one Conservative as its representatives to Westminster.[30] Birmingham proved equally inhospitable to overt political anti-Catholicism, but the story was otherwise in small-town Lancashire, Murphy's prime stamping ground that year and also the region in which the percentage of Irish immigrants was largest. There the Conservatives defeated Gladstone personally and scored their greatest victory in 1868; Murphy's lectures were widely regarded as an important reason for that outcome.[31]

When Murphy sought to renew his lecture campaign in the spring of 1869, Gladstone's Liberal government was in power. A lecture by Murphy at Tynemouth in Northumberland inspired some 250 Irishmen from the vicinity to march in military array toward the Oddfellows' Hall in which Murphy's meeting was being held. They were armed with sticks and hammers, and their battle cry was "We'll Kill Murphy!" The police barred the door against them while most of the audience fled through a smaller door at the opposite end of the auditorium. In the meantime, Murphy and his remaining followers armed themselves with chair legs to meet the impending Irish charge. The police were unable to stop the attackers from smashing the auditorium windows, but they did prevent actual bloodshed.

Murphy thereupon attempted but failed to hire halls in other Northumberland towns. When he sought a return engagement in Tynemouth and an even larger troop of Irishmen threatened to converge upon the town by train to stop him, the mayor looked for legal deterrents. On the basis of the advice of the new home secretary, Henry Austin Bruce, who in turn had consulted the Treasury solicitors, the mayor appealed to an act dating back to the French Revolution to bar Murphy from speaking. The hired hall was closed, and Murphy was threatened with a one-hundred-pound fine if he sought to lecture; members of his audience were threatened with a fine of twenty pounds each if they tried to attend. Murphy was outraged. How could "An Act for the more effective Suppression of Societies established for Seditious and Treasonable Purposes, and for the better preventing of Treasonable and Seditious Practices" apply to him? He was a loyal British subject who, unlike many Roman Catholic priests, did not connive at Fenianism, view Anglicans as heretics, or judge the English people to be heathens. It was quite untrue that he went about the country exciting violence "for no good purpose whatever." His followers caused disturbances only when they had received more than adequate provocation. Murphy was prepared to put forth his legal case in detail, but the home secretary refused to grant him the personal interview he sought.

When in June a meeting was scheduled in Birmingham to discuss the pending bill for the disestablishment of the Irish church, Murphy proclaimed in widely distributed placards that he expected to participate in the meeting and to denounce the encouragement to Roman Catholicism implicit in the measure. Remembering the riots of two years before, Birmingham's new mayor decided to act. He gave instructions to his chief of police to order Murphy to stay away lest a breach of the peace take place. If Murphy insisted on attending, he was to be taken into custody until the next day. "Believing I can find a justification of my conduct in the moral law," the mayor explained, "I seek it not in the Statute law. If I have done Mr. Murphy any wrong I am willing that a jury should assess the damage." Murphy was placed under arrest and did not enter the auditorium, but the meeting ended in tumult anyway.[32] He was released the following morning, and he did subsequently sue both the mayor and the police chief. Although Murphy eventually won the case, the Warwickshire jury limited the damages to forty shillings; thus, in the judgment of the Liberal *Daily News*, "they wisely refused to declare that the vindication of personal rights might be practically assisted by violent and disorderly action."[33]

A number of members of Parliament found disquieting the government's apparent approval of the manner in which Murphy had been silenced in Tynemouth and Birmingham and was now deterred from speaking anywhere else. Newdegate acted as chairman of a meeting of fourteen hundred people at London's St. James's Hall to protest this attack on the principle of free discussion. Newdegate still did not consider himself a "Murphyite," and, although Murphy was present, the two men did not meet. The principle transcended the individual, Newdegate insisted, and, however rude of speech Murphy might be, his manner did not justify either violent personal assaults upon him or breaches in the law in order to silence him. Newdegate received support from John Arthur Roebuck, the veteran Radical M.P. who had retired from Parliament less than a year before. Roebuck was quite willing to grant that Home Secretary Bruce looked upon Murphy as "a pestilential agitator." "That too," Roebuck surmised, "was the state of mind of Leo X, when he thought of Luther."[34]

On 23 July 1869, Newdegate introduced a resolution into the House of Commons affirming "the right of free speech [as] one of the most important safeguards of good Government and . . . attacks upon this right [as] therefore, dangerous to the welfare of the State." The resolution went on to censure the home secretary for acting to curb freedom of discussion in both Tynemouth and Birmingham. Speaking in support of his resolution, Newdegate taunted the government of the day, headed as it was by a prime minister "who is, *par excellence*, a Liberal," with having dug up from the graveyard of disused laws a statute that the party's spiritual father, Charles James Fox, had denounced as "an act of tyranny," a statute whose repeal that same government had recommended earlier in the session. Could Murphy truly be equated with the French Revolution as a threat to English society when the only thing anyone who did not wish to hear him had to do was *not* buy a ticket and *not* listen to his lectures? Why could not Bruce emulate the conduct of his predecessor, Hardy, who had refused to intervene? Bruce's attitude smacked too much of "salus populi suprema lex, . . . a maxim which has been used to cover acts of tyranny of the blackest dye."[35]

In the ensuing debate, Newdegate found a number of allies, including Dr. Thomas Chambers, the Liberal M.P. for Marylebone. Chambers was as unhappy as Newdegate with the government's apparent contention that "if the people who disagree with you are numerous enough and strong enough and unscrupulous enough, wherever you go, to combine together for the purpose of putting you down, there is an end to free speech and the exercise of the rights of a British citizen." Murphy might well be an unworthy individual, but was it not in the nature of great constitutional questions to be fought over unworthy representatives?[36]

The Liberal M.P. for Northampton, Lord Henley, disagreed. "Freedom of discussion," he observed, was as likely to be injured "by being abused as by being arbitrarily interfered with." Since Murphy's lectures had clearly not been "of a very proper kind," there could not have occurred any "straining of

John Arthur Roebuck, a parliamentary veteran best remembered as an early Victorian Radical (from a scrapbook in the University of Illinois Library).

the law on the part of the Home Secretary." Bruce defended his actions by providing a lengthy review of the circumstances at Tynemouth. The home secretary did not find it surprising that the impeachment of the morality of Roman Catholic priests and laity manifested in the notorious lecture on the confessional should lead to deplorable consequences. Bruce admitted that he had misgivings about the particular law he had been forced to rely on, but so long as it was in the statute book, he would use it to preserve the public peace. If a Roman Catholic lecturer had

gone about the country "inflaming the public mind, and leading
to violence, destruction of property and bloodshed," then,
Bruce insisted, he would have been equally ready to use the law
to silence him. Newdegate, the home secretary suggested,
would not have been so evenhanded. Bruce denied, moreover,
that he had ever given Birmingham's mayor legal advice. When
Newdegate sought to amend his motion to eliminate the reference to Birmingham, the house refused him permission to do
so, and the resolution of censure subsequently went down to
defeat by voice vote.[37]

The Murphy lectures posed a genuine dilemma for Victorian Englishmen. In his *Culture and Anarchy* (1869), the Liberal
critic Matthew Arnold cited governmental toleration of Murphy's actions at Birmingham and elsewhere as an example of the
drift toward anarchy. He discerned "at the bottom of our English hearts a very strong belief in freedom, and a very weak
belief in right reason."[38] Many men who, like Bruce, were not
themselves Catholics, proved, however, to be fully prepared to
silence Murphy if they could find a plausible method. At the
time of the Birmingham riots in 1867, *The Times* had congratulated the mayor on refusing Murphy use of the town hall. If the
Birmingham authorities had the "legal power to silence him . . .
they should exercise it firmly," the paper advised. If they did
not, *The Times* conceded, "he must be protected against brutal
violence, however provoked." "In a free country," declared the
chief Liberal party organ, London's *Daily News*, "it is simply
intolerable that the common right of public meeting and public
speaking should be abused by a professional agitator, whose
stock-in-trade is rioting and disorder."[39]

Murphy was obviously not a gentleman, either by birth or
behavior. He did not, in Gladstone's words, abide by "the laws
of English debate."[40] He gave publicity to unsavory matters,
and, finally, he represented a threat to the peace. If asked to
choose between abstract liberty, on the one hand, and social
order, on the other, many mid-Victorians would have regretted
the necessity of the choice, but they would nonetheless have
given the nod to order over liberty, especially if they could do so
in the name of morality. A student of the Hyde Park riots of 1867
has concluded that mid-Victorian Liberals were more sensitive
to the right of popular assembly than were mid-Victorian
Conservatives,[41] but a survey of the Murphy riots suggests that
overarching principles were readily reinterpreted in the light of
particular circumstances. Conservatives appear to have been
more sensitive to the rights of sponsors of private indoor meet-

ings as opposed to public outdoor demonstrations. Admittedly, they were also, at that time, less dependent upon Roman Catholic electoral support.

To suggest that the mid-Victorian years did not constitute a golden age for abstract freedom of speech is not to deny that that concept involved philosophical difficulties[42] or to imply that such abstract liberty was more secure elsewhere in the world. In any event, the problems that he encountered in 1869 did not discourage Murphy altogether. In April of the following year, he gave a series of nine lectures at Woolwich. Again there were disturbances: the windows of the lecture hall were broken, and Murphy was knocked down in the scuffle. Extra police had to be called to the scene. When he sought to begin a new series of lectures at Greenwich (the constituency that the Prime Minister, William Ewart Gladstone, then represented in Parliament), the trustees of the literary institution that had let the hall to Murphy reneged on the deal. Murphy sought in vain to lecture on the building steps and on nearby Blackheath Common; he did succeed in leading his followers in a rousing rendition of "Rule Britannia" while marching back to the railway station. The Protestant Evangelical Mission and Electoral Union protested this new assault on what it saw as the cause of free speech. "Englishmen are being deprived by a *Military Despotism* at the *dictation* of ROMISH PRIESTS. Such is the tyranny and cruelty to which Loyal Protestants are exposed under the il-Liberal Government of our pro-Popish Premier."[43]

The *Pall Mall Gazette* of 13 April 1870 had a rather different concern. How much longer did Murphy deserve police protection of the size or scope that he had received at Woolwich? Surely, policemen had other and more important duties than guarding "a mere firebrand, as irrational as he is dangerous. . . . We presume that it is not intended to give him a body guard during the term of his natural life, should he insist so long in shocking the feelings of a considerable portion of the population of this country."[44]

The term of Murphy's natural life turned out to be more limited than the *Pall Mall Gazette* had anticipated. In April 1871 he was scheduled to give several lectures on "The Seven Sacraments of the Catholic Church" at the Oddfellows' Hall in Whitehaven, Cumberland. The first of these was broken up by a group of Irish miners. The next night more than two hundred people marched to Whitehaven from nearby Cleaton Moor, and half an hour before Murphy's talk was scheduled to begin, they seized him in a lecture-hall anteroom, dragged him downstairs,

JEDDO AND BELFAST; OR, A PUZZLE FOR JAPAN.

JAPANESE AMBASSADOR. "THEN THOSE PEOPLE, YOUR GRACE, I SUPPOSE ARE HEATHEN?"
ARCHBISHOP OF CANTERBURY. "ON THE CONTRARY, YOUR EXCELLENCY: THOSE ARE AMONG OUR MOST *ENTHUSIASTIC RELIGIONISTS!*"

The Murphy riots in the mid-nineteenth century caused parts of England to resemble Northern Ireland in the twentieth (from *Punch*, 31 August 1872, p. 89).

and struck and kicked him repeatedly until he lay bloody and unconscious. A group of policemen finally came to his rescue; five of the assailants were eventually sentenced to twelve months' imprisonment at hard labor, and two others received lesser sentences. Murphy was brought back to Birmingham where he and his wife had made their home; although his condition improved for a time, he never fully recovered from the attack, and on 12 March 1872 he died.[45]

For his immediate followers he became a martyr.

> There rest thee, Christian warrior, no longer shalt thou roam
> 'Mid hostile crowds in a foreign land, for thou art safe at home
> The envious tongue of slander can never touch thee more,
> Nor hireling's polluted guile its venom on thee pour
> No more shall trained assassin in ambush for thee lie,
> For thou art gone to that blessed land where none can ever die.[46]

Although the *Irishman* could take comfort in the fact that the tirades of "the arch renegade and appointed antagonist to Catholicity" had been stilled at last and although the Irish

Nationalist leader, Timothy Michael Healy, was sure that "the authorities felt small regret,"[47] the *Daily News* was temporarily abashed. "His murder is a stain upon our system, a stain, the darkness and magnitude of which are not in any way diminished by the nature of his unlucky crusade, or the extravagance of his language."[48] Newdegate, for one, did not doubt that Murphy had "been actually murdered by a Roman Catholic mob, aided by Papal emissaries." Whatever minor imperfections might be found in the conduct of men like Mackey and Murphy, Newdegate felt certain that these "will be overlooked in a sense of indebtedness to them as exponents of those rights which the Constitution and laws of this country ought to ensure."[49]

A full narrative of Murphy's relatively brief career would require a careful survey of provincial journals; some of the details will always remain uncertain. He was evidently a powerful and skillful platform lecturer who did much to arouse and, at the very least, to reconfirm latent anti-Catholic sentiments among working-class and lower-middle-class Englishmen, many of them already troubled by the self-assertive Irish minorities recently established in their communities. What have been described as the Murphy riots were, in the first instance, anti-Murphy riots, though Irish Catholic attacks were almost invariably followed by English Protestant counterattacks. Despite the accusations of men like Whalley, it is doubtful that the Roman Catholic clergy directly inspired such attacks. More often than not, they sought to quell the storm. At the same time, they could derive comfort from the manner in which members of their flock had sprung to the defense of their besieged church in an alien land.

The activities of William Murphy created a troublesome dilemma for respectable Englishmen, many of whom at bottom shared his distrust of Catholicism, but who were repelled by his lack of gentility, by the blatant style of his placards, by his self-advertisement—by his Irishness. For a man like Newdegate, by definition a gentleman, Murphy posed a special problem: he was the wrong man in the wrong places saying, fundamentally, the right things. The manner in which, with the endorsement of a Liberal government, Murphy was repeatedly silenced in 1869 and 1870 seemed to confirm Newdegate's fear that the power of Roman Catholicism was indeed continuing its irresistible advance and that an Englishman's freedom to speak out against that advance was in peril.

8. The Great Convent Case

Early in 1869, just as the indefatigable William Murphy was embarking upon yet another speaking tour designed to alert his artisan and middle-class countrymen to the perils of Roman Catholicism, the legal case of the decade alternately fascinated and scandalized the citizens and newspaper readers of the nation's capital and beyond. An Irish-born Roman Catholic nun from a convent near Hull was suing her mother superior and assistant mother superior for libel and slander and for "wrongfully and maliciously conspiring" to drive her from the order in which she had found a spiritual home for more than ten years.

Even though Susanna Mary Saurin (Sister Mary Scholastica Joseph) had assured that same mother superior: "I would rather die than leave the convent of my own free will," she had ultimately been "expelled and driven disgraced and degraded upon the world," and she insisted upon a compensation of five thousand pounds.[1]

The case, *The Times* predicted, "promises to excite an unusual degree of public interest," and so indeed it did. The setting was the Court of the Queen's Bench in Westminster Hall; the presiding judge the Lord Chief Justice of England, Alexander Cockburn; the attorney for the plaintiff, the dashing and eloquent John Duke Coleridge. Coleridge had just been named solicitor general in Gladstone's new Liberal ministry, but that appointment did not bar him from continuing to handle occasional private cases. Every spectator seat in the court was filled for the duration of the trial, and few of the visitors dared leave during the luncheon recess lest their places be taken by others. The duke of Norfolk, England's premier Catholic layman, was a frequent attendant, as was a contingent of nuns who sat still as statues, patiently resigned to the possibility of persecution for their convent sisters. Hundreds of additional spectators clustered outside ready to cheer or hoot at the trial participants— and to serve as occasional victims for pickpockets. A force of policemen was required to keep clear the way to the entrance door. A majority of the spectators was clearly sympathetic to the plaintiff, and whenever Mary Saurin entered the courtroom, a thin figure draped in black, hidden behind a thick veil, and surrounded by relatives, they cheered her. The spectators cheered and applauded as well when she or her attorney made a particularly telling point. "Let there be no more of that," warned the Lord Chief Justice. "The court is not to be turned into a theatre."[2]

Yet the trial was theater. It was, indeed, long-run theater; as the Lord Chief Justice was despairingly to admit on 15 February, it was "the longest cause on record—the longest that has ever been tried within these ancient walls."[3] In the course of the proceedings, both the judge and the opposing lawyers were inundated with letters of comment and advice. The counsel for the plaintiff expressed the hope that, like all good Victorian plays, the trial would teach a sound moral lesson. Disclaiming any desire to arouse emotions or to criticize convents or judge their inmates, he did give voice to one solemn prediction: that the trial

> will teach those ladies that, although they may shroud themselves in their seclusion, and seek to shelter themselves under the shade of religion, English justice has eyes that can pierce through all their veils, and English law has power enough to protect their victims.[4]

And it was, indeed, a sad tale that Mary Saurin unfolded— the story of a woman eager to remain a nun who had been falsely accused of all manner of derelictions before an investigative commission appointed by the local Roman Catholic bishop. Since she was permitted no explanation that reflected on the character of her superiors, she could provide that commission with no evidence on her own behalf nor could she cross-examine any witnesses.[5] "She was set to scrub floors, clean the hearth, and do every kind of menial work," Coleridge declared, "the apparent intention being to make her life miserable and break down her bodily strength."[6] On at least one occasion, as a form of penance, she had been forced to wear a dust cloth as a head covering, on another to apologize for arriving late for an assignment by kissing the floor. (The degradation in status implicit in a lady being condemned to such drudgery and such self-abasement may well have been found more horrifying by the middle-class spectators than was any possible danger to Mary Saurin's health.) Moreover, Coleridge insisted, worse was yet to be revealed. During her final seven months in the convent, after she had steadfastly refused to depart, she was condemned to complete silence, restricted to a single room, and assigned to a bed with too few blankets. Mail addressed to her was withheld, letters she sent not forwarded. Her food was unfit to eat.

"She was unable to get over her dislike to mutton given

"The Convent Scandal Case—Examination of Miss Saurin" (*Illustrated Weekly News*, 20 February 1869, p. 965).

from day to day," her defense counsel assured the court. The Lord Chief Justice was sympathetic: "Having mutton, and nothing else, might well give a distaste for it." "No doubt, my lord," Coleridge concurred, "and there is good mutton and bad mutton—hot mutton and cold mutton—fat mutton and lean mutton. She had only the bad, the cold, the fat, and—at last—the leavings of the plates of others."[7]

Even Coleridge's eloquence paled beside the description her Jesuit brother had sent to the Catholic bishop four years earlier when he had visited his sister and heard her confession. "Her story," he wrote in a letter introduced as evidence, "is equal to anything I saw in the *Lives of the Saints*, and the horrors of which she has been made the victim far surpass anything that has entered the mind of the most fanatical enemies of the convents. . . . Her crimes are those of Christ, my lord, by whom she is ever physically sustained. She is starved and naked, for even her covering by night and day is gone."[8] During one dreadful night, the other nuns had, indeed, snatched away her convent habit and had substituted secular clothes. When the bundle of clothes she had worn as a nun was brought into the court, the result was a sense of shock. They looked so old and so sordid and they were so far past mending that their state "might satisfy the most rigidly interpreted vow of poverty."[9]

The defense had yet to present its case, but *The Times* had had enough. The "amazing disclosures" thus far revealed sufficed to inspire an editorial in which *The Times* cautioned young ladies between the ages of seventeen and twenty against the lures of the convent. With its rules and offices, its habits and services, its fasts and penances, and with "its intimate communion with the POPE, and its guarded intercourse with us poor 'externs' of the outer world," convent life might seem to be a heaven on earth, but it was not so. Perhaps the England of 1869 did not provide enough vocational opportunities for the increasing number of young women brought up as ladies, and the convent doubtless seemed like a splendid scheme "for converting all the female waste into a glorious fabric meant for the Heavenly Jerusalem," but the trial was teaching otherwise. Such alternative occupations as teaching or writing or serving as governess, as operating boardinghouses and watering places, and even "ordinary old maidhood, with its dulness, its weakness, its vicissitudes, and its want of just estimation in the vulgar world" might yet prove preferable after all.

Take away the titles, the bells, the Gothic windows, and the medieval door knockers, and what was a convent? No more than a very human institution, a collection of women who "cannot live together without coming into collision, and without a continual contention as to precedence, command, and submission." Men would not submit to perpetual bullying and would settle their differences both more quickly and more violently, but women acted differently: "Theirs is an infinity of pettiness." The trial revealed the story of a young lady "having to endure for a long period a series of hardships, ignominies, insults, and vexatious annoyances, which none but women could inflict, and none but women, it must be added, could endure." It was an environment in which every example of liberty of thought or action turned out to be a sin. "Indeed feminine ingenuity seemed almost to exhaust itself in devices for doing that which a NERO or a TIBERIUS would have done more terribly."

At last they had learned what convent life was truly like, the life that the young ladies of fashionable Belgravia were supposedly dying for. "This is the promised escape from that miserable house of bondage, the dull old Church of England, with its

TWO GIRLS OF THE PERIOD.

Ritualistic Priest. "THERE, MY CHILD, OBSERVE THAT EXAMPLE OF HUMILITY AND DEVOTION. HOW SWEET TO CHANGE THE VANITIES OF THE WORLD FOR A LOT SO HUMBLE!"

Fashionable Convert. "OH, BUT THAT IS NOT AT ALL WHAT I EXPECTED!—AND WEAR SUCH AWFUL SHOES? AND—— OH REALLY, ON SECOND THOUGHTS, I SHALL STICK TO BELGRAVIA."

The reality of convent life often fell short of the romantic expectations of middle- and upper-class girls (from *Punch*, 20 February 1869, p. 7).

family life and its homely ways. They that fly should have a refuge; they that would avoid the storm must have a harbour; but we don't see it here."[10] The lawyers for the defense immediately complained that *The Times* editorial had been prejudicial to their cause. The Lord Chief Justice, although concurring that newspaper comment on cases in progress was inadvisable, ruled that the trial should continue. The jurymen had not read the article, and neither had he.[11]

The portrait of Mary Saurin presented by the defense was far different: it was that of a young lady who had utterly mistaken her vocation. She had sworn vows of poverty, obedience, and chastity, and yet she had repeatedly violated the first two and had acted in defiance of the spirit of the third. According to the rules of the order, the sisters were pledged "to obey the Mother Superior as holding her authority from God." They were, moreover, "without hesitation [to] comply with all the directions of the Mother Superior, whether in matters of great or little moment, agreeable or disagreeable."[12]

Sister Mary Joseph (described in the trial report as "Mrs. Star") had served as mother superior of the convent in Hull from 1855 to 1867; three times she had been elected superior by the voluntary vote of the community sisters. All had been happy under her stewardship except the plaintiff, who during her youthful years had been difficult only on occasion and who had often but vainly promised to correct her faults. By 1862 her fellow sisters had come to see her as the odd woman out, as a cross for the community to bear. No other community would accept her, and yet the bishop in authority was for long unwilling to agree to her expulsion from the order. What were her faults according to the testimony of Mrs. Star, Mrs. Kennedy (Sister Mary Magdalene, the assistant mother superior), and other members of the order? Mary Saurin was a thief; she made written records reflecting on the character of her fellow sisters; she beat the schoolchildren and stole their food; she lied when found out; she was vain about her dress; she repeatedly pledged repentance but as repeatedly broke her vows.[13]

The details, as set forth in the evidence of Mrs. Star, involved for the most part "matters of . . . little moment," but they did provide a multidimensional portrait. On one occasion, Mary Saurin ate so little at mealtime that the mother superior asked a physician to examine her. When he found her in good health, Miss Saurin, who was then in charge of the convent refectory, was discovered to be eating so much in secret between meals that, not surprisingly, she had little appetite at dinner time. Mrs. Star testified that "on going into the pantry one day I saw her before a ham. I asked her a question and she could not answer me, her mouth was so full—and the lower part of her face was besmeared with grease." "Did you speak to her?" inquired the judge. "When she saw me she turned pale." The spectators burst into laughter.[14]

"Mrs. Star" (Sister Mary Joseph) testifies (from *Vanity Fair*, 1869).

On another occasion, Mary Saurin was found eating straw-
berries in the pantry between meals. "Do you not all sometimes
eat some?" asked Coleridge while cross-examining Mrs. Kerr,
another of the sisters. "Yes, but not with cream," replied the
witness. "If she had leave to eat them, would not the pantry be
the place?" "Yes," acknowledged Mrs. Kerr, "if she had leave to
do so there." Coleridge waxed poetic: "You know the pantry is
the place where the queen 'eat the bread and honey' [*sic*]." The
audience laughed, and the Lord Chief Justice corrected the
solicitor general: "No, it was in the parlour." The audience
laughed again. "Now did you think it a very grave offence,"
asked Coleridge. "Oh, I did," replied the witness, "very bad

indeed; it was so contrary to what I had been taught." "But was it bad in itself to eat a strawberry?" insisted Coleridge. "It is not a great sin," admitted Mrs. Kerr, "but eating an apple is not so either, and you know what has come of eating an apple once." The audience was delighted. "There the sin was not the eating of the apple, but disobedience," Coleridge observed. The witness agreed: "Here there was disobedience also."[15]

Nor was eating without permission the plaintiff's only fault. She was perpetually "borrowing" thread and scissors, pencils and pens, ink and notepaper from her fellow sisters without permission. She even stole a medal from the body of a dead sister. When caught in the act, "her powers of misrepresentation," according to Mrs. Star, "would raise an edifice of falsehood on the least foundation of truth." At one time, Mary Saurin had deliberately cut holes in her clothes to justify getting a new habit. She added extra pockets to her petticoats in which to house small treasures. She was guilty of "the spirit of appropriation."[16] She lit lamps in her room without permission, and she even set the clock back when she found herself late for an assigned duty.

As a teacher at the convent school she had proved equally ineffective. Not only was she deficient in spelling, but she would at times beat the children without cause and would sometimes steal their food. On other occasions, she would speak to them unnecessarily; she would even inquire about their romantic infatuations. Might she not merely have asked about their sewing, wondered the Chief Justice. "No," replied one witness, "I don't think it was, the children seemed so pleased."[17] Mary Saurin also repeatedly found excuses to talk to nonmembers of the community, to so-called externs. In the morning she would rise early without permission to go into the garden, explaining that she was looking at birds' nests. "Were the birds externs?" wondered Coleridge.[18]

The mother superior in due course demoted the nun from the convent school to the convent laundry. Mrs. Star admitted that Miss Saurin's writing implements had been taken away after she was found jotting down critical comments about her fellow sisters. She conceded also that Miss Saurin's correspondence with her relatives was censored when found "too worldly." The tone of her letters to members of her family seemed unduly "tender and affectionate." "We are taught," Mrs. Star observed, "that the natural affections should be moderated and subdued by religious reserve." According to convent custom, outside visitors might be entertained only once a month for a quarter of an hour, but Mary Saurin repeatedly sought longer visits from her relations, and yet each such visit made her more troublesome.[19]

According to the other inmates, the mother superior had been remarkably lenient with their errant sister until the latter's conduct compelled her to be strict. The punishments were standard ones. Mary Saurin had been asked to wear the dust cloth only after failing to heed repeated reminders to do her duty. She was asked, as penance, to wear the dust cloth only for an hour, but she had then defiantly insisted upon wearing it during religious services as well. "As to kissing the floor, we all do it."[20] When asked whether such punishments did not represent "indignities," Mrs. Kennedy concurred: "All punishments are indignities in a sense, but not if deserved."[21]

The sisters had often marveled at the mother superior's patience with Mary Saurin, but at length that patience ran out. As early as 1862 Mrs. Star had asked the bishop to remove the offending nun, and by 1865 her continued presence was making the mother superior physically ill.[22] In a letter to the bishop, Mrs. Star insisted that the community was in so disturbed a state that "it is plain that either Sister Mary Scholastica or I must yield. . . . I feel as one paralysed, without heart, mind, or spirit for anything." The sisters "are, with one exception, docile, simple, self-sacrificing, and laborious. They love God, love each other, love their rules, love the poor."[23] Then at last did the bishop in authority, Dr. Cornthwaite, since 1861 the Roman Catholic bishop of Beverley, ask Mary Saurin's brother to remove her from the convent. When the latter refused, Bishop Cornthwaite appointed a commission of inquiry to recommend a solution; the body was to be "in no sense a judicial proceeding," but it was charged with the task of "the discovery of truth." Miss Saurin's uncle, Father Mathew, was invited to nominate some of the members of the commission. Father Mathew at first gave his sanction to the commission and was, in effect, allowed to serve as his niece's lawyer at the hearing, but when the commission overwhelmingly found against her, he described the proceedings as "a cruel and offensive farce."[24]

Although Mary Saurin denied before the commission most of the charges against her, the members of the commission (with one exception) judged her in the wrong. "I am of the opinion," declared Canon Walker, the commission president, "that the charges against Miss Saurin are abundantly proved, but that she made some important explanations, which, if true, may be justly deemed greatly to mitigate some portion of her offenses. I found it impossible to resist the concurrent testimony of so many respectable deponents, nor could I place much confidence in the hesitating, confused, and indecisive statements of the accused." Canon Walker "was drawn strongly to a conclusion that morally and intellectually she was warped."[25]

Bishop Cornthwaite, who had independently decided that Mary Saurin must be "not quite right in her mind," received his commission's report in June 1866. He thereupon asked Father Mathew to take his niece away. When he refused, the bishop at length decided to exercise his authority to order her removed from the community. "A good cause of removal," he explained to the court, "would be conduct such as would tend to the ruin and destruction of the community, even though in the individual there was not necessarily any great fault." For this purpose, it was not necessary to release her from her conventual vows, though eventually he did free her from them. A full seven months elapsed between the time that she was ordered to leave the convent and the time that she finally departed. The case for the defense seemed plain: "I shall submit, my lord," declared Charles Russell, the chief counsel for the convent, "that there cannot be a legal right to remain in a convent."[26]

All the witnesses having been examined and cross-examined, there remained only the summing up by the counsels for the defense and the plaintiff and the Chief Justice's charge to the jury. A Mr. Mellish, an Anglican by religious affiliation, summed up for the defense. He dismissed as absurd the charges of assault and imprisonment, libel, and conspiracy that had been brought against his clients. The only "assault" reported had been an occasion on which Mrs. Star had asked Miss Saurin to remove some of her petticoats with unauthorized pockets, but this so-called stripping accorded with rules that Mary Saurin had voluntarily accepted. Inasmuch as Miss Saurin was free to depart at any time, there could have been no "imprisonment." As for the charge of libel, had a single sister supported Mary Saurin in charges against her superiors? Why then should Miss Saurin have brought suit? Because she was clearly unfitted for convent life but was unwilling to admit it. Convent life involved certain voluntarily accepted restrictions and required of its members an appropriate attitude of mind. "The mind of Miss Saurin was not so constituted, and to one like her a convent must be intolerable, and she must have made the convent intolerable to herself and to everyone else." But the fact that Miss Saurin was a misfit did not entitle her to manufacture grievances or to cast aspersions on ladies of "unimpeachable and unim-

paired character." Far from wishing to create a scandal, Mrs.
Star and Mrs. Kennedy had sought quietly to ease Miss Saurin
out of a life for which she was unsuited. Had she seen fit, the
plaintiff could have appealed her expulsion to Archbishop Manning or even to the pope. Instead, she refused either to obey her
bishop or to appeal to his episcopal superior. To sue in the
secular courts "was not, according to the rules of the plaintiff's
own Church, the proper course to pursue." Having been law-
fully expelled from her convent but refusing to leave, Miss
Saurin was naturally not treated as a privileged nun. The sisters
did not wish to appeal to the police; they did not wish to create a
disturbance. They deserved the jury's sympathy, not its
condemnation.[27]

John Duke Coleridge, the counsel for the plaintiff, necessarily saw the affair in a different light. The details of the case
might be petty and contemptible, he conceded, but to Miss
Saurin, they were far from trivial. Was she to be allowed to
continue the vocation to which she had devoted her life and to
which she yet desired to consecrate herself, or was she to be
flung back upon a world that she had expected to leave forever
and for which she was now totally unfitted? Was she not only to
remain the unavenged victim of cruelty and oppression but also
to endure a permanent stain on her character? The case transcended Mary Saurin in exposing to English eyes the realities of
convent life. True, the story revealed no trace of "what is com-
monly called 'scandal,' " but it stripped from the so-called religious life every shred of sanctity. Protestants and Catholics alike
believed in feeding the hungry, clothing the naked, teaching the
ignorant, attending the sick, and praying to God, but such
activities did not require a convent, an institution that encouraged the basest and meanest temptations, an institution in
which one found "little sins created by silly rules foolishly
enforced; childish penances for childish faults, . . . all independence of mind crushed out under abject humiliation." What
a dull, unattractive, unsuitable life for modern times!

The immediate question at issue, to be sure, was not
whether convent life was good or bad per se, but whether the
rules, which the plaintiff had admittedly accepted voluntarily,
were "honestly and fairly worked out." If they were, her case
must fail. If the rules were dishonestly perverted and abused in
order to drive her out of her house and her order, her case must
succeed. It was hardly surprising, Coleridge suggested, that the
convent sisters all supported their mother superior in their

testimony; they were all sworn to obey. Mary Saurin's willingness to challenge the rest was in itself "no small guarantee of her sincerity." How petty were the proofs of Miss Saurin's supposed faults was demonstrated by the reluctance of the bishop to take them seriously. How uncharitable the sisters were was demonstrated by the manner in which Mrs. Star forced Miss Saurin to admit her faults in writing and then employed that very letter to help secure her ultimate expulsion. If Miss Saurin was so unsuitable for convent life, why had there been so little complaint of her for almost ten years? People unfitted for a life tended to shrink from it rather than cling to it. Even the counsel for the defense had hesitated to mention the most serious charges—such as that of stealing the medal from the dead sister—because the proof was so scanty. Almost all the detailed charges turned out to be vague or petty—when they had not been refuted. There was evidence aplenty that the nun had been well liked by her schoolchildren and by the Roman Catholic laity. There had never been a bona fide inquiry—all was exaggeration and hostility. Miss Saurin had been made a scapegoat, but the jury could redeem her. The issue of religious prejudice was in no sense involved because the plaintiff and her relations were fully as much Catholics as were the defendants. Admittedly, a verdict in her behalf would be popular, but "do not you be afraid," Coleridge told the jury, "of doing what is right and just because it chances to be popular. . . . You are Miss Saurin's last sole refuge! Through you alone can she obtain reparation or compensation for the wrongs she has suffered."[28]

Cockburn's charge to the jury suggests that England's Chief Justice had been more impressed by the case for the defense than by the case for the plaintiff. Had "this monster case" dealt with any institution other than a convent, Cockburn noted, these "miserable squabbles" would never have attracted the attention they clearly had. Convents had indeed become matters of great public concern, the Chief Justice conceded, but the all-male and presumably all-Protestant jury was warned to guard itself against anti-Catholic prejudice. They all might well believe that withdrawing women from their proper roles as wives and mothers was "contrary to the voice of nature and to the ordinance of God." This was not, however, a case involving a Protestant daughter inveigled into a convent, and the jury should look upon the case as would any twelve Roman Catholics who fully accepted the convent ethos. The case for the defense was that the plaintiff had, in effect, assented to all the acts of which she complained, and yet no convent regulation would warrant personal violence, imprisonment, or conspiracy. The Chief Justice dismissed the counts of assault and imprisonment as unproven. That left conspiracy as the key charge. That the plaintiff was treated "with great severity and great harshness" from 1864 on was clear, but if the plaintiff perpetually resisted the authority she had sworn to uphold, then even that count "becomes very infinitesimal." The Chief Justice next called attention to the inconsistency implicit in the plaintiff's attempts to account for the origins of the supposed conspiracy against her. Her letters, introduced as trial evidence, were written in a tone of mingled humility and self-assertion; they suggested "a sort of vacillating, ill-conditioned, ill-regulated, ill-balanced mind."[29]

Miss Saurin had been the beneficiary of having had her case stated first and last by that most skillful of barristers, John Duke Coleridge. Cockburn considered Coleridge's summing up to have been "one of the most able and eloquent speeches that he remembered in the whole course of his experience." Cockburn went on to review the evidence, both pro and con, on the humiliations that had allegedly been heaped upon Miss Saurin. Perhaps some of the penances were unduly rigorous, "but faults which looked very petty in the face of day appeared in very magnified proportions when seen through the medium of dim convent light." If Mrs. Star's conduct originated in the rebellious behavior of the plaintiff, the case for conspiracy was defeated. And unless the plaintiff's story had impressed the jury as the more creditable, he saw no reason why they ought not to believe the witnesses for the defense, women "who had devoted their life to visiting the sick, instructing the poor, and other acts of piety." That the sisters owed obedience to their superiors was clear, but the Chief Justice doubted that "in our age" the obligation to tell the truth would be "totally obliterated from their minds"—especially under cross-examination.[30]

Whatever implications might be read into Cockburn's summing up, the jury of London businessmen, after deliberating for two and a half hours, found in favor of the defendants on the counts of assault and imprisonment and for the plaintiff on the counts of libel and conspiracy. They did not, however, conclude that the humiliations imposed upon her required damages of five thousand pounds. Five hundred pounds would have to do, and since that amount included the three-hundred-pound dowry, which the convent had, in any case, agreed to return, the punitive damages were assessed even more lightly. When the crowd outside Westminster Hall heard the news, it gave vent to "a loud and long-continued and right hearty English cheer."[31] According to the London *Express*, elderly and middle-aged men and women "chuckled and shook hands as if they had won something for themselves." Where were the convent sympathizers, the paper wondered, inasmuch as every face wore a smile.[32]

Ninety out of a hundred, the *Express* predicted, will see the verdict as a "famous victory," and a survey of newspaper editorials suggests that the *Express* was right. An award of a mere five hundred pounds might seem prosaic, *The Times* agreed, but the law had now declared that "no Mother Superior on English soil can be suffered with impunity to exercise authority as Mrs. STAR exercised hers."[33] For the *Globe*, "the details . . . were simply sickening. . . . May we and our dear ones be evermore delivered from conditions of existence so degrading, so tormenting, and, we will add, so corrupting." Convent life had been exposed as "sordid" and "melancholy," the *Morning Herald* was convinced. All that the case showed, according to the *Pall Mall Gazette*, was "a set of rather spiteful, not very trustworthy, and thoroughly commonplace ladies engaged in making each other wretched, and living in systematic defiance of all the strongest and healthiest instincts and principles of human nature."[34] Although mid-Victorian Englishmen had often voiced suspicion of convents because they believed that their inmates had pledged blind obedience to Roman Catholic priests, in this instance they conceded what some defenders of convents asserted: that they were in truth "female republics." But if a striving for female autonomy constituted a part (a generally unacknowledged part) of the appeal of convent life, then the case of *Saurin* v. *Star* reconfirmed the conviction of most mid-Victorians that female self-government did not and could not work.

"Oh, Don't Be a Nun!" became a favorite music-hall ditty, and *Punch* was inspired to print "The Chant of the Convent Bell." Two of its verses follow:

> Here, from constant dissipation,
>   You will find a nice retreat,
> Of the flesh mortification;
>   Mouldy crusts of bread to eat;
>   Fat mutton if you hate,
>   Fat mutton on your plate.
> Come where holy maceration
>   Shall take down your self-conceit.
>
>   . . . .

> If you have in your possession
>   Bit of rag, or candle end,
> That will be a dire transgression;
>   Or, a letter should you send,
>   Though to relations near
>   Them if you call too dear,
> Such misdeeds will need confession
>   Penance too, when you offend.[35]

In a separate note, *Punch* suggested that nuns who, according to the trial testimony, wore the same vest for ten years or more would make excellent wives if released by their bishops from their vows of celibacy. Such a woman "would be just the wife for a poor philosopher who remains single because he is deterred from matrimony by the fear of linendrapers' and milliners' bills."[36]

For a man like James Grant of the Scottish Reformation Society, *Punch* was too frivolous. The "most important ecclesiastical cause that was ever brought before a British tribunal," a case that exposed "the true nature of Popery," deserved more than transient commentary. The society therefore had the entire transcript of the trial printed and circulated in order "to deter many well-meaning, amiable, but grievously mistaken young ladies from immuring themselves in the dark and dismal cells of a convent." It made no difference that the case involved a nun who desperately sought to remain within her order rather than to escape from it.

Another goal that the circulation of the trial transcript was expected to attain was the passing of a parliamentary statute authorizing the periodic inspection of convents by a duly appointed commission.[37] This was a goal upon which Charles Newdigate Newdegate had long set his heart.

9. Mr. Newdegate Tastes Victory

The main interest of the parliamentary session of 1869 lay neither in the affairs of William Murphy nor in the travails of Sister Mary Saurin but in Gladstone's mammoth bill to disestablish the Church of Ireland. The election of December 1868 had confirmed what the parliamentary division of April 1868 had promised, that the Liberal majority in the House of Commons was now prepared to disestablish and, in part, to disendow the Irish wing of the Anglican church. Although the new organization was to be as independent of the Church of England and of the crown as if it had been a separate Nonconformist denomination, it was ultimately allowed to retain three-fourths of its endowed wealth. Of the remainder, £732,000 was awarded to the Presbyterians and £366,000 to the Roman Catholics (as a permanent substitute for the annual Maynooth grant), while lesser sums went to secular charities.[1] Charles Newdegate fought the measure every step of the way, acknowledging at no time, as did some Conservatives, that any change in the status quo was called for. "Gentlemen on my side of the House have always objected to confiscation," he recalled, "and we do not think it is any additional recommendation in favour of confiscation that the confiscated property of the Protestant Church is to be applied to the purposes of the Roman Catholic religion."[2]

The provision in the measure that would have provided a degree of "concurrent endowment" to Roman Catholic priests and Presbyterian ministers as well as to Anglican clergymen in Ireland was ultimately dropped, but Newdegate became no happier with the bill for that reason. He found unpersuasive the argument that Roman Catholicism was the religion of the majority of the inhabitants of the Emerald Isle and that the religion of a minority ought no longer to be given official preference. The Warwickshire M.P. denied "that the value of a religion can be measured by the number of its adherents. Were I to admit that, I must assume that Christianity in the days of its blessed founder was an imposture." The Liberals were exercising the power of "a tyrant majority" in favor of a proposal that originated not with the Irish people but with the papacy. History had taught the English people that times when Protestantism had to maintain itself without the protection of law "were times of trouble and discord." Needless to add, all Newdegate's efforts, including an amendment designed to protect the role of the laity in the now to be self-governing Church of Ireland, proved vain.[3]

Newdegate was not alone in predicting that the disestablishment of the Protestant Church of Ireland "would pave the way for, and must entail, the establishment of the Roman Catholic Church in its stead."[4] This was a prospect that Disraeli looked upon with resignation and the Vatican with delight. "England is hastening, almost without perceiving it, towards Rome," proclaimed *Osservatore Romano*, the official papal journal, "and the day is not far off in which Great Britain will return obsequiously to the chair of Peter."[5] The act was, in Newdegate's mind, only one more triumph for Archbishop Manning, "that most insinuating of priests," who counseled the Roman Catholic M.P.s daily in the lobby of the House of Commons.[6] The act also led to a political parting of the ways between Newdegate and his longtime Liberal ally, George H. Whalley, M.P. for Peterborough since 1859. Whalley had, in Newdegate's view, discredited the cause of withholding government financial support from the Roman Catholic seminary at Maynooth by rendering that cause "a laughing-stock," and Newdegate began to suspect that the member for Peterborough was a Jesuit in disguise. Whalley, in turn, charged the solemn Newdegate with an "affectation of superiority and supremacy."[7]

Newdegate had both personal and public cause for solemnity in the later 1860s. His beloved mother had died on 21 January 1868, and his stationery, for half a decade thereafter, featured thick black borders. She had demanded his attention. She had served as his confidante. More than twenty years earlier, he had promised her—"I'm the strength of your old age"—and the promise had been kept. In the words of the anonymous author of Newdegate's own obituary,

> One of the most beautiful traits in his character was his deep affection, amounting to homage, of his mother. . . . The attachment existing between them was of a most touching character, and her death was one of the greatest blows Mr. Newdegate experienced in the course of a long and useful life. After her demise, the establishment at Arbury became strictly that of a bachelor, although visitors who chanced to find Mr. Newdegate at home were always sure of a hearty welcome.[8]

The ears of a majority of his countrymen, however, seemed as deaf as ever to his doleful warnings. For moderate journals like the *Spectator*, Newdegate was the prime example of a parliamentary "impracticable" in search of will o' the wisps. Lord Granville, Gladstone's colonial secretary (and after 1870 his foreign secretary), preferred to characterize the squire of Arbury Hall as "The 'Prince Chevalier' of the House of Commons."[9] Newdegate often felt his isolation, and, suspecting that parliamentary reporters under Roman Catholic influence might minimize or ignore his contributions to debate, he hired his own reporter to take notes in the press gallery. *Hansard*, which in the mid-Victorian years often provided no more than summaries of speeches by back-benchers, utilized those notes to record Newdegate's contributions as fully as those of members of the cabinet.[10]

Newdegate saw himself as a spokesman for "the rights and privileges of the subject," whether it be the right of an evangelically minded Anglican to continue to attend services free from Romish church innovations or the right of any subject to send telegraphic messages through the facilities of a company that had not become part of a "dangerous" government monopoly.[11] It was within the framework of traditional English liberties that Newdegate saw himself battling against the pretensions of Rome, and, if his efforts often went unappreciated within the walls of Westminster, they received the applause of most of his constituents. His files contain numerous letters like that from "Emmanuel Lexton, Weaver," who wrote in 1868: "I must Say it done My heart and Soul good to think I had such a Nabiour that whold try to keep me from the Bonds of popery and Slavery." Lexton accompanied his praise with a small gift.[12]

Newdegate's attempt in February 1869 to persuade the House of Commons to establish a select committee to determine whether Roman Catholic communities had properly registered their property trusts with the government and had properly reported all burials in Roman Catholic cemeteries met with little support. Newdegate reminded the house that England was now dotted with more than 1,200 Catholic churches, chapels, and meeting places, with 18 Roman Catholic colleges, 214 convents, and 67 monasteries, and that the total value of conventual and monastic property alone might well add up to more than three million pounds. But his motion, after cursory debate, was voted down by a vote of eighty-five to forty-six.[13] An attempt later in the session to have the government provide an official return of all Roman Catholic property enrolled during the previous three years was similarly defeated.[14]

Early in the spring of 1870, Newdegate returned to the fray once more by introducing a motion asking the House of Commons to set up a "Select Committee to inquire into the existence, character, and increase of Conventual or Monastic Institutions or Societies in Great Britain, and into the terms upon which income, property, and estates belong to such Institutions or

"The Capuchin Monastery at Peckham" . . . "but one of the many proofs of the
money which the priests have been able to collect, and are continually collecting
in England from all who are foolish enough to be deluded by them" (*Illustrated
Weekly News*, 6 March 1869, p. 995).

Societies, or to members thereof, are respectively received,
held, or possessed."[15] Newdegate reminded the house of his
previous attempts to check whether Roman Catholic institutions generally, and convents in particular, were enrolling their
property according to English law. He feared that they were
evading the law against *mortmain*. As in the Middle Ages, he
suspected, property was being withdrawn permanently from
the marketplace, and succession duty was being paid once but
never again.

Why, asked Newdegate, ought Roman Catholic convents
to be outside the purview of the law? They were not so in
Catholic France. All Continental experience demonstrated indeed that "a vast increase of monastic and conventual establishments does not contribute to the national welfare," yet since
1830 they had grown in England at an extraordinary rate. At
times they might promote public education, to be sure, but as
visitors to the kingdom of Naples had discovered, where convents and monasteries were most rife, there popular ignorance
was most dense. Even Gladstone had applauded the fact that
the new kingdom of Italy was using the property of suppressed

monasteries for educational purposes. The Liberal prime minister was "a bright ornament of Christ Church, Oxford, of which I am a humble member; and whence, I ask, came the funds which provided for the education of the right hon. Gentleman and myself, but from suppressed monasteries?"[16] In the debate that followed, neither Newdegate nor his supporters seemed altogether clear as to whether they were asking for immediate convent inspection or merely, as the resolution stated, for an inquiry as to whether such inspection was necessary.[17]

The same John Duke Coleridge who a year before had been the passionate advocate of Mary Saurin's claims in the great convent case had said at that time: "When you recollect that all this was done towards Miss Saurin in the name of God, you have a proof" of John Bunyan's passage "that 'he saw there was a by-way to Hell from the very gates of Paradise.'"[18] Now, as solicitor general, Coleridge found himself in the paradoxical position of opposing Newdegate's motion on behalf of the government. He observed merely that "most people were of the opinion that Roman Catholics should be at liberty to follow out the principles of their religion, where they did not interfere with the general well-being of the State, and should be responsible to the Almighty alone for the particular forms which their belief might take." Coleridge conceded that if Roman Catholicism were making "considerable progress" among the mass of the English population, Newdegate might have some cause for the alarm he had expressed, but Coleridge perceived no such growth and consequently saw no useful purpose in the inquiry that Newdegate advocated.[19]

Newdegate received strong support from several Liberal back-benchers, however, including Dr. Thomas Chambers, M.P. for Marylebone, a cosponsor of the resolution. Was the government aware, asked Chambers, that monasteries, of which there were by then sixty-nine in England, were prohibited by the Catholic Emancipation Act of 1829? "What other denomination would be allowed so to violate the law?"[20] A twentieth-century Catholic historian concurs that the flamboyant and self-confident Italianate orders introduced into England in the 1850s and 1860s—Redemptionists, Passionists, and Oratorians—gave "Protestant bigotry . . . plenty to feed on."[21]

In summing up the debate, Newdegate returned to a theme that clearly moved him as much as, or more than, the alienation of English property, namely, the religious seduction of English womanhood. Petition after petition had descended upon the House of Commons asking protection for convent inmates,

Charles Newdigate Newdegate, M.P.—"Statesmen No. 59" (*Vanity Fair*, 13 August 1870, p. 66).

pleading that young and inexperienced girls not be permitted to subject themselves to an unknown but rigorous discipline under which they were forbidden to communicate with friends, placed in dungeons, and even smuggled out of their homeland.[22] Petitions requesting government inspection had indeed been sent to Parliament in increasing numbers by a variety of public meetings and by numerous Anglican and Dissenting groups. Ninety-five petitions bearing more than sixteen thousand signatures had been submitted during 1865; a comparable number had been sent in 1869; 134 petitions bearing over thirty-three thousand signatures had been submitted early in 1870. The petitions told repeatedly of "much suffering and helpless privation," of "no legal means of escape," of unreported "deaths and interment," and of "the deprivation of personal liberty and property."[23]

When the votes were counted, Newdegate, a melancholy Cassandra well acquainted with the experience of defeat in the division lobbies, discovered to his own astonishment that his motion had won by a vote of 131 to 129. He had won the support (counting tellers) of forty-four Liberals as well as that of eighty-eight fellow Conservatives. Only four Conservatives had voted against him. As on comparable previous divisions, his party leader, Disraeli, had failed to participate.[24]

What factors account for Newdegate's success in 1870 in the face of his defeats in similar attempts in 1865 and 1869? Part of the answer certainly lies in an increased popular awareness of the growth of Roman Catholic convents and monasteries in Great Britain. Another seventy-one convents and fourteen monasteries had been founded since 1863 alone, and the Scottish Reformation Society had prepared a map "which showed Lancashire, Warwickshire, Middlesex, and Lanarkshire literally black with crosses and other emblems marking spots where the Roman Catholics had established places of worship, instruction, or conventual retirement." In the words of the *Spectator*, "half the dislike still entertained in England towards the theological system [of the Catholics] is based upon a traditional suspicion of the monastic establishments."[25]

The popular impression of what such institutions were like was very much influenced by the works of Victorian painters. During the early and mid-Victorian era, there was scarcely an annual exhibition by the Royal Academy or the British Institution that did not include at least one portrait of a nun or the depiction of a convent scene. The nun as symbol of spiritual docility or of repressed sexuality or as victim of disappointed love or physical cruelty constituted a subject of perennial fascination for Victorian artists.[26] One case in point was the giant painting displayed by the Royal Academy at a Trafalgar Square exhibition in 1868. The canvas portrayed a beautiful young girl being walled up by a number of grim-faced monks while observed by compassionless old nuns. The impression of hopelessness was relieved only by the figures on the right-hand side of the picture, a gallant young knight in full armor bursting into the chamber with his followers to rescue his beloved. The painter had appropriately entitled his painting *Not a Whit Too Soon*. "Oh, how dreadful!" exclaimed one viewer, the young bride of an Anglican clergyman. "Why are such things tolerated? Can't the Government interfere?" Her husband's reply was a guarded "I am sure I don't know." Outside the exhibition hall, a young boy was hawking *Revelations of a Convent; or, The Story of Sister Lucy* at a shilling a copy.[27] Catholic apologists sought to explain that even the most damning medieval sources referred to perpetual imprisonment rather than walling up alive, but nineteenth-century authors had imprinted the vision of horror upon the popular mind. Thus Sir Walter Scott:

> And now the blind old Abbot rose
> To speak the Chapter's doom
> On those the wall was to enclose
>   Alive within the tomb

and Elizabeth Barrett Browning:

> A nun in the east wall buried alive,
> Who mocked at the priest when he called her to shrive.[28]

Although the details of the *Saurin* v. *Star* trial of the previous year had hardly confirmed the preconceptions illustrated in *Not a Whit Too Soon* or in such examples of romantic poetry, they had borne out the assumption of many Protestant readers that the atmosphere of the convent was degrading and demoralizing.[29] If *Saurin* v. *Star* had also inadvertently demonstrated that Roman Catholic nunneries lay within the purview of English law as it then stood, the case may at the same time have whetted the public appetite for further convent horror stories. In August 1869 *The Times* gave appropriate publicity to the case of Barbara Ubryk, "the nun of Cracow," whose superiors had shut her in a dungeon where she had been kept for years on end without heat or clothing. The *Tablet* sought to explain the case as one of insanity—the victim, who sought to destroy all clothing and furniture within reach, had been well fed—but *The Times* was certain that this revelation of "diabolical" events in Austria-Hungary would "tend to confirm the repulsion with which Protestants regard these institutions."[30] At the same time, J. R. Digby Beste, a popular author of the day, recounted the story of how his adopted daughter had entered a Roman Catholic convent and how he had found it impossible to locate her despite appeals to Cardinal Wiseman and the lord chancellor as well as to the local police. According to Beste, it was only after the church authorities learned that "she was not entitled to any large property" that she was at once given up.[31] During the same year the Protestant Evangelical Mission and Electoral Union found occasion to republish the far more inflammatory, twenty-five-year-old account by one William Hogan, an apostate priest educated at Maynooth. His disenchantment with the Catholic faith began, he reported, when as a young priest he was attached to a nunnery. There a convert from Protestantism revealed to him that she had become pregnant. Had she revealed this fact to her episcopal confessor, asked Hogan. It was that very confessor, the bishop, she explained, who was the guilty party. The young woman had afterward died of a poison administered by her mother superior in order to effect an abortion. Hogan subsequently emigrated to the United States where during the 1830s he had been excommunicated by the bishop of Philadelphia.[32]

Yet another event that caused parliamentary opinion to veer in Newdegate's favor was the widely publicized conversion to Roman Catholicism late in 1868 of John Patrick Crichton-Stuart, the twenty-two-year-old third marquess of Bute, one of the wealthiest landowners in all of Great Britain, who was just embarking upon a career that would make him "the greatest private patron of architecture in British history."[33] Orphaned at age twelve and the subject of a notorious legal custody struggle, Bute had persuaded himself that the Reformation had been a gigantic mistake and that, if he remained in the Church of England, "I should be making myself an accomplice after the fact in a great national crime and the most indefensible act in history." The loss of so eminent a member of the aristocracy (and a Christ Church graduate into the bargain) excited new alarm in the press that "the shameless machinations of 'jesuitism' " were precipitating a new wave of conversions to Catholicism. So fumed *The Times*, while the *Daily News* lamented that Bute "had taken up his honours, wealth and influence, and laid them in the lap of the Church of Rome." The young nobleman had no desire to be the focus of controversy and left the country

for half a year. In the meantime, the *Tablet* exulted in the voluntary "martyrdom" that not Bute alone but "hundreds, if not
thousands, here in this matter-of-fact, money-making, and
money-loving London, are deliberately accepting, and cheerful-
ly suffering for the love of God, and for the happiness of belonging to His Church."[34]

Benjamin Disraeli, who had shown his awareness of the
powerful spiritual attraction of Roman Catholicism in earlier
novels like *Contarini Fleming, Sybil*, and *Tancred*, utilized the
conversion of the marquess of Bute as the basis of his novel
Lothair (1870). Disraeli, who felt that Archbishop Manning had
stabbed him in the back in 1867–1868 during the parliamentary
negotiations designed to set up a Roman Catholic university in
Dublin, transmuted Manning in his novel into Cardinal Grandi-
son, "a wonderful study of asceticism, devotion, high breeding,
tact, delicacy, and unscrupulousness."[35] According to a twentieth-century appraisal, *Lothair* described "the last chapter in the
reign of the English territorial magnates." Contemporaries were
more struck by "its very clever and damaging exposure of the
arts of the Roman clergy" and suggested that the novel's immediate object was "to hold up the whole body of English
Roman Catholics to derision." The *Morning Post* dubbed it "A
Romance of No-Popery." It may be more accurate to view
Lothair as an attack neither on Roman Catholic ceremony nor on
the character of the quietist English Catholics who had doggedly
adhered to the faith of their fathers but as an assault upon
converts like Manning who had forsaken their own religious
tradition in favor of an imported faith at once exotic, exclusive,
and subversive.[36] For the moment, Disraeli appeared to have
given up his hope of winning the Roman Catholic vote for the
Conservative cause. It is fair to add, however, that the converted marquess of Bute remained politically a Conservative
and that, two years later, Disraeli attended his wedding.

The factor that had contributed most to what the *Spectator*
called "the thrill of anti-Catholic panic" was no new revelation
of convent life or any well-publicized conversion but "what
was, in every sense, the crisis of the nineteenth century, the
Vatican Council."[37] The gathering of Roman Catholic clerics in
1869 and 1870 had been carefully arranged so as to lead to a
preordained climax: the declaration of papal infallibility. As
Britain's unofficial emissary to the Vatican, Lord Odo Russell,
privately predicted to his uncle, Earl Russell, the former prime
minister: "It will all be so organized and managed as to render
the expression of any individual and independent opinion on

the part of the foreign Bishops quite impossible,—and they will be disagreeably surprized to find themselves compelled to sanction what they intended to condemn!"[38]

The opposition within the episcopate to the doctrine of infallibility was crushed by a margin of five to one, and the *Spectator* was caused to marvel: "No Pope has ever succeeded like this Pope." "Nothing but the audacity of blindness," thundered *The Times*, "can have impelled the Roman Church, at this crisis in European history, to proclaim formally this monstrous proposition."[39] It was especially distressing to the London press that English Roman Catholics like Manning were, unlike their French counterparts, in the vanguard of the movement for papal infallibility and thus forsaking "that cause of freedom which our forefathers had in common with all other Teutonic races."[40]

At a time when *The Times* saw the propapal party committing the Roman Catholic church to "a mortal war with civil society" and when the bishops of Lincoln, Ely, Guildford, and Gloucester were urging the archbishop of Canterbury to issue a ringing "Manifesto to the World in Opposition to Romish Error,"[41] Newdegate had no lack of company in his avowed hostility to papal pretensions. "The action of the Papacy has come to this," he concluded, "that every State in Europe is compelled to resist the Pope."[42]

Gladstone's Liberal government of 1868–1874 had begun on a note of cooperation with Roman Catholics, a policy manifested not only in the measure to disestablish the Irish church but also in a decision henceforth to offer new peerages to Roman Catholics "with equality in proportion to their numbers." Archbishop Manning would hardly have acclaimed the elevation of so principled a political liberal as Sir John Acton, one of the first two men to be nominated, but, aside from several dormant peerages revived in the 1830s, they constituted the first new additions in several centuries to the ranks of those Catholic peers whose titles had survived the hazards of Reformation and post-Reformation politics.[43] Gladstone's spirit of amity toward domestic Roman Catholicism did not extend to the proceedings in Rome. Until overruled by his cabinet, he had indeed considered a joint international intervention in the Vatican Council in 1870. He confided to his friend, Dr. Ignaz von Döllinger, the German Roman Catholic theologian, his fears that Christian belief generally was being "exposed to subtle & frightful danger" by the actions of the Vatican Council.[44]

Though Gladstone had voted against Newdegate's pro-

posed inquiry—according to the London *Standard*, Newdegate
had indeed carried his motion "in the teeth of the whole power
of the Government"[45]—the prime minister clearly derived wry
satisfaction from this manifestation of English hostility toward
Vatican presumption. "The undeniable fact," wrote Gladstone
privately, "is that the proceedings at Rome are producing effects
in this country very unfavourable to our Roman Catholic fellow
subjects. . . . Those who extend religious authority or the
claims of it into the civil sphere must be prepared for the *lex
talionis*."[46] Through the agency of Lord Odo Russell, Gladstone
made it clear to Manning how high were the costs of unbridled
ultramontanism. "How sad it is for us both," Gladstone wrote
to his onetime friend, "that the things which the one looks to as
the salvation of faith and church, the other regards as their
destruction."[47]

In the later years of Gladstone's public life, his views were
often to diverge from those of his monarch, but on the potential
threat of papal claims they were largely at one. "I can see that
she has strong anti-Catholic feelings," noted Gladstone's home
secretary on first meeting Victoria, and the queen's correspondence with her eldest daughter, the crown princess of Prussia,
reveals how the two ladies confirmed one another's predilec-
tions. "Here also," the queen wrote in 1869, "people will not see
the danger of encouraging the R[oman] Catholics which is too
foolish. You can never conciliate without their encroaching."[48]

Once the immediate domestic and international climate of
opinion is kept in mind, the general welcome that the British
press extended to the prospect of a parliamentary inquiry into
convent life becomes less surprising. As recently as August 1869
the *Catholic World* had suggested that Newdegate was "building
castles in the air" if he expected his motion to carry.[49] Back in
1864 *The Times* had expressed its shame at the support that
Newdegate's anti-Catholic harangues were attracting, but now
its approach was far more sympathetic. Why did Roman Catholicism remain so unpopular in mid-Victorian England? Why did
Roman Catholics continue to find it so difficult to gain a seat in
the House of Commons or even in a town council or parish
vestry when representatives of other religious minorities like
Jews and Quakers were making substantial progress? It was not
because of the speculative opinions of Roman Catholics, *The
Times* suggested, and if the cause be prejudice, "there is seldom
a prejudice without a reason." English Protestants were upset
not by Catholic doctrine but by Catholic discipline in matters
such as clerical celibacy, enforced confession, and conventual

vows. Why ought convents, whose vows had no standing in English law, to be treated with greater indulgence than trade unions? A deep-rooted suspicion of the entire system was characteristic, *The Times* now concluded, not merely of narrow-minded evangelicals but also of all Englishmen, religious or secular, who were devoted to the supremacy of English law and committed to individual freedom.[50]

The *Daily News*, which advertised itself as "A High Class Liberal Paper" and boasted the largest circulation of the day, felt sure that "MR. NEWDEGATE by his perseverance may have succeeded in conferring a real benefit upon the community." It was hardly possible, after all, for the state to renounce "the duty of protection which it owes to every individual under its allegiance."[51] The *Daily Telegraph*, which a year before had asked the state to ensure that conventual discipline did not turn into an instrument of religious terrorism, now expressed the hope that convent leaders would open their doors to state inspection just as mine owners and factory owners had done earlier.[52] It is "a most righteous and proper inquiry," added the *English Independent*, a voice of religious Nonconformity. After all, observed the staunchly Conservative *Morning Advertiser*, "If lunatic asylums are bound to admit a Government inspector, why should a nunnery, which is but another sort of lunatic asylum, be left altogether uncared for and unwatched?"[53] The more moderate *Spectator* stressed another aspect of the matter, that an official inspection might well "relieve the convents of a load of obloquy under which they are now quite needlessly content to remain."[54] As Charles Newdegate read such comments in the public press, he had genuine cause to wonder whether a man so often accused of tilting against dragons of his own invention had not at last been recognized as the savior of his nation's institutions.

10. Papists, Protestants, and Mr. Gladstone

It was not in the nature of an English Roman Catholic community led by men like Henry Edward Manning and William Bernard Ullathorne to turn the other cheek toward the expression of anti-Catholic sentiment embodied in Charles Newdegate's successful motion. The archbishop of Westminster and the bishop of Birmingham were both in Rome at the time of the vote, and their absence may help to explain the relatively lackluster opposition that Roman Catholic M.P.s had provided. The laity had felt too confident. As the duke of Norfolk explained to Gladstone, they had "believed that Mr. Newdegate's motion was too monstrous to obtain any formidable support, and did not think it necessary to argue against a palpable injustice."[1] Once the motion had passed, however, cries of protest began to be heard throughout the land.

The Times was filled with letters like that from "A CATHOLIC" who described the parliamentary resolution as "an irreparable personal insult, as a gross piece of injustice, and as an infringement of the liberty of the subject." If the government were to allow the projected investigation to proceed, he warned, it would lose the support of every Catholic M.P.[2] The firesides of nuns, agreed "INDIGNANS," deserved to be "as inviolate as the traditional 'castle' of every Englishman."[3] In a letter to the *Daily News*, "A NUN" was willing to concede Newdegate's sincerity as a self-appointed "knight-errant to deliver the oppressed," but the fact that Protestants failed to understand the motives that caused women to adopt a religious vocation did not give Parliament the right to infringe on their "liberty of conscience" or to violate their "common rights as Englishwomen." Surely, the House of Commons had more important business than to interfere with those who had dedicated their lives to tending the sick, praying for the sorrowful, teaching the poor, guarding the aged, and reclaiming the fallen. "Why not have a Committee to investigate the condition of English families?" Many of them were reputedly unhappy.[4] Convents had no wish to hold by force nuns who became indifferent to their calling, and those who had lawful reasons to leave could obtain lawful dispensations from their religious superiors.

One former nun who had received such a dispensation was the daughter of the marquess of Queensberry, Lady Gertrude Douglas. In a letter to *The Times*, she revealed that she had spent three years in a convent as a novice and two more as a nun before seeking and being granted release from her vows for personal reasons. Even if she had not obtained such ecclesiastical release, she would not have sought relief from the civil law because she was convinced that "no authority from God could rest with any but the priests of the Holy Catholic Church." A nun neither needed nor sought any other court of appeal. No one had ever prevented her from communicating with friends and relations by letter or in person. The nuns she had known had all been carefully prepared for their chosen life and had found joy within that life. "There reigned about one and all of them, without exception, a spirit of simple, childlike confidence and attachment for their Superior; a warm devotion to their work and their Order. I never in the course of those five years heard an expression of discontent upon the lips of any of the sisters. . . . They all seemed happy, really and truly happy."[5]

The proposed committee did stimulate a mood of genuine anxiety among many of the Catholic clergy,[6] and the *Dublin Review* of October 1870 was moved to devote a long article to a thoughtful defense of the convent system. The anonymous author poured scorn on the notion that any association of religious women would wish to retain a reluctant inmate against her will or that, if such a desire existed, it could be carried out in Victorian England. It was, the journal suggested, a thousand times easier for Newdegate to hide away a black-sheep family member in his spacious Warwickshire country house than for the average convent to do the same. Its grounds were far less spacious and its non-Catholic neighbors far more suspicious. Admittedly, a professed nun who broke her vows and left the convent had committed a sin, but so did every wife who left her legal husband. Did that imply that all wives ought to be regarded as prisoners in their own homes? The article concluded that, although much anticonvent feeling was founded "upon a misunderstanding of the real character" of such institutions, a modicum of hostility was likely to continue.[7]

A far more lively and intense attack upon the Warwickshire M.P. and his followers was launched by Father Peter Gallwey in his *The Committee on Convents—The Nun's Choice: Newgate or Newdegate*. Gallwey was a young Irish-born Jesuit priest who, during the previous decade, had converted numerous young English women to Catholicism and who shared with Manning the reputation among Roman Catholics as one of "the two best preachers of their generation." The fierce aggressiveness and scornful humor that characterize his sermons are also evident in

his anti-Newdegate tract.[8] "Hard Times! Hard Times! Are You
Come Once More?" asked Gallwey on the title page. Would the
parliamentary inquiry prove "nugatory"? Not at all, retorted the
author; it would prove "Newdegatory"—and even a parliamentary decree that the old Tower rack and thumbscrew be restored
to use and "that one Nun or two should be tortured every week
or every fortnight" would be preferable to "this Newdegatory
inquiry with which our Nuns are menaced." Completely ignor-
ing the remarkable composure and verbal skill with which witnesses in the Saurin case had faced cross-examination, Gallwey
went on to assert that the nuns of England were terrified by the
prospect of an inquiry, fearful that they might damage their
community by saying either too much or too little. Admittedly,
the committee would eventually find that there was no case
against the nuns, but by then the damage to their spirits and
their communities would have been done. It was therefore the
solemn duty of Catholic laymen to prevent the nuns from ever
being brought before the committee as "criminals against whom
there is a presumption of guilt." One step of state interference
would inevitably lead to another until all nuns and monks, as
once before, would be compelled to leave the island. And if the
nuns departed, "will Mr. Newdegate provide for our orphans
and our aged poor?" Will he "furnish funds, and teachers, and
nurses?"

Devils must be at work in the land, Father Gallwey felt sure.
Otherwise parliamentary committees would be appointed not
to investigate the lives of holy Catholic women but rather "to
purify the theatres of London, to watch over the press of England, to check the voluptuous extravagance and dishonest
speculation that beggars the families of England and condemns
the young men and young maidens of England to accept a life of
unholy licentiousness instead of the happy and holy home of
Christian marriage." Resistance at all costs was Gallwey's in-
junction, because inspection was no more than a prelude to
confiscation. In the business of inspecting convents Newdegate's "immediate predecessor" was none other than Henry
VIII's agent, Thomas Cromwell. What weapons should the re-
sisters employ? They should utilize spiritual weapons, such as
prayers and fasting (and an especially frugal meal to be known
as "the Newdegate dinner"), as well as every type of parliamentary stratagem. Let no nun face the members of the committee
unless she had been forcibly brought before them by the police.
Once there, let the nuns keep silent even at the risk of jail. It
would be better by far "to undergo the horrors of Newgate than

to yield to what the Irish would call the deluding tongue of Mr. Newdegate."[9] As his biographer observes, Father Gallwey had a gift for Irish fantasy as well as for sardonic humor.[10]

One senses in Gallwey's pamphlet and in other public statements that the Roman Catholic hierarchy was not altogether unhappy at the prospect of a mild dose of English persecution—one just sufficient to strengthen the faith and to increase the financial support of the faithful. In Rome, Manning boasted to Lord Odo Russell (who informed Gladstone) that unless Newdegate's inquiry were quashed, Roman Catholic army and constabulary officers in Ireland were determined to resign their commissions.[11] For the moment, however, the hierarchy concentrated upon a massive campaign of prayers and petitions against the establishment of the committee. In the absence of the leading archbishops, a meeting of eminent Catholic laymen was convened at the Stafford Club in Piccadilly with the duke of Norfolk presiding. It was the largest such meeting that those present could remember, and it involved numerous members of Parliament including Sir John Simeon, the sole Catholic then representing an English constituency. It also included numerous peers and army officers, a few clergymen, and Sir Charles Clifford, the eminent barrister with whom Newdegate had tangled before. Clifford strongly opposed the notion that a parliamentary inquiry would set to rest the slanders that had been spread concerning convent life. Those who believed that "knew but little of the cunning malignity and of the tactics of the enemy." If there were to be an investigation, at the very least let it be conducted by a statutory commission with the power to put witnesses under oath. In the meantime, he urged his fellow Roman Catholics to do everything in their power "to defeat the unconstitutional, abominable, and tyrannical action." The earl of Denbigh agreed that English Catholics were "on the brink of a social persecution such as they had not had in their time before," and the meeting subsequently resolved to send a personal deputation to the prime minister and to condemn the proposed committee "by which practical malignity, morbid curiosity, and reckless calumny are, for the first time in the history of this country, publicly recognized as sufficient grounds for the persecution of private individuals." The proposed inquiry, the resolution concluded, "must and will be regarded as a declaration of war against the Catholics of the United Kingdom."[12]

A deputation did call upon both Gladstone and Granville and, with the blessings of the hierarchy, a vast petition cam-

The duke of Norfolk, the youthful premier Roman Catholic layman in England
(from a scrapbook in the University of Illinois Library).

paign was organized. A model petition form was drawn up by
the duke of Norfolk, A. Langdale, and Sir Charles Clifford and
posted to every Catholic priest in England whose address could
be found. Each was asked to gather signatures in support of the
demand that Newdegate's proposed committee be halted in its
tracks. As a result, petitions with over 100,000 signatures arrived in the House of Commons within a week; within three
months, the total was to reach 284,664. The petitions came
exclusively from Roman Catholic sources—churches, colleges,

convents, and specially convened public meetings—and with scarcely an exception, all petitioners signed the same model petition. It described the proposed inquiry as "an infringement upon their rights as British subjects, and an impeachment of the honour and security of those whose welfare and liberty are already thoroughly guaranteed."[13]

A petition campaign that could obtain in a few weeks the signatures of half the adult Roman Catholic population of England and Scotland demonstrated a very high degree of organization. A few petitions also arrived from Ireland, which was not included in the proposed inquiry although it supplied some 50 percent of the inmates of English convents.[14] The militant tone and broad scope of the Catholic reaction startled both Newdegate and many of the newspapers that had hailed the House of Commons vote. Newdegate and his supporters felt compelled to launch a petition campaign of their own. Their petitions publicly regretted that such powerful efforts were underway to prevent the naming of a committee whose inquiries were "necessary for the protection of freedom." Pro-Newdegate petitions poured into Parliament from a wide spectrum of English society: Anglican churches and Congregationalist, Wesleyan, and Baptist chapels were well represented. So were the organizations that took a highly specific interest in limiting the expansion of Roman Catholicism in Great Britain: the Protestant Alliance, the Protestant Association, the Scottish Reformation Society, various chapters of the Protestant Defence Association, and the Lord's Day Observance Society. Among English communities, London, Birmingham, Liverpool, Sheffield, Spitalsfields, and Wolverhampton were most strongly represented in the pro-Newdegate campaign, as was Paisley in Scotland. Within a few weeks, a total of 985 petitions bearing 253,470 signatures upholding the Protestant cause had reached Westminster.[15]

Newdegate also sought to stem the epistolary storm with his own letter to *The Times* and with repeated explanations to the House of Commons. If the members of the Stafford Club sincerely expected members of Parliament wantonly to insult any inmate of any convent, they must have a very low opinion of the members of the House of Commons. Or were their professions of regard for the feelings of their conventual sisters no more than a smokescreen to avoid any investigation of the law? Roman Catholics apparently claimed "a total immunity from all secular or civil control" that was granted to no other denomination and was altogether opposed to the spirit of the age.[16] At the

same time, papers like the *Church Times* (High Church Anglican)
agreed that Lady Gertrude Douglas and the Stafford Club indignation meeting had taken the wind out of Newdegate's sails,
and the *Saturday Review* was moved to wonder whether Newdegate intended his committee to prepare a new *Confessional Unmasked* and to appoint the notorious William Murphy as convent
inspector.[17] The Conservative *Morning Post* agreed that it would
be foolish to ignore the sense of injury that the proposed inquiry
had aroused among Roman Catholics.[18]

In contrast, the Conservative *Standard*, the independent
Times, the Liberal *Daily News*, and the Radical *Pall Mall Gazette* all
agreed that the Roman Catholics were protesting too much.
Their language, suggested the *Standard*, was "childishly extravagant and violent, and most offensive to the laws and institutions of the country. . . . The greater the outcry against examination, the stronger will be the impression that there exists
something in these religious institutions which it is not conve-
nient to have examined." Surely a Parliament that had just
disestablished the Protestant Church of Ireland and was engaged in relieving the condition of Irish Catholic tenant farmers
by means of a new land act merited less hostility from the
Catholic community. If Lady Gertrude was right, observed *The
Times*, and nuns were neither cajoled nor coerced nor tyran-
nized nor cut off from the sympathy and support of their friends
and relations, then why should they fear an inquiry from a
committee of gentlemen of high character and social position?
Such an inquiry might well dispel the anti-Catholic prejudices
"still to be found among the lower portion of our population"
upon which foul-mouthed lecturers like Murphy fed. It remained fair to acknowledge that in his "jealousy for the supremacy of our national Law, and a still stronger jealousy for
individual freedom, and for the protection of the weak and the
impulsive," Newdegate had at his back not merely the ultra-
Protestants "but also a formidable array of outside supporters"
covering the entire political and religious spectrum.[19]

The *Daily News* wondered how "a natural and reasonable
demand for information" could constitute "a violation of the
common rights of Englishwomen?" The *Standard*, while conceding that in theory the conventual veil, like death, leveled all
social ranks, wondered whether Lady Gertrude Douglas would
have fared quite so well as a nun had her father not been a
marquess. The *Pall Mall Gazette*, in contrast, was quite willing to
concede Lady Gertrude's observation that most nuns were content with their lot. "Why, indeed, should it be otherwise? Most

women take naturally to being placed under strict regulations, relieved from worldly anxieties, and having a daily task laid upon them sanctioned by strong religious motives." Yet a community whose members all abjured secular intervention as profane almost required some kind of inspection. Moreover, the convent life that Lady Gertrude depicted in such glowing colors surely deserved publicity; "perfect people and perfect institutions are so rare in this world that it becomes almost a duty for them to court inquiry." What a coup for Lady Gertrude if "a stern inspector appointed by Mr. Newdegate—or even Mr. Newdegate himself— were to be converted to the True Church by the touching spectacle presented to him!"[20]

However the pros and cons of convent investigation may be evaluated, the Warwickshire squire had clearly succeeded in raising at least a minor whirlwind. In the opinion of the *Illustrated Times*, his motion "has agitated the country more than it has been agitated for a long time."[21] But gaining parliamentary approval for an investigative committee was one thing; appointing that committee and setting it to work was another. As Newdegate soon discovered, his parliamentary path was not yet clear of pitfalls. Although his self-confidence had been bolstered by the unexpected compliments of London's leading newspapers and his sense of personal courage confirmed by the cries of indignant outrage from the champions of English Catholicism, Newdegate decided to proceed cautiously. The House of Commons had approved the appointment of a committee, but the members of that committee had yet to be chosen. Newdegate remembered that back in 1854, when Parliament had given analogous approval in principle to a committee to investigate convents, such approval had given way to practical defeat when the house failed to agree on any of the names proposed. The Warwickshire M.P. was determined to avoid that pitfall. Ordinarily, a back-bencher who successfully moved for the appointment of a select committee was expected to go on to propose the members of that committee and to nominate himself as chairman. Instead on 8 April 1870, Newdegate moved that the Committee of Selection nominate both the committee's chairman and its membership.[22]

William Cogan, since 1852 a member for county Kildare, Ireland, decided to take advantage of Newdegate's action to introduce an amendment asking that the proposed committee be discharged altogether. He could not believe that the vote of 29 March had been anything but a fluke and insisted that it did not express the true feeling of a majority of the House of Com-

mons. Injecting into the debate the sense of outrage that had
been missing a week and a half earlier, Cogan accused the
supporters of Newdegate's motion of inflaming religious fanaticism and of flooding the country with the vilest calumnies
against those noble women who cared for the young and nursed
the aged. Besides wishing to subject those brave and angelic
ladies to a reckless "inquisition," Newdegate apparently expected English monks called before his committee publicly to
incriminate themselves, because he was fully aware that the
Catholic Emancipation Act of 1829 had left male orders illegal.
Besides, once the House of Commons had thus violated the
sanctity in England of what were in truth private houses, was it
prepared to extend its inquiries into Ireland and thereby add
more fuel "to the flame of discontent and danger which un-
happily existed now in that country?" Cogan appealed to "the
honour, the chivalry, and the love of fair play of the House of
Commons" and pleaded with the house to reverse its earlier
verdict.

Sir John Simeon, who seconded Cogan's amendment,
could recall no question that had "so deeply stirred the feelings
of his Catholic fellow-countrymen." Henry Matthews, the M.P.
for Dungarvan who was sixteen years later to become the first
Victorian Roman Catholic appointed to cabinet office, agreed
that in no other land would such a Protestant inquiry be projected. In Catholic lands, convents might receive closer legal
supervision, but they also possessed far greater legal
privileges.[23] Newdegate's problems were compounded when
one member of the Committee of Selection expressed his distaste for the task that Newdegate wished to assign to himself
and his colleagues and when the Liberal home secretary, Henry
Austin Bruce, reminded Newdegate that his original motion
"had raised religious passions, which could not be easily
allayed." Newdegate could derive a degree of comfort, however, from the fact that a motion to adjourn—in truth a test of
parliamentary sentiment on the issue—went in his favor, 110 to
76.[24]

Eventually, the debate did have to be adjourned for the
day, and Newdegate did not find another spot on the Commons' agenda until three weeks later. On 28 April, he defended
both his honor and his proposed approach. Could people of
education and social position truly believe, he wondered, that
the House of Commons was about "to commit some monstrous
outrage on some of Her Majesty's subjects"? He had no desire to
invite an invidious debate on each name that he proposed.

Nomination by the Committee on Selection freed both the house and himself from any imputation of unfairness. Again the debate dragged on. Again the home secretary reminded the house that national excitement on the subject was so intense that "it was impossible to discuss it with moderation." A test vote again went in Newdegate's favor—by a margin of 173 to 128—but ultimately the debate had to be adjourned once more.[25] It seemed clearer than ever that sooner or later the Liberal ministry in the person of the prime minister would have to take a hand.

Although it would be misleading to suggest that the convent issue presented Gladstone with a political problem of heroic proportions, it did pose for him the neat dilemma: how to sail the ship of state between the Scylla of Charles Newdegate and his temporary majority and the Charybdis of Archbishop Manning and his English flock. The member of that flock who was most persistent in urging the prime minister to act was the duke of Norfolk. If the ministry could not stop the inquiry altogether, the duke asked Gladstone on 4 April, could it not have the task performed by a tribunal that, unlike a select committee of the Commons, could examine witnesses under oath? It should be made possible to indict such witnesses for perjury and to sue them for slander. Gladstone was skeptical: did Norfolk truly seek such a statutory commission or had he put the suggestion forward as a debating point?[26] Within a week, two more alternate possibilities had been called to Gladstone's attention: to withhold from the select committee the power to compel the attendance of women, and to transform the proposed committee into a joint Lords–Commons body. The government was prepared to support whichever of these alternatives the duke and his committee of Catholic laymen preferred. What it was not in a position to do was to rescind Newdegate's resolution outright. The vote of 29 March had not been altogether accidental; it reflected genuine parliamentary concerns. In any event, Gladstone observed, his ministry had been charged with responsibility for resolving "other and greater questions." It dared not risk defeat on this matter.[27] Outright rejection is what the duke of Norfolk would have much preferred, however. Prior to calling on the prime minister once more on 25 April, Norfolk forwarded yet another series of Catholic pronouncements on the convent issue: "These declarations will shew you what our feelings are; they were deep and earnest from the first and mature reflection has intensified them."[28]

At the same time that Gladstone was seeking to assuage
Catholic feeling, he was reminded by *The Times* that most Englishmen had a deep-rooted suspicion of convents and would
be pleased "to see Convent doors open to some public commissioner, and the race of Confessors, Superiors, and the rest
brought under control."[29] In the meantime, Newdegate was
himself seeking to explain to Gladstone, both in person and by
letter, the scope of the proposed investigation and to obtain his
assistance in making certain that the obdurate opposition of a
few Roman Catholic M.P.s would not foil the express intent of
the House of Commons. "There is a growing feeling," he told
Gladstone, "that the Conventual and Monastic Institutions are
being treated by the House of Commons as if they were exempt
jurisdictions, subject to Papal Authority, but . . . exempt from
the authority of Parliament."[30]

By 2 May 1870 Gladstone had decided on his course. On the
one hand, he publicly regretted the decision of the house to set
up the committee and sympathized with the Committee on
Selection's reluctance to take on the task of manning such a
committee. On the other hand, he acknowledged a precedent
for parliamentary concern with monasteries and convents, and
once the house had charted a course, it believed in following
through. Yet Newdegate had been less "lucid and effectual"
than Gladstone had hoped in making a prima facie case for
investigating the "internal anatomy" of such institutions, and
the prime minister could hardly believe that the house would
permit women to be dragged before one of its committees in
order to be examined and cross-examined as to "the feelings of
their hearts, their principles, their motives, their conduct, their
habits and rules of life." There was a case for an inquiry into the
way that such institutions were endowed with property,
however. Gladstone therefore recommended that the house
adopt Cogan's amendment that the proposed committee be
discharged on the understanding that he would immediately
thereafter introduce a substitute motion. Newdegate protested
at once that the order for his committee should not be rescinded
in defiance of thousands of petitions from England and Scotland
merely because the House of Commons had "been threatened
in violent terms by a small section of the community and their
representatives." The house, crowded as it ever was when the
fate of a ministry was at stake, agreed, however, by a margin of
270 to 160 to heed the prime minister's advice.[31]

Gladstone thereupon proposed that a select committee be
appointed "to inquire into the state of the Law respecting Con-

ventual and Monastic Institutions or Societies in Great Britain, and into the terms upon which income, property, and estates belonging to such institutions or societies, or to members thereof, are respectively received, held, or possessed." The substitute committee was not directly to be concerned with the "existence, character, and increase of" such institutions but with their legal position. Newdegate regretted that the new committee would be "incapacitated" by the changed definition of its scope, but he preferred Gladstone's committee to none at all. Henry Matthews, speaking on behalf of the Roman Catholic M.P.s, admitted that the most odious portion of Newdegate's motion had been removed but indicated that they would still feel compelled to oppose. Matthews and his colleagues found themselves in a lonely minority, however, as Gladstone's compromise proposal won acceptance by a vote of 348 to 57.[32] *The Times* acquiesced in the compromise since it upheld "the right of the Legislature to control every institution and every person within its territorial jurisdiction," but a number of religious journals ironically congratulated their Roman Catholic brethren on their lucky escape from detailed parliamentary scrutiny. For the staunchly evangelical *Record*, the Gladstone compromise represented a Catholic victory, a victory achieved "by violent language, by menaces of disobedience, and by a reversal of a solemn vote of the House of Commons."[33] The *Illustrated Times*, in contrast, stood amazed at Gladstone's mastery as a political captain. "After the manner of Nelson he broke the enemy line."[34]

Inasmuch as the victorious resolution had the ministry's support, it became the ministry's task to nominate the resultant committee, and, on 10 May, Gladstone proposed a fifteen-man committee to the House of Commons for its approval. The nominees included nine Liberals and six Conservatives, but since one of the so-called Liberals, Matthews, regularly sat on the opposition benches, the political makeup of the committee was hardly lopsided. As the anti-Catholic press was soon to point out, there was a distinct irony in having a committee designed to investigate the conventual and monastic law in Great Britain (but not in Ireland) include only a single Scot, Sir John Ogilvy, but four "Irish Roman Catholics," Henry Matthews, William Cogan, The O'Conor Don, and David Sherlock. Matthews, though representing an Irish constituency, was by birth and education an Englishman; the prime minister was clearly intent, however, on including a sizable contingent of Catholics on the committee. Another of the committee's members, Joseph Whitwell Pease, was a Quaker, and yet another, George Jessel, was a Jew. The best-known member of the committee was Charles Villiers, an M.P. since 1835, a minister in the 1850s, and brother to the earl of Clarendon, Gladstone's foreign secretary until his death in 1870. The Liberal contingent, though dominated by non-Anglicans, also included Newdegate's ultra-Protestant associate, Dr. Thomas Chambers. The Conservatives on the committee were a relatively inexperienced lot, since, aside from Newdegate, all the others—Edward Howes, Edward Pemberton, Robert Bourke, John Gilbert Talbot, and George Gregory—had been elected to Parliament for the first time in 1868. Seven of the members were trained lawyers—four of them queen's counsels—and those, such as Newdegate, who were not, were likely to have served as justices of the peace.[35]

Since the select committee was to hold its first meeting within a few days of receiving formal parliamentary sanction and was to continue to meet at regular intervals until the session ended in early August, the late spring and summer of 1870 was to prove a busy time for the Warwickshire squire. Although one of his correspondents bemoaned the fact that however well or wisely Newdegate might speak, "England has become indifferent to the encroachments of Roman Catholics," Newdegate could take comfort in the fact that the legislative gears were grinding at last. Even *Vanity Fair* had at last recognized him as a statesman worthy of a full-page caricature. That the accompanying paragraph suspected him "of being a Jesuit in the disguise of a politician" did no more than illustrate anew for Newdegate how a serious age was compelled to tolerate a leaven of frivolity.[36]

11. The Committee Investigates

The House of Commons Select Committee on the Law Respecting Conventual and Monastic Institutions met for the first time on 17 May 1870 and on fourteen subsequent occasions during May, June, and the hottest days of July. Its hearings concluded only when Parliament adjourned for the year. In the process, the committee examined twenty-nine witnesses: of these, four represented the Charity Commission, four served as legal advisers to Roman Catholic communities, five were specifically invited by other members of the committee, and sixteen were specifically invited by Charles Newdegate. The Warwickshire M.P. was given the opportunity to chair the committee, but he preferred to give that distinction to Charles Villiers, the committee's senior member in parliamentary service and ministerial experience. Yet, as Villiers was subsequently to recall, Newdegate "took a prominent part in the inquiry; in fact, he was regarded as being the most remarkable member of the body."[1] According to another member of the committee, Newdegate asked precisely 1,222 questions in the course of the committee's hearings.[2] Newdegate also had the distinction of missing not a single meeting. The attendance records of three of the committee's Roman Catholic members—Henry Matthews, David Sherlock, and Myles William O'Reilly (who replaced The O'Conor Don after the first day)—and of the chairman were almost equally good, but one of the committee Conservatives, Edward Howes, dropped out after three sessions. The greatest disappointment for Newdegate must have been the failure of his presumed Liberal ally, Dr. Thomas Chambers, to be present on more than two occasions.[3]

The chief purpose of the committee, as prescribed by Gladstone's resolution, was presumably to clarify the state of the law respecting monasteries and nunneries and the property given to such institutions. Did the laws of England permit charitable trusts designed to support Roman Catholic activities? The evidence presented by Peter Erle, chief commissioner of the Charity Commission, and by several Roman Catholic solicitors confirmed that the answer to that question was cloudy. The Catholic Emancipation Act of 1829, which had opened nearly all offices of state to professing Roman Catholics, had not specifically removed the taint of illegality from charitable trusts set up to maintain the Catholic religion. An act of 1832 (2 and 3 Will. 4, c. 115) had placed Roman Catholic schools, churches, and charities on the same legal footing as those of Protestant Dissenters, but the case of *West* v. *Shuttleworth* (1835) had distinguished between legitimate and illegal charitable purposes. Charities that violated the ban on "superstitious uses" (for example, the saying of masses for the dead) remained null and void since, according to a statute of 1714 (1 Geo. 1, c. 50), all property given for such purposes automatically reverted to the crown.[4]

The Charity Commission was one of the triumphs of the early Victorian administrative revolution. Before 1853 any citizen who suspected that a charitable trust was being misapplied had to take the case to the Court of Chancery, a tedious and expensive process. Thereafter all he had to do was to alert the charity commissioners, who kept a record of all charitable trusts, who exercised a general supervision over them, and who investigated all complaints about them without fee. Each year the commission received reports from more than eighteen thousand charities indicating how much money they had received and how they had administered income from earlier endowments.

Roman Catholic charities had been exempted from the original act of 1853, but an act of 1860 enabled Roman Catholic charities to be enrolled with the commission; indeed, all charities established later than 1735 were required to be so enrolled. Some four hundred enrollments had been made in consequence, and Commissioner Erle was happy to provide the committee with a list of Roman Catholic trust deeds. The Charity Commission, Erle admitted, had "the most imperfect information" in regard to Roman Catholic endowments; moreover, it had scarcely any occasion to investigate them. Although initially he could advance no reason why mid-Victorian Roman Catholics should wish to conceal trusts, he afterward conceded three possible reasons: the trust might be held to violate the law of superstitious uses, which had not been affected by the act of 1860 though its abolition had been recommended by a parliamentary committee years earlier; the trust might be held to violate the medieval law of *mortmain*, which prohibited the permanent alienation of land to corporations that were by legal definition perpetual; or the trust might violate the Roman Catholic Emancipation Act of 1829, which maintained the illegality of monasteries in Britain. A trust to maintain a monk would therefore be an illegal trust and so, Erle suggested, would a trust to maintain a group of nuns that did not spell out a specific educational or charitable function.[5]

What Peter Erle suspected, William Bagshawe, a Roman

Catholic solicitor, was more than willing to avow: monasteries were utterly illegal according to English law, and the legal status of convents was dubious at best. Their property was not therefore held as a charitable trust. Instead, a community of monks would buy a house as joint tenants; the property would be transferred by successive deeds from one set of owners to another. This method was disadvantageous for purposes of taxation and for obtaining mortgage loans; moreover, should a monk leave the order and demand his share of the property, his fellows could not legally resist him because the law did not recognize the order as a separate entity. In questioning Bagshawe, Roman Catholic M.P.s tended to stress the legal problems that monastic orders faced, while Protestant M.P.s repeatedly asked for instances in which the penal section of the Catholic Emancipation Act had been enforced. Bagshawe conceded that he knew of none. Newdegate alone apparently derived enormous satisfaction from having the witness admit time and again that monasteries were illegal under English law.[6]

George M. Arnold, another Roman Catholic solicitor, confirmed the manner in which monastic and conventual property was transferred from one group of joint tenants to another; most property was sold before death in order to avoid succession duty. Arnold stressed that all such property was legally held and represented no evasion of the law; it simply caused a great deal of inconvenience that could readily be avoided if only convents and monasteries were granted the same rights that other voluntary clubs in England possessed. Unfortunately, they were prevented from being regarded as voluntary clubs by the unrepealed section of the Catholic Emancipation Act (10 Geo. 4, c. 7), which declared it "expedient to make provision for the gradual suppression and final prohibition of Jesuits and other religious orders of the Church of Rome bound by monastic vows." Newdegate objected to the manner in which Arnold described the act against monasteries as a penal law. For Arnold, it was clearly such inasmuch as residence in England per se constituted an offense, even though the person involved was a subject of Queen Victoria, paid his rates and taxes, and acted as a law-abiding citizen. But, Newdegate asked, had not a recent Catholic writer conceded that "the Roman Catholic Church has more liberty in this country than in almost any other state of Europe?" "I should not think so," replied Arnold, "the present inquiry is rather in the opposite direction." Replied Newdegate, "An inquiry is not legislation."[7]

James Cuddon provided precise information about the role

that religious orders played in English and Scottish communities. They supplied parish priests for 121 missions responsible
for some 279,000 people; they helped to teach some 92,000
schoolchildren, and they operated ten colleges educating 1,192
young men in England. "We like our country," Cuddon insisted, "and much prefer that they should be educated here."
Even though the statutes had not been enforced, Roman Catholics regarded it as "a most terrible grievance" that their religious
leaders, "members of the first families of the country," should
be regarded by law as common criminals. Why should such
restrictive laws not be struck from the statute book, asked Cuddon. Why should faithful Roman Catholics not be allowed to
endow their colleges in the way that Oxford, Cambridge, Eton,
and comparable "ancient institutions" could be endowed?
George Jessel reminded Cuddon that no modern institutions,
whether Anglican, Nonconformist, or Catholic, possessed such
special legal privileges. "But it is exactly those very exceptions
that I think are unfair," responded Cuddon. "Merely because
they are ancient, they ought not to be exceptions, and they were
ours once, you know."[8]

But were not foreign rules imposed upon these religious
orders, asked Newdegate. Were they not bound by the rules of
their order? Their consciences were bound, Cuddon admitted,
but "their vows impose no obligation in point of law; they are
merely registered in heaven, that is all; nowhere else. . . . Our
laws are not affected by anything that comes from Rome." Was
not Cuddon aware, Newdegate insisted, that the law of *mortmain* had been passed because of the enormous accumulation of
property by medieval monasteries? How was that relevant to
the England of 1870, replied Cuddon. "It is nothing to me what
was the custom or the practice in 1470. I submit to you, monasteries are different now." They were not contemplative and idle;
their members went out into the world to do educational and
missionary work. Of thirty monasteries, no more than one or
two were secluded from the world. These thirty monasteries
were inhabited by 476 monks, 300 novices, and 200 lay brothers
acting as servants. They owned only 2,432 acres with an annual
rental income of thirty-four hundred pounds. "People run away
with notions of immense wealth, which are quite absurd."[9]

All that Cuddon sought, he reiterated, was equality of
treatment. "Then you say that all religious bodies should be
treated alike?" asked Joseph Whitwell Pease. "I say so."
"Would not that involve you in the toleration of Mormonism
and its rites?" wondered Pease. "I should not call Mormonism

religion but socialism," answered Cuddon. "Who is to judge where religion ends, and socialism begins?" Pease went on. Cuddon was ultimately forced to concede that the state would have to be the final judge.[10] In regard to monasteries as to other institutions, Scottish law turned out to differ in degree from English law. Neither a law of *mortmain* nor a law against superstitious uses interfered with the establishment of male religious orders in Scotland, but the legal obstacle against religious orders erected by the (in this respect ironically named) Catholic Emancipation Act of 1829 loomed as large north of the Tweed as further south.[11]

James Vincent Harting, another Roman Catholic solicitor, outlined the position of the 216 English convents and the 17 Scottish convents with their twenty-five hundred full-fledged members. The Carmelites operated several contemplative convents, but four-fifths of the establishments were involved in teaching, in the care of children, in visiting the sick, and in the "reclamation of penitent women."[12] The prime purpose of the orders, according to Harting, "was to meet the wants of modern society and modern times, arising from the great increase of poverty, great increase of population, great increase of crime, and all those many things which have to be considered and provided for in a great community." Some sixty-five thousand children attended schools taught by members of female religious orders. "The simple fact is," explained the *Dublin Review*, "that the first endeavour of a Catholic priest engaged in gathering into a congregation a number of poor and long-neglected Irish Catholics in one of our towns, is to try whether he cannot get the assistance of some nuns. If he succeeds, then one more is added to the list of new communities, and there is a new outcry from Mr. Newdegate, echoed back by a leader in *The Times*."[13] A century later, an Anglican historian was to provide a yet more generous appraisal: "This pastoral motive derived strength from the sight of Roman Catholic nuns in slums or hospitals or orphanages. . . . Unmarried women were necessary to care for orphans, prostitutes, female prisoners, helpless old, and the sick. Beyond other ages early Victorians knew that gentle ladies could only work in Stepney or nurse cholera if sustained by grace beyond the common lot."[14]

The income of the convents was obtained from the proceeds of investments (derived in part from the dowries paid by the nuns) and from the school fees paid by the better-off. The convents were far from wealthy: they owned scarcely half an acre of land per person and could expect an annual income averaging no more than £6 13s. 6d. per head. Even collectively, nuns owned much less property than did the average Briton, because, as the *Dublin Review* was to point out, if the entire island of Great Britain were divided by its population, that would leave 1¾ acres per individual.[15] Although convents, unlike monasteries, had not been specifically outlawed by the Catholic Emancipation Act of 1829, Catholic lawyers assumed that "the whole policy of the law" remained hostile. Like monasteries, convents were dependent on secret trusts and therefore on the honor of the de facto owners. If all the joint tenants died without replacement, the property would formally descend to the legal heir of the last surviving joint tenant, and the community would have no recourse at law. Harting knew of no instance in which convents had suffered in this way, but, like the other Catholic representatives, he pleaded for statutory relief. "You would not object to these institutions being recognised by the law?" asked John Gilbert Talbot. "I should not object at all," responded Harting. "If that is what you desire, and these institutions were recognised by the law, I suppose you would not object to their being under proper inspection like other institutions?" "That," replied Harting, "is a totally different question." He had no objection, however, to the legalization of trusts on behalf of Catholic religious orders so that they might come within the purview of the Charity Commission.[16]

Harting was no more willing than was any other Catholic witness to concede that Roman Catholic orders were subject to any foreign law. They all did their best, he insisted, to abide by English law, "the law of the land," and sought no special privileges or exemptions. All they wished for was the removal of those last remaining disabilities that prevented Roman Catholics from practicing their religion as freely as did members of other English religious denominations. As Baron Clifford of Chudleigh phrased the matter:

> I can only state that the country for nearly the last 200 years has been passing these [anti-Catholic] laws and has now repealed almost every one as being utterly futile and unjust, except for the few fragments which still remain, and which we have tried over and over again to get repealed.[17]

From Newdegate's point of view, the hearings were going from bad to worse: what had been intended as a demonstration of Catholic duplicity was increasingly being made to appear as a case of Protestant injustice. Even one of the non-Catholic witnesses, Charity Commissioner Arthur Hobhouse, recommended the removal of the legal checks that inhibited Roman Catholics from enrolling all their charities with the Charity Commission. The taking of vows, he added, was a matter that ought to be left to people to judge for themselves—as long as the state was not asked to enforce them. The law in regard to superstitious uses ought to be repealed so that individuals might decide for themselves what practices were or were not superstitious, though Hobhouse was willing to exclude religious criminal bands like the Indian "Thugs" from such liberty. In general it was the desire of the Charity Commission to interpret the law liberally and to tolerate all manner of eccentric endowments. The current legal position of Roman Catholic religious orders was, however, an utter muddle. "That the state of the law can be satisfactory to anybody, I cannot conceive."[18]

Although the prime function of the committee was to investigate the state of that law, it became bogged down on several occasions in the problem of defining the institutions whose legal status it was exploring. Was the Roman Catholic oratory at Brompton, for example, a monastic institution? Since several of Newdegate's witnesses had information concerning the oratory, the Warwickshire M.P. was eager to have the committee so define that community. It ultimately did so by a vote of six to five, relying largely on the fact that the annual *Catholic Directory* listed the Oratorians under the heading "Religious Communities of Men." The Reverend William Anthony Johnson, who served as the directory's editor as well as secretary to Archbishop Manning, was startled to discover that the *Catholic Directory* had become a veritable Bible to Newdegate. Johnson explained that the Oratorians were an association of secular priests and that it had been an error to rank them with the monastic orders. "If I had had any idea, and if any one connected with this matter had had any idea that the Directory would ever be brought as evidence in any important question, of course every word would have been well weighed." Newdegate remained suspicious. Did not the volume's frontispiece bear the authoritative words, *"Permissu superiorum"*? Its Latin imprimatur notwithstanding, Johnson insisted, the phrase meant not that the book was "official" but only that the religious authorities did not object to its publication.[19]

Although Newdegate had to his own satisfaction established the relevance of the Brompton Oratory to the committee's proceedings, he was not as readily able to establish the relevance of the evidence provided by his witnesses. Albert Smee, the medical officer of the Bank of England who had aroused

Newdegate's sympathy back in 1864, was one of these. Smee remained as obviously unhappy in 1870 as he had been in 1864 that his brother-in-law William Hutchison had left his estate to the Brompton Oratory rather than to Smee's wife. Smee felt certain that Hutchison had given his property to the Oratorians "under a vow of poverty" and had therefore challenged the will on the grounds that it had been illegal, that Hutchison had not been of sound mind when he had written it, and that Hutchison's fellow Oratorians had subjected him to undue influence. Smee had taken the case to court, and the judge had held against him. Only lack of money had deterred Smee from appealing the judgment, and he remained as certain as ever that the law of the land had been violated. William Cogan was not impressed: "Then you simply come here now to try and defeat the decision of the judge?"[20]

A majority of committee members was no more impressed with the evidence of the Reverend James H. Harrison, whose son had joined the oratory at age eighteen; thereafter, he "was completely under the control of Father Faber. . . . He seemed to have no control over his own actions." John McDermott, an erstwhile member of a lay class within the oratory who had reconverted to Protestantism in 1859, remained under the impression that the priests at Brompton were as much monks as were members of other male religious orders. The Reverend William Thomas Gordon, the oratory superior, pointed out that the decision of ten secular priests to live together and to share the costs of meals and lodging no more made them a monastic order than it made monks of members of a club or college who had entered upon a similar arrangement. The priests were "bound by no vows, oath, or promise of any sort." It was quite true that William Hutchison had presented the oratory with a library, but he had made large donations to other institutions as well. "He simply spent the whole of his property upon good works."[21] As Edward Pemberton, one of Newdegate's Conservative committee colleagues was to protest, what did the grievances voiced by Smee, Harrison, and McDermott have to do with the committee's charge?[22] Would the House of Commons have concerned itself with Hutchison's wealth, wondered the *Dublin Review*, if he had merely indulged his own pleasure?[23]

The committee also came to the conclusion that the Anglican sisterhoods—six in the 1840s and nine more in the 1850s—that had been established under the inspiration of the Oxford movement in general and under the influence of Edward Bouverie Pusey in particular lay outside its purview. The Protestant Evangelical Mission and Electoral Union had denounced such "Popish establishments" where "the errors of *confession, Mariolatry, prayers to the saints,* and *masses for the dead,* are taught and practiced."[24] As Charles Freeman, the solicitor for one such sisterhood, pointed out, however, communities such as the Clewer House of Mercy—of which Gladstone was a trustee—required "no formal life vows," did not insist that their members give up all private property, and did not prevent any member who wished to leave from doing so. There was no legal barrier to trustees receiving or administering land on behalf of a community such as the Clewer sisterhood, which managed a school, an almshouse, and an orphanage. This type of Anglican activity made Newdegate distinctly uncomfortable, and several members of the committee found it difficult to believe that such institutions did not owe their ultimate loyalty to the Roman church. The majority of committee members took what comfort they could in the conclusion that none of the Anglican sisterhoods "appear to be bound by religious vows," though, as a matter of fact, precisely such vows had been adopted by several of the groups.[25] Newdegate was also shocked by Freeman's assumption that the Church of England was not fundamentally Protestant. Under questioning, Freeman conceded that "if Protestant means protesting against the doctrines of the Church of Rome, then, I suppose, that there are some doctrines of the Church of Rome which the Church of England protests against, and to such an extent it may be Protestant. . . . But there is not a word in the Prayer-book to show that the Church of England is Protestant."[26]

The 1870 parliamentary session came to a close before the committee could agree upon a report but not before Newdegate felt the force of one more parliamentary rebuff. The government's University Tests Bill was about to open all Oxford and Cambridge posts and fellowships to non-Anglicans, and Newdegate was appalled by the casual manner in which the measure was being allowed to sail through Parliament. It was generally seen as a bill to benefit Dissenters, but were those Dissenters not aware that henceforth Roman Catholics might legally be appointed to the highest professorships at those venerable institutions, and at a time when the Church of Rome was in the process of subordinating all other dogmas to that of obedience to the pope?[27] The House of Commons was not swayed by Newdegate's eloquence, however, and approved the bill by voice vote.

For its part, the new kingdom of Italy was not swayed by

the spiritual eminence that the Vatican Council was about to
confer on Pope Pius IX. The Italian nation took advantage of the
Franco-Prussian War of 1870–1871 by marching its troops into
the Papal States and by making Rome rather than Florence its
new capital. For Archbishop Manning, Rome was more than the
capital of any one country—it was the "capital of the whole
Christian world"—and he publicly deplored such "sacrilegious
robbery."[28] English Roman Catholics pleaded with Gladstone's
government to assist their spiritual leader, and the prime minister wrote a private letter to an Irish M.P. that stirred a temporary
furor. "Must we be constantly startled by the epistolary eccen-
tricities of Prime Ministers?" asked *The Times*. What did he mean
by calling the now landless pope a "Sovereign Pontiff" and by
expressing his concern for "the adequate support of the dignity
of the Pope"?[29] In the House of Commons, one of the members
for Belfast wondered whether Gladstone, by recognizing the
spiritual functions of the pope, had not pledged his government
"to a policy inconsistent with Protestant principles." His ministry had no desire to meddle with the pope's spiritual functions,
responded the prime minister, "but the Government believe
that the liberty of the head of the religion of many millions of our
fellow subjects—his liberty and personal independence—is a
legitimate matter for the notice of this Government." Newdegate reminded Gladstone that back in 1848 the British government had specifically pledged itself to deal with the pope only as
the temporal ruler of the Papal States and not "in his spiritual
capacity." Did Gladstone now think it "his duty to violate the
intention of the law?" "I said that we had no relations whatever
with the spiritual functions of the Pope," responded Gladstone;
the government merely had the right to take note of "his freedom and independence in the exercise of them." Newdegate
was left in bewilderment: "The right honourable Gentleman's
definition is so fine that really my blunt vision cannot perceive
it."[30]

Since the government did not find it necessary to supplement the prime minister's words with gunboats or to give refuge
to the pontiff in Malta, Gladstone's supposed desire to be "the
Protestant protector of the Pope" was gradually forgotten.
Newdegate did protest once more when the Prince of Wales
paid a courtesy visit to the pope in 1872, and he attempted but
failed to prevent the Liberal ministry from using one Clarke
Jervoise as unofficial envoy to the Vatican.[31]

In the meantime, Newdegate and his cohorts had been
roused anew by the government's decision to scrap the twenty-

year-old Ecclesiastical Titles Act. Gladstone had at the time opposed that expression of legislative anger at the papal bull of 1850. The provision prohibiting Roman Catholic priests from adding English place-names to their titles had never been enforced, moreover, and, as Gladstone was to recall some years thereafter, in 1871 the measure "silently closed its unwept existence."[32] Silence was certainly not the manner in which Charles Newdegate greeted a measure of repeal that seemed to ignore the pretensions of the Vatican Council and that seemed specifically designed to exalt the position of the so-called archbishop of Westminster, Henry Edward Manning, so "that he may in this metropolis carry out this doctrine as to the Pope's supremacy in all matters, whether private, public, or political." The measure was only one more sign of the Liberal government's apparent political dependence on the Roman Catholic hierarchy. "It seems to me a picture of the geese led by the foxes." One Liberal M.P., Charles Gilpin, ridiculed Newdegate's fears; the fact that Catholic prelates wished to give themselves territorial titles worried him no more than would Newdegate's decision to style himself "the Cham of Tartary." The repeal measure was given a second reading in the Commons by a vote of 137 to 51. Only the discovery that the Ecclesiastical Titles Act unwittingly invalidated the clerical titles of the leaders of the newly disestablished Protestant Church of Ireland persuaded the House of Lords to concur in the act's repeal.[33]

Of more immediate concern to Newdegate than the Ecclesiastical Titles Act was the select committee of the previous year whose meetings he had attended so assiduously but which, in his judgment, had gone so badly astray. When Chairman Charles Villiers asked the House of Commons on 17 March 1871 to reappoint the committee so that it could complete its report, Newdegate immediately moved an amendment expanding the committee's jurisdiction so that it might inquire not merely into "the existence, number, increase, and regulation of Conventual and Monastic Institutions in Great Britain," but also into the income, property, and estates of these communities and finally into "whether adequate legal securities or means exist for ensuring the personal freedom of the inmates thereof." The previous year's committee had been badly handicapped by its restricted instructions, Newdegate insisted, and he had not been able to obtain from the Roman Catholic witnesses the precise names of the nominal owners—the secret trustees—of these communities or details of the precise value or location of their properties; their claim of legal privilege meant in effect that the House of Commons had been defied. Newdegate went on to review tales of individual nuns that demonstrated the necessity of including concern with their personal freedom among the committee's charges. Was the House of Commons aware that English coroners had not thus far held an inquest upon a single nun? With thousands of convent inmates, was it plausible that there should not have been a single death deserving such inquiry? Surely, the experience of Continental nations ought to teach England the necessity of bringing these communities within the purview of the law at a time when they were increasing more rapidly in number than ever before.[34]

Villiers had little patience with Newdegate's complaints. By becoming a member of the committee, Newdegate had tacitly acquiesced in the defined scope of its inquiries, and yet he had repeatedly insisted on inquiring into irrelevant matters. Newdegate had failed to mention the true source of his unhappiness with the previous year's committee: of the M.P.s whom he had expected to support his views, "some did not attend, and others did not altogether agree with him." Newdegate must surely "recollect that general surprise was felt and expressed by the Committee at the small number of witnesses and the meagre nature of the evidence he produced, considering the large expectations he had raised in the House and the country." Two other members of the committee were equally hostile. His fellow Conservative, Pemberton, complained of the vague and uncertain evidence that Newdegate's witnesses had put forward, and Pease sternly denied Newdegate's implication that the previous year's committee had labored in vain. Newdegate's amendment was decisively defeated, 196 to 79, and Villiers successfully moved for the reappointment of the committee of the previous year. Newdegate refused to participate on that condition, and since Howes also dropped out, the number of committee members was reduced from fifteen to thirteen.[35]

With Newdegate retired from the committee, in order, so Sherlock suspected, to leave himself free to attack its ultimate report, Villiers waited until June to summon it once more.[36] The committee then decided to hear no more witnesses but to adopt a report. Pemberton, the Conservative M.P. from East Kent, and Matthews, the Liberal representative for an Irish constituency, offered alternate drafts. The committee preferred Matthews's draft to Pemberton's, and with minor amendments, it was transformed, after three meetings, into the committee's official report.[37] Matthews was one of several M.P.s who, in Newdegate's judgment, scrupulously followed the directions of the Roman Catholic hierarchy and thereby facilitated "the rapid political progress—of the Papacy in this country."[38] That such a man should draft the report of a committee originally designed to expose the iniquity of Roman Catholic institutions must have impressed Newdegate as an irony almost too poignant to be borne. The cogent and intelligent manner in which the Roman Catholic solicitors had presented their evidence had apparently impressed several members of the committee deeply,[39] and Matthews's draft provided a similarly clear summary of the state of the law. Members of all English religious groups had the right to enroll themselves in religious communities and to take monastic vows except for those associated with the Church of Rome. Roman Catholic monasteries remained illegal. All gifts of land or property to such institutions remained similarly illegal as were all gifts given to procure prayers for the dead. An unrepealed section of an act of 1791 also left gifts to convents a matter of doubtful legality. Since, in a technical sense, monasteries and convents were not charities, they did not fall under the supervision of the Charity Commission, and Roman Catholic founders had necessarily hesitated to enroll any legal trust that the statutes cited earlier might render void.

Matthews's report went on to describe how novices joined religious orders and how they divested themselves of all private property once they took their solemn oaths of poverty, chastity, and obedience. Since their communities were not recognized by law as corporations, "a universal practice appears to have grown up of conveying to several individuals as joint tenants all property which is meant to be enjoyed in common by such institutions" and no trusts, either open or secret, were declared. The welfare of the community depended therefore on the honor and goodwill of such joint tenants. Although no specific example had been reported of a community suffering from this mode of handling property, numerous witnesses had described the state of the law as "inconsistent with the principles of religious liberty." The religious orders performed highly valuable educational and social-welfare functions, and it was held to be a sore grievance by several witnesses that such useful members of society "should be treated by the law as criminals."

Matthews's report, thus far, was an obvious prelude to a recommendation that the law be changed, and this is precisely what Matthews proposed in his final paragraph. Though acknowledging that such legal alterations "would probably be of a very different kind, according to the point of view from which the subject is surveyed," he went on to recommend the removal

from the statute book of the antimonastic clause of the Catholic
Emancipation Act of 1829, of the clause in the act of 1791 that
threw doubt on the legality of convents, and of the several
statutes against superstitious uses. The committee, which had
gone along with almost all Matthews's premises, balked,
however, at accepting his apparently logical conclusion. The
report therefore ended inconclusively: "A complete discussion
of the position, if any, which Conventual or Monastic Institutions ought to have in our law . . . would lead to much difference of opinion, and might exceed the limits of our inquiry, and
we have therefore abstained from recommending any . . .
alterations."[40]

The Times, which had strongly backed Newdegate the year
before, recognized that the committee he had brought into
being had paradoxically enabled Roman Catholics "to urge a
strong plea for a further removal of their disabilities." The
existing law was not merely inefficacious; it defeated its own
ends by, in effect, exempting convents and monasteries from all
legal cognizance and control.[41] The Saturday Review was similarly
persuaded by the report that legal limitations on Roman Catholic practices should be ended. As it stood the law was "dis-
figured by the two worst faults that a law can have. It is tyrannical, and it is impotent."[42] The Globe had warned the previous
year that an inquiry confined to property law could "benefit no
one but those whom it is intended to rebuke," and so, the St.
James's Chronicle agreed, matters had turned out; the report
showed "an evident leaning towards Roman Catholic
interests."[43] "We can afford to thank Mr. Newdegate for the
good that has come out of his evil intentions towards us,"
declared the Catholic Times.[44]

No immediate change was in the offing, but the unanimous
committee report—from which Newdegate completely dissoci-
ated himself—had clearly presented Roman Catholic religious
orders as victims rather than villains. Even as legislators hesitated, judges grew bolder. In the case of Cox v. Manners, the
husband of Mrs. Frances Manners challenged his wife's decision to will part of her estate to the Dominican convent at
Carisbrooke and another part to the Sisters of Saint Paul at Selly
Oak. In a judgment announced late in the summer of 1871, the
court upheld the right of Mrs. Manners to grant gifts to convents, which were defined as legal voluntary associations. Thus
the first legal judgment since the Reformation on the validity of
gifts to Roman Catholic convents gave convent defenders an
additional triumph.[45] How quickly, Newdegate must have felt,
the hopes of the spring of 1870 had faded.

12. The Protestant Crusader

Charles Newdegate had lost too many battles in the course of his political career to be unduly surprised that the apparent victory of 1870 had turned into apparent defeat a year later. He felt confirmed in his oft-expressed fears of the political influence that Roman Catholicism had already achieved on English soil and of the blindness of contemporary English liberalism to the power of the "totally illiberal" Roman Catholic church.[1] Whatever the vicissitudes of each year's parliamentary session, by the 1870s Newdegate had achieved a special position within the precincts of the House of Commons. When he died, *The Times* was to describe him as "a Tory of Tories, a regular attendant in his place in Parliament, and a safe and certain vote on the Conservative side."[2] A regular attendant he certainly was, but a regimented Tory he never became. Newdegate liked indeed to refer to himself as a Whig of 1688, a champion of constitutional monarchy and Protestantism. In *Dod's* he listed himself as a Conservative, if only because people were too likely to make the point that the word *Tory* was "of Irish origin, and not Protestant in character."[3] First and foremost, Newdegate saw himself as an independent member.

As the decade opened, the *Spectator* described the Tory party as consisting of a head, a body, and a tail.

> Whereas the Liberal head and centre and tail are all strictly continuous, and connected by the proper vertebral arrangement, the Tory party is afflicted by a certain discontinuity between its head and its body, and between its body and its tail—the head (Mr. Disraeli) being decidedly severed from the trunk, though still able—as French physiologists maintain that all guillotined heads are—to observe and criticize what is going on in the body; and the tail (Mr. Newdegate), though still following the body at a certain interval, being similarly circumstanced, so far, at least, as tails can be said to have percipient faculties at all.[4]

Yet, as the Liberal *Daily News* was to concede, on many matters Newdegate's staunch Conservatism "was tempered by a shrewd common sense." Newdegate viewed himself as sufficiently above narrow partisanship, as well as sufficiently expert in parliamentary procedure, to qualify as successor to John Evelyn Denison as speaker of the Commons in February 1872. He had turned down the ministerial posts offered by Derby and the peerage offered by Palmerston; Gladstone was not, however, to give him the opportunity either to refuse or to accept the speakership.[5]

Newdegate saw himself first and foremost as a preserver of the English Constitution, and more often than not he deplored those for whom

> The Constitution was intended
> For nothing else but to be mended[6]

In regard to measures of social reform, he was ever the champion of local rather than national supervision. "I have not the same feeling against parochial authorities," he declared in 1872, "which seems to prevail among modern reformers. My belief is that the parishes are, on the whole, well governed; and I own that I am afflicted with the ancient prejudice—a prejudice which many generations of Englishmen have entertained—that public freedom is best secured by local authority, so subdivided and limited as to area of population and locality that it shall be brought within the command of such a number of the population as can consult with each other and thus effectively act upon the mind of the authority."[7]

Newdegate was aware that some of his colleagues viewed him as a funeral bell and others as a "Knight of La Mancha,"[8] but, in the words of *Vanity Fair*, "he hears unmoved the laughter of the indifferent and the jeers of the ribald."[9] However lugubrious Newdegate might appear as the Jeremiah or "the Melancholy Jacques" of the House of Commons, he never became its laughingstock. His manner was too earnest and his temper too imperturbable to make him truly a figure of ridicule. However narrow his vision, his motives seemed too obviously disinterested and his impulses too clearly well-intentioned to be idly dismissed. Even to a Liberal parliamentary correspondent, he appeared to ride "as straight to the truth as to the hounds."[10]

Nor was Newdegate a poor speaker. His manner could be long-winded, and despite (or because of?) the lessons in execution he had imbibed, his gestures were unduly mechanical; "he would sweep the air with his arms, he would fold them across his breast, then he would shake his forefinger warningly." Yet his voice could alternately soar toward the rafters and descend into the cellar. On occasion, the Warwickshire squire would so lose himself in his subject that he would mistake for a table top the black hat of the member sitting in the row immediately beneath his own, and he would emphasize a point by bringing a clenched fist down upon it with full force. After a fellow Conservative, Clare Sewell Read, had his brand-new hat driven deep over his nose as the result of one such declamatory onslaught in 1878, Newdegate found the bench immediately below his emptying whenever he rose to speak.[11] The corner seat on the fourth row below the gangway on the Conservative side of the house became Newdegate's own to such a degree that, when an unwitting intruder claimed it, Newdegate found an unlikely defender in Col. Francis Plunket Dunne, an Irish Roman Catholic M.P. Dunne was a professed advocate of the "Three Fs" for Irish tenant farmers—fair rent, free sale, and fixity of tenure—and Newdegate, Dunne declared, represented an Irish principle, "fixity of tenure."[12]

Newdegate saw himself, understandably, as a firm English patriot and as an upholder of the Church of England. Even in the 1870s, the representative of North Warwickshire found it as difficult as had the Anglican divines of the age of Elizabeth I to disentangle the English church from the English state. "The Church of England," declared Newdegate in 1874, "comprehends the majority of the nation, and how then can it be either fair or appropriate to speak of them in such terms as to raise the presumption that they are distinct bodies, and not merely different phases of the same community?"[13] And what did the Church of England represent to Newdegate? It represented a Christianity devoted to Bible reading but not hamstrung by sabbatarian legislation. The church was to be open to the influence of the laity. Newdegate's opposition to the abolition of church rates (local property taxes to pay for parish church repairs) was immediately related to his desire to preserve the influence of the parish vestry. By ending the church rate, he warned the Protestant Dissenters, the strongest advocates of church-rate abolition, you "leave us, the laity of the Church, at the mercy of the clergyman. You virtually take the parish churches from us, the laity of the Church of England, to whom they have always hitherto belonged, and vest them in the clergy who are irremovable by law."[14] The Dissenters had triumphed on that question in 1868, but how ironic it was, Newdegate noted a few years later, that the same people who had argued that it was unfair to make non-Anglicans pay for the upkeep of churchyards that were of no use to them now demanded not merely the right to bury their dead in such churchyards but to have the funeral services conducted by a Dissenting minister. Such a burials bill was yet another step in the direction of disestablishment, and yet for Newdegate it was the fact of establishment—meaning regulation by parliamentary statute—that served as a safeguard to the Anglican laity against clerical despotism.[15] The matter was a serious one, and it was not Newdegate who told the story of the Anglican clergyman who, when asked whether he would bury a Dissenter in his parish churchyard, replied, "Bless you, I should like to bury them all."[16] George Osborne Morgan, the Liberal who had introduced the burials bill, compared the anguish a Baptist might feel at being buried by an Anglican clergyman with the horror that Newdegate would feel at the idea of being buried by a Roman Catholic priest. Newdegate questioned the analogy; he had, in any event, "no wish to be buried before my time in due course of nature; but I certainly had much rather be buried by a Roman Catholic priest than be baptised by a Roman Catholic priest."[17]

It was not the Dissenters but the Church of Rome that for Newdegate continued to pose the most severe threat to his beloved Church of England, and he could take satisfaction in the fact that in 1871 the London branch of the Scottish Reformation Society had joined forces with the Protestant Association to form a joint Protestant Educational Institute that by means of lectures, courses, and tracts was continuing to instruct "the People in the Principles and History of the Reformation," "defending our Protestant Constitution and Institutions," and "Opposing Papal Aggression throughout the Empire." Newdegate was one of thirteen presidents, a distinction he shared with three other M.P.s, two earls, and a total of seven privy councillors. The twelve patronesses included a duo of duchesses. The organization prided itself on having trained seventeen thousand students between 1867 and 1872 and on having distributed twenty-two million tracts. It had also continued to support a parliamentary agent to alert unwary M.P.s to Catholic plotting, if only, the institute reported, because "with honourable exceptions, the public press is against us."[18]

In Parliament Newdegate could discern the tentacles of Rome directing the maneuvers of the advocates of Irish home rule and (more surprisingly perhaps) the activities of the supporters of parliamentary votes for women. With regard to Ireland, Newdegate could claim the support of the former Liberal prime minister, Earl Russell, who declared in 1873 that the government of Ireland was one "conducted entirely according to the orders and inspiration of the Roman Catholic Church." As Russell had confided to Newdegate the year before, "although I have differed with you on many political questions there is one in which I cordially agree with you—I view as you do with distrust & dislike the progress of the influence of the Jesuits in this country." Irish members like Isaac Butt who

sought home rule were apparently prepared to have the imperial Parliament abandon its regulation of Ireland's domestic
affairs. Were they equally prepared, Newdegate wondered out
loud, to have Irish M.P.s cease their interference with the internal affairs of England and Scotland? That prospect was in no
sense displeasing to Newdegate. Speaking in the same debate,
Gladstone noted that Newdegate had put his finger upon the
chief difficulty in any home-rule scheme thus far advanced, that
men invested with an exclusive power over Irish affairs might
continue to meddle with matters fundamentally English and
Scottish.[19]

Newdegate was equally suspicious of Jacob Bright's measure to extend the parliamentary franchise to female householders on the same basis that it had been granted in 1867 to male
householders. The measure might seem conservative in that it
gave the vote only to property-owning spinsters and widows,
yet, for Newdegate, the very notion flew in the face of natural
law. It would, moreover, lead rapidly to universal adult suffrage: no man would stand for exclusion from the vote once any
women at all had been admitted to the polling booth. That
universal suffrage led to despotism, to empires founded upon
plebiscites, had been demonstrated by recent Continental history. The works of the French historian Jules Michelet had
demonstrated, moreover, that if women were ever to constitute
the political majority in any country in which Roman Catholicism was the dominant religion, the result would be priestly
tyranny. Bright's better-known brother John felt compelled to
agree that women's suffrage would greatly increase the influence of priest, parson, and minister—especially in Ireland.[20]

During the 1870s the dangers of Roman Catholicism for
Newdegate became embodied increasingly in the person and
the pronouncements of Henry Edward Manning, the Roman
Catholic archbishop of Westminster, and Newdegate therefore
came to be one of the most avid students of Manning's sermons.
Was it not Manning who had described England as "the cess-
pool of nations" and who had declared "that no man who really
loves his country can desire that it should remain the centre of
an Empire"? Was it not Manning who was making revolutionary speeches in favor of Joseph Arch's farm laborers' union,
forgetting that it was the existence of that very empire that
enabled farm laborers and others to migrate, if they wished,
from one liberty-loving land to another?[21]

In the autumn of 1873 Newdegate became involved in a true
epistolary slugging match with the redoubtable Manning. It

began when the archbishop challenged a report in the *Coventry Standard* of 24 October 1873 according to which Newdegate had said:

> This Dr. Manning has published another sermon, a sermon which he published ten years ago, and has republished, and in that sermon he lauded the conspirators of the Gunpowder Plot, who sought the destruction of the King, Lords, and Commons, by one fell conspiracy. He states in that sermon that Guy Fawkes, Garnett, and the Jesuits who were allied with him, although they were arraigned as culprits in the dock, now stand arrayed in bright robes, and at the right hand of Christ.

What was Newdegate's authority for such a statement, demanded Manning.

In reply, Newdegate's lawyers cited a recent sermon by Manning that had been printed in *The Times* of 20 October 1873 and the *Sermons on Ecclesiastical Subjects* published by Manning in 1863 and 1870. In a letter to *The Times*, Newdegate supplemented this response with a citation from one of those sermons in which Manning had contrasted the "short fair season" of Mary Tudor with the tempest-tossed reign of Elizabeth I. Only the disciples of Saint Ignatius Loyola had sought to stem the tide: "At length the tempest burst, and the storm fell upon his [Loyola's] sons. One by one they went to the scaffold and the rack. The rack groaned and the scaffold dripped with gore, and they ascended to a martyr's crown. What a tale is the history of these 300 years! a twofold history, written both in earth and heaven; by the wise and worldly here on earth entitled 'The Execution of Justice;' in Heaven the roll of martyrs. On earth they wore the garb of felons; in Heaven they stand arrayed in white, and crowned. Here they were arraigned in the dock as malefactors; there they sit by the throne of the Son of God." The implication was clear enough.

It was not clear enough to Manning, however, who considered Newdegate's reply "wholly insufficient and evasive." Where in any sermon had Manning specifically praised the Gunpowder Plot conspirators? It was not the first time that Newdegate had had an erroneous statement called to his attention and had refused to withdraw it. Manning could not regard the matter as personal, his solicitors wrote *The Times*; he saw Newdegate's slanders rather as "an attack on the Catholics of England, and an endeavour to renew false accusations and the bitter hates of past times." When Newdegate's solicitors simply referred Manning's lawyers to their earlier letter, Manning accepted this reply as a public acknowledgment by Newdegate

Henry Edward Manning, archbishop of Westminster, 1865–1892; named cardinal in 1875 (reprinted from Shane Leslie, *The Oxford Movement, 1833–1933* [Milwaukee, 1933], by permission of the Macmillan Publishing Company of New York).

that he was unable to back up his charges: "The Archbishop has thereby placed Mr. Newdegate before the honour and justice of the country, as uttering unfounded and slanderous statements against his neighbours." He would therefore take no further

legal action and would let Newdegate stew in his own igno-
miny.

Newdegate wondered privately if Manning's letter provided a sufficient case for a successful libel suit; his solicitors
thought not. He therefore went ahead to brand Manning's letter
as far more slanderous than any statement that the archbishop
could possibly attribute to him. Manning's implications notwithstanding, the dispute was very much a personal matter
between Newdegate and Manning and was in no sense an
attack on English Catholics as a body. Newdegate felt sure that
most Catholic laymen then as now deplored the attempt by
Jesuits and their allies to blow up Parliament, but Manning had
never denied, nor did he now deny, the presumption that he
approved of such an action, an "inference, which, in my opinion, may fairly be drawn from his published sermons." Manning had never denied telling his fellow Catholics that "we have
to subjugate and subdue, to conquer and rule, an imperial
race"—the English nation. And on what types of men should
the prospective conquerors of England model themselves?
According to Manning's sermons, upon men like Anselm and
Thomas Becket, who "crossed the will of the world in its pride of
place and set a bound to its pretensions. They were the shadows
of a Superior, and the ministers of a higher, law." Other models
that Manning presented were the purposeful Jesuits who,
though rebels against the state, now sat as martyrs by the side of
the Son of God. In none of his sermons had Manning exempted
from his praise the Henry Garnett who had served as English
provincial of the Jesuits at the time of the Gunpowder Plot and
who had been found guilty for his role in the conspiracy. Could
there be any doubt that Manning had publicly justified in these
sermons "rebellion, treason, and attempted wholesale murder" as means for effecting the subjugation of England, an
England that "like Rome, pagan of old, has become," according
to another sermon, "*Sentina gentium*—the pool, into which the
evils of all the earth find a way."

Newdegate's professed purpose had been to call public
attention to the kind of ecclesiastic who served as spiritual ruler
of the Roman Catholics of England. Although his plodding
inferences could hardly match Manning's prose in vividness of
metaphor, Newdegate felt certain that he had emerged triumphant in the epistolary duel. He therefore had the entire correspondence published as a twelve-page pamphlet.[22]

However many shadows might, in Newdegate's judgment,
be cast by the Church of Rome as an entity, it was the threat

posed by its religious orders that remained his foremost concern. But early in 1872 he found the parliamentary initiative temporarily taken by others. In February five Irish Roman Catholic M.P.s decided to give teeth to the committee report of the previous summer by introducing a private-member bill designed to legalize monastic orders, to repeal the law on superstitious uses, and to open the offices of lord chancellor of England and lord lieutenant of Ireland to non-Anglicans. The lead was taken by Sir Colman O'Loghlen, the member for county Clare, who had served Gladstone's ministry as judge advocate general in 1869 and 1870. The penal clauses had not been enforced and could not be enforced, O'Loghlen declared; let them therefore be repealed. The ban on "superstitious uses" was similarly mistaken; if he wished to leave money for masses to be said for the repose of the soul of Charles Newdegate, why ought the law to prevent him? When the crown had taken over the rule of India back in 1858, Queen Victoria had proclaimed the qualification for administrative office there to lie in ability rather than in religious belief—"all shall alike enjoy the impartial protection of the law." O'Loghlen wanted the same precept to hold sway at home. One of[23] O'Loghlen's fellow Irish M.P.s strongly concurred: the so-called safeguards of the Catholic Emancipation Act were no longer needed; "there had been substituted the undoubted loyalty and attachment of our Roman Catholic fellow-subjects to the Throne."[24]

The opponents of the measure dominated the debate. Thomas Chambers reminded the Catholic M.P.s that emancipation had been granted to them back in 1829 as a gift subject to conditions; it was hardly fair to accept the gift and now to dispense with the conditions. In regard to "superstitious uses," the question was not whether or not it was right to say masses for souls in purgatory but whether "if the doctrine were honestly believed by a dying person, and if that person were reminded of it, it was not likely that property would be bequeathed away from those who were justly entitled to it."[25] James M. Holt failed to understand why "the law of the land ought to be altered to suit the convenience of those who were in the habit of breaking it."[26] The debaters frequently alluded to the conflict with the Catholic church that Bismarck was waging in Germany as well as to the "Syllabus of Errors" and the doctrine of papal infallibility. Newdegate himself cited Dr. Ignaz von Döllinger, the most famous Catholic theologian to break with his church over the doctrine of infallibility, on the manner in which the pope had fallen under Jesuit influence, and, Newdegate added, "there was no Communism so pronounced as the Communism of the Society of Jesus." A time when doctrines subversive of English independence abounded was hardly propitious for a further weakening of the kingdom's legal defenses.[27]

Several opponents of the measure, though not Newdegate, observed that the subject was not one for which a private member's bill sufficed; but it was not until the end of the debate that the government intervened in the person of Home Secretary Henry Austin Bruce. He was sympathetic to O'Loghlen's intentions, Bruce observed. Now that the lord chancellor had ceased to be "the keeper of the Royal Conscience" and the lord lieutenant had ceased to advise on ecclesiastical matters, it did seem unnecessary to specify their religion. The penal clauses of the Catholic Emancipation Act were clearly "the relic of a barbarous time," and he doubted that even Newdegate condemned the government for failing to enforce them. There was merit in a well-considered repeal of the Superstitious Uses Act. Yet, Bruce observed, O'Loghlen had combined three somewhat separate matters in a single bill, and he had found "the sense of the House" indifferent. Not a single Nonconformist M.P. had supported the measure. As Bruce confided to his wife, he found it difficult to argue against a proposal with which he was sympathetic but which was opposed "by all parties in the House except the Roman Catholics." Bruce concluded his public comments by suggesting to O'Loghlen that he should remain satisfied with the discussion he had elicited.[28] Two weeks later, after the attorney general had given a legal opinion that Roman Catholics *were* eligible to serve as lord chancellor and as lord lieutenant of Ireland, O'Loghlen withdrew the bill.[29]

Newdegate was as certain in 1872 as he had been in 1870 that monasteries and convents required investigation rather than legalization, and in April he introduced a resolution asking for a royal commission to look into these institutions. Protestant societies had been rather slack in providing petitions in support of the motion—petitions with only fifty-five hundred signatures had arrived—but Newdegate had been much encouraged by a meeting with four thousand Scots in Glasgow's city hall during the previous winter and by a more recent meeting in Sheffield. He spoke, he declared, on behalf of tens of thousands of Britons who had been made uneasy by the rapid increase of these institutions. Almost all Continental lands had regulatory laws to keep such communities in check. The United States admittedly did not, "but there is a rough kind of justice there of considerable power. It does not wait for tedious legal proceedings. If a sufficient number of the American people suspect that anyone is confined in a monastery or convent against his or her will, they make short work of it, and by means of a Vigilance Committee speedily open the doors which had been closed against them, and set the prisoner free." Newdegate was not suggesting direct emulation, but unwilling nuns deserved assistance in Britain; once freed, nuns should be aided by the government to emigrate to the colonies. Since the recent census had revealed such a sharp disparity between the sexes in Great Britain—750,000 more women than men—it would be desirable for his proposed commission to look into this problem as well.[30]

Newdegate's motion received the support of a handful of back-benchers: one of them suggested that nuns deserved as much legislative protection as Irish tenant farmers; another repeated that convents had as much reason to be inspected as did lunatic asylums.[31] Two of Newdegate's erstwhile fellow select-committee members were less charitable. Henry Matthews recalled that Newdegate, though he had taken up hour after hour of the committee's time, had failed to come up with "one single grievance, evil, or act of wrong-doing" in regard to property held by monasteries and convents. "Since the days of Torquemada no one had exhibited such a genius for inquisition as the hon. Member." Matthews's Conservative colleague Edward Pemberton was equally scathing in regard to Newdegate's role on the select committee of 1870: "A more wanton waste of time was never incurred, and a weaker case was never brought before a Committee of the House of Commons, without so much as a tittle of evidence to support the charges."[32]

Though Newdegate's resolution was introduced and briefly discussed, the representative of North Warwickshire failed to obtain an opportunity to return it to the parliamentary calendar before the end of the session. He had to take whatever comfort he could find in meetings the following November in Aberdeen and Dundee. At Dundee, by overwhelming margins, resolutions were passed hailing the Reformation, celebrating John Knox, and viewing with uneasiness the multiplication of unsupervised and uninspected convents. Newdegate recalled his efforts to control the last-named menace and how he was at length forced to resign from a select committee "whose futile inquiries merely served to delude the people of the country." At this very time German Jesuits were flocking to Britain—though illegal there—because they were unwilling to obey German laws. "You all know," Newdegate recalled, "that I have been treated for years as the blindest of bigots, because I have upheld the policy upon which Germany now acts. . . . Is Bismarck a bigot?—is Bismarck a fool?"[33]

During the 1873 parliamentary session, Newdegate reintroduced his resolution in favor of a commission with the power to investigate convent inmates upon the scene and under oath. All other institutions were inspected or regulated; why should monasteries and convents be exempt? Let five commissioners be named, suggested Newdegate, one by the lord chancellor, a second by the speaker of the House of Commons, a third by the Lord Chief Justice of the Queen's Bench, and two more by the Roman Catholic Poor School Committee. A sixth commissioner might well be named by the Lunacy Commission "because they are in the habit of dealing with the affairs of families without exposing its affairs to needless publicity or inflicting unnecessary pain." Since the government had refused to act, the House of Commons would have to act on its own; the problem was becoming ever more serious. In 1870 there had been 233 convents; now there were 260. In 1870 there had been sixty-nine monasteries; now there were seventy-seven. According to historians of medieval England, 300 religious houses had been built during the reigns of Henry I, Stephen, and Henry II. "We are approaching the same number now." The monarchs of the later Middle Ages had been compelled to regulate and ultimately to supress those houses. Such regulation was needed once again. No doubt he would once again be accused of wishing to insult or annoy nuns, but he did not intend to enter a single convent "except as authorized by Her Majesty's Commission." If he entered under any other auspices, he would "become the object of those depraved accusations which exhibit a foulness of mind on the part of those who utter them totally unworthy of gentlemen."[34]

The historical sweep of Newdegate's reflections was indeed vast, admitted Joseph Whitwell Pease, another select-committee colleague. Yet Newdegate had failed to lay the foundation for such an inquiry; there was no prima facie case. As the Lord Chief Justice of the Queen's Bench had pointed out just a few days before, "a small piece of paper from that Court would open the door of any convent in England." Not since the days of the Stuarts, declared Henry Matthews, had a parliamentary proposal so flagrantly violated every principle of personal liberty and constitutional right. According to McCarthy Downing, Newdegate was afflicted by monomania. Let Newdegate

produce a single petition from the inmate of a single convent—
or her relations—suggested David Sherlock; then he would be
entitled to ask for such a commission. John Martin, the representative of an Irish county and a recent Catholic convert, conceded that Newdegate "did not intend to do injustice or injury
to anyone. The hon. Member was moved simply by pure
bigotry."[35]

Newdegate had supporters as well, such as Edward
Greene, who charged all the Irish Catholic M.P.s with being the
delegates of priests, and James M. Holt, who saw the new
inves'igation as a necessary supplement to the partial inquiry of
three years before.[36] No prestigious M.P.s were prepared,
however, to support a measure whose purpose was, as Newdegate explained in his summing up, to assure "that an Irish
domination shall not be established in England and in Scotland."

When the votes were counted, Newdegate's proposal had
gone down to defeat, 131 to 96.[37] Newdegate was supported by
twenty-six Liberals, almost half of them from Scotland or Ulster,
and opposed by five Conservatives; otherwise the vote followed
party lines. "Mr. Newdegate," marveled *The Times*, "is indefatigable in his exertions to protect the liberty of Roman Catholics." That he succeeded in attracting almost a hundred votes for
his proposed inquiry into convents and monasteries "is a proof
of the strong dislike entertained by Englishmen to such institutions, and of the incurable suspicion which attaches to them."
Ultimately the legal status quo was probably the best solution.
No large portion of the nation was likely, after all, to reconvert to
"an exploded superstition" like Roman Catholicism; those who
had done so would "be gradually overcome by the increasing
enlightenment of the people."[38] It was not in Newdegate's nature to feel so sanguine about the age in which he lived.

13. Three Prime Ministers Lend a Hand

"In almost every European country," wrote J. M. Capes in 1872, "there are signs of a renewal of that passionate identification of theological and political animosities which so terribly embittered the hostilities of the sixteenth and seventeenth centuries."[1] A year later Queen Victoria wrote privately of "the *universal struggle*, which has begun between the Roman Catholic Church and Protestant Governments in general."[2] For Charles Newdegate, to whom such sentiments represented ancient truths rather than novel appraisals, 1874 was to prove a paradoxical year. In his immediate aim of rearousing the concern of his countrymen in the the growth of Roman Catholic convents and monasteries in the United Kingdom, the Warwickshire M.P. was to obtain but indifferent success. In his efforts to hal' the tendencies toward "Romanization" within the Church of England, however, he was to receive the support of his party's leader, Benjamin Disraeli. In his concern with the Roman threat to all Europe, he was to forge a bond of union with the erstwhile Liberal prime minister, Earl Russell. In his attempts to awaken fellow Britons to the dangers posed by the Vatican, he was to obtain the unexpected but firm alliance of the current champion of British liberalism, William Ewart Gladstone. What G. F. A. Best has termed "the presumed neuroses of Newdegate"[3] were to receive at least temporary validation from the mouths and pens of the mighty.

Before all these matters would reach fruition, a new general election had to be held. Such an election, Mitchell Henry had warned Newdegate the year before, would clearly separate "the friends and foes of liberty."[4] It was not presumably the purpose of Henry, an Irish Roman Catholic who had hitherto called himself a Liberal but who now labeled himself an Irish Home Ruler, to distinguish friend and foe in precisely the same fashion as did the sponsor of the late William Murphy, the Protestant Evangelical Mission and Electoral Union. That organization recommended that parliamentary candidates be opposed or supported on the basis of whether they would protect the nation's Roman Catholics from tyranny and fraud at the hands of the pope's agents, whether they would pledge protection of the law to nuns imprisoned in convents against their will, and whether they would be willing to repeal the Catholic Emancipation Act of 1829, a measure that had permitted Roman Catholic priests "to subvert our National Institutions in the interest of the Pope."[5]

When the election of 1874 was over, the Conservatives had become the majority party in the House of Commons for the first time in thirty years. They occupied 350 seats, as opposed to 250 for Gladstone's Liberals and 57 for Isaac Butt's Home Rulers, with whom the Liberals shared the opposition benches. The outcome has been attributed in part to the defection of numerous Irishmen from the Liberal banner, their appetites whetted rather than appeased by Gladstone's numerous measures to "pacify Ireland." It has been attributed also to the apathy of Nonconformists dissatisfied with the compromise with Anglicanism entailed by the National Education Act. It was attributed by Gladstone himself to the "torrent of gin and beer" with which irate pub keepers and their clients had retaliated against the promoters of the restrictive public-house Licensing Act of 1872. Conversely, the outcome has been seen as a triumph of both Conservative electoral organization and the appeal of Disraeli's threefold rallying cries of Monarchy, Empire, and Social Reform. In 1872 Disraeli had aptly compared the Liberal front bench to "a range of exhausted volcanoes"; for the moment, clearly, the aims of Liberal reform had been achieved, and the electoral pendulum had swung.

For Newdegate, the general election of 1874 was peculiarly peaceful and almost relaxing. He faced no meaningful Liberal opposition, and he was able to boast to his local supporters about his recent newspaper triumph over Archbishop Manning. His political principles, he admitted, were the same as when first elected. "He was prepared to meet a change of circumstances by altered measures, but always with the object of securing to his fellow countrymen those advantages which had made England the envy of the world." The Liberal *Warwick Advertiser*, which had opposed him in the past, awaited his reelection this time with acquiescence. Newdegate had been an obstacle to progress in years gone by, but "notwithstanding these defects Mr. Newdegate has justly acquired a firm hold upon the esteem of his constituents by estimable qualities of mind, by cultivated intelligence, by laborious attention to public business, and by manly independence of conduct."[6]

The election outcome in North Warwickshire was Charles Newdegate (Cons.), 4,672; William Bromley-Davenport (Cons.), 4,322; and George Frederick Muntz (Lib.), 3,187. Though pleased by his victory and by that of his party, Newdegate retained numerous reservations about the character and the principles of Benjamin Disraeli. He could not feel altogether sanguine about the prospect of having the wily novelist, acerbic wit, and baptized Jew serve as Her Majesty's first minister for the indefinite future. There was now no question, as there had been with Derby, of a tender of office—even if only to give Newdegate the satisfaction of turning it down. Gladstone's personality, if not his program, was in some ways more appealing to the squire of Arbury Hall, and *Punch*'s parliamentary reporter records that on the first day of the new session, Newdegate, after depositing his top hat on the same corner seat on the government side that he had hitherto occupied on the opposition side, wandered aimlessly to and fro—still unhappy with the state of the world.[7] Gladstone, who regarded the House of Commons of 1874 as "the most reactionary, the most apathetic, and the least independent in which he ever sat,"[8] was, to be sure, no happier.

In March, Newdegate, together with his associates Thomas Chambers and James M. Holt, introduced a new monastic and conventual institutions bill asking the Disraeli government to appoint an investigatory commission. The bill won the support of a number of religious journals and worried the duke of Norfolk sufficiently to cause him to request a special meeting with Disraeli.[9] Newdegate found it difficult, however, to obtain a place for a discussion of the measure on the crowded Commons calendar, and in June he embarked upon an alternate tack, a formal request that the government collect all laws regulating convents and monasteries in France, Germany, Austria, Russia, Italy, Sweden, Norway, Belgium, Spain, and Switzerland. Scarcely had he begun to explain the utility of such an assemblage of information to the house than Sir George Bowyer called the attention of the speaker to the fact that there was no quorum (to note publicly the presence of less than forty members was known as "counting out the house"). To Newdegate's distress, a group of Irish members chose that moment to leave the chamber and to block the doors to M.P.s seeking to come in. The speaker, seeing no quorum, promptly adjourned the house. Newdegate regarded Bowyer's parliamentary maneuver as a shabby abuse of parliamentary privilege, while Bowyer afterward explained that he had simply saved the Warwickshire M.P. from the ordeal of "making one of those dreary speeches which we have heard from him so often."[10] *Punch* found the episode amusing.

> CHILDE NEWDEGATE mounted his hobbye so blacke,
>   To ride at the monke and the nun.

But a Bowyer sly hath his shaft let fly,
  And the Childe with a count foredone!

"Now foul thee fall, thou false Bowyer,
  That shoot'st from behind Rome's wall!"
But the Bowyer laught—"Nay," quoth he, "my shaft
  Flew not for Rome, but all!

"For hot was the night and heavy the weight,
  And O but his hobbye was slow;
And the SPEAKER was crouse, and glad the House
  For the shooting of my bow!"

And members all did a blessing call
  Upon the Bowyer gay,
Who CHILDE NEWDEGATE'S hobbye did hamstring,
  And sent the House to play![11]

Three days later, a frustrated Newdegate tried yet another tack. Having given up hope of bringing his own measure to the floor, he sought to amend a routine government resolution to have the house transform itself into committee to discuss the budget by substituting the words: "it is expedient that Her Majesty's Ministers should introduce a Bill appointing Commissioners to inquire as to Monastic and Conventual Institutions in Great Britain." The land was as unprepared legally for the onslaught of Roman Catholic religious orders in the 1870s, he declared, as it had been unprepared militarily for the onset of the Crimean War twenty years earlier. At a time that the German Empire had taken the most active steps to regulate such institutions within its borders, it seemed absurd for Great Britain to remain satisfied with so flimsy an investigation as that of 1870. The laws of the kingdom were being publicly flouted, and yet the duke of Wellington could hardly have intended the ban on Jesuits in the Catholic Relief Bill of 1829 to be treated as a dead letter. Too many reports involving the mistreatment of nuns had, moreover, come to public attention to justify continued neglect of these subjects by "the English House of Commons, an assembly of English gentlemen."

William Henry O'Sullivan immediately arose "to defend the honour of those pure and holy women"; Newdegate's resolution was a political trap for Disraeli into which he trusted the prime minister would not fall and a wanton insult toward Irishmen, an insult that they would not take lying down. Sir George Bowyer similarly defended convents as no more deserving of inspection than were private homes. Foreign analogies were hardly to the point, he ingenuously observed; "England and

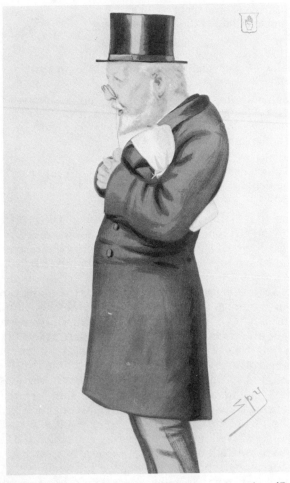

Sir George Bowyer, a leading Roman Catholic lawyer and member of Parliament (*Vanity Fair*, 1876).

America were the only countries where the true principles of civil and religious liberty were properly understood. From Germany, in that respect, they had nothing to learn for its Government was founded on a military despotism."[12]

Gathorne Hardy, the secretary of state for war, was given the task of pouring oil upon the waters of religious militancy on behalf of the government. He complimented Newdegate on the sincerity, honor, and consistency that he had demonstrated throughout his public career. "But it has not been a successful career, and it is rather hard upon the Government, when he has withdrawn his own Bill, because he found that it did not command sufficient sympathy in the House, that he should bring forward a Motion calling upon us to take up the very same Bill." "I hope the Government will produce a better Bill," interrupted Newdegate. "I am sure," Hardy continued, "that my hon. Friend does not think that a better Bill than his own can be introduced." He reminded Newdegate that neither Wellington nor Peel had sought to enforce the ban on monastic orders when in office after 1829; concern with theoretical implications must be balanced against the danger of unnecessary interference where the ordinary law sufficed to prevent abuses. "In a country so divided in religious feeling as this, we must exercise the greatest tolerance towards each other." Newdegate's resolution met defeat by a vote of 237 to 94.[13]

However decisive his defeat, Newdegate could take comfort in the degree of interest that the question had once again aroused outside the House of Commons. In the course of 1874 some 1,343 petitions with 211,335 signatures descended upon the House of Commons seeking an investigation of convents and monasteries; 633 petitions bearing 202,327 signatures opposed such action.[14]

In the weekly journal *Public Opinion*, a very lively correspondence developed that revealed more pointedly than did the debate in Parliament the sexual concerns that lay behind the arguments of at least some of the proponents and opponents of convent regulation. O'Sullivan broke a House of Commons taboo by suggesting bluntly that, if Newdegate's resolution carried, there would result "an inspection of convents, which would include the underclothing of the nuns—[Oh, oh!]—and the ascertaining of the fact whether any of them were of the colour which seemed to inflame bulls, turkey-cocks, and Protestants alike—[Oh, oh!]."[15] One of the letter writers to *Public Opinion* called attention to the obverse implication: Roman Catholic priests were but men, after all, and if they persisted in opposing the investigation of convents to which they had regular access, then "they can scarcely be surprised if the idea crosses our minds that, instead of a convent being a *Maison d'Education*, it may be a *Maison de Plaisir*."[16] For other letter writers, convents provided a refuge for a girl not suited to become a materfamilias: refined Christian women escaped to such homes in order "to escape the horrid unreality of modern fashionable society." A writer signing himself "CENSOR" had known girls forced into matrimony but never girls forcibly immured within convent walls. There was the possibility of dispensation from convent vows, but what hope was there for a young woman tied down by an unsuitable marriage—only "death, or the worse alternative of divorce." A self-designated "IRISH PRIEST" reminded the journal's readers of one of the pronouncements of the Council of Trent: "If any one says that the conjugal state is to be preferred to the state of virginity or celibacy, and that it is not better or more blessed to remain in virginity or celibacy than to be joined in marriage, let him be anathema." Marriage was good enough for ordinary folk, but a select few continued to have "a higher and holier calling."[17] The opponents of convents were equally explicit. Robert Bruce M'Combie declared: "I take the opportunity of uttering a protest against the unnatural, unscriptural, and pernicious practice of immuring men or women in a convent." Another writer castigated the government for burying its ostrichlike head in the sand and for failing to realize that intelligent and healthy English girls were being discouraged from becoming wives and mothers. The Roman Catholics were the greatest offenders by far in encouraging "the growth of non-producers."[18]

During the same month that such correspondence was gracing the pages of *Public Opinion*, the government mollified Newdegate by assembling in the House of Commons a comprehensive collection of foreign laws and regulations concerning conventual institutions. Speaking on behalf of the ministry, Robert Bourke added that, though this material was now in the Commons library, it had been deemed an unnecessary expense to translate and print all the documents. The minister "thought there was scholarship enough in the House to obviate the necessity for translations."[19]

Although Disraeli's ministry did not share Newdegate's concern with the the growth of monastical institutions, it more than lived up to his hopes in the support that it gave to the Public Worship Bill of 1874. For several decades, numerous groups within the Church of England had been fearful of what the *Quarterly Review* called the efforts "to bring our worship into harmony with that of the Romish Church, and especially to assimilate Holy Communion with the Mass by 'histrionic' means."[20] Anglican ritualists lit candles, held processions within the church, sprinkled holy water, invoked the Virgin Mary, and practiced auricular confession, and Roman Catholics like

Dr. Herbert Vaughan were hailing the ritualists as Roman Catholics in every respect except the acknowledgment of papal authority.[21] Queen Victoria agreed that such High Church ritualists were "R[oman] *Catholics at heart*, and *very* insincere as to their professions of attachment to the Church." The English church, she observed, should concern itself with the danger of the papacy instead of using Roman practices that estranged it from fellow Protestant communions.[22] Under the circumstances, the queen warmly applauded the measure introduced into the House of Lords in April 1874 by the archbishops of Canterbury and York. Their bill proposed a system whereby members of the church might appeal to an episcopal board of assessors made up of both churchmen and laymen against Anglican clergymen who instituted such untraditional liturgical practices. Upon Lord Shaftesbury's recommendation, a special ecclesiastical judge, to be appointed by the two archbishops with the approval of the crown, was substituted for the board of assessors.

The measure passed the House of Lords, and, after initial hesitation, Disraeli's ministry decided to make it a government measure in the House of Commons. The proposal was to divide both major political parties, and it placed Gladstone in a special difficulty. He was generally reputed to be sympathetic to the High Church position, but as he had assured Queen Victoria the year before, he had never taken on "any party designation whatever in religion."[23] Initially he opposed the Public Worship Bill on the ground that it implied lay interference with the liberty of Anglican clergymen. He conceded that a variety of liturgical practices had grown up within the Church of England, but he did not believe that "they ought to be rashly and rudely rooted out." Disraeli was happy enough to tackle Gladstone's scruples at their source. He had no desire to abolish all divergent tendencies within the church, he insisted. The High Church, the Low Church, and the Broad Church—attitudes respectively embodying ceremony, enthusiasm, and free speculation—all had their proper role to play, but, he reminded Gladstone, the Church of England was a national church established by parliamentary statute. He had no desire to mock the religious practices of avowed Roman Catholics; "What I do object to is Mass in masquerade." It was time, therefore, "to put down Ritualism."[24] It was impossible, the prime minister declared, "to conceal from ourselves that the great struggle between the Temporal and Spiritual power, which had stamped such indelible features upon the history of the past, was reviving in our own time." One of the objectives of the Public Worship Bill was to rally the nation and its church, the Church of England, "on the broad platform of the Reformation."[25]

Though uncertain about the details of the bill, Newdegate was delighted with its tenor and purport. He proudly presented numerous petitions favorable to the measure, and he used it to illustrate the manner in which Conservatives were prepared to remedy abuses. "If I believed that Conservatism meant merely the preservation of abuse, I could not be a Conservative," he asserted. It was for Newdegate the proper function of Parliament to ensure that the Church of England did indeed remain a national church faithful to its theological foundations.[26] The Public Worship Bill eventually passed its second reading without a division. Its approval, Disraeli confided to Victoria, "proved the Protestant spirit of the new House of Commons, fresh from their constituents."[27] The measure was hailed by the *Observer* as a sign that Englishmen, however tolerant, would not permit their national church to serve as a cloak for practices and ceremonies that they found repugnant and by the *Scotsman* as a major contribution to "that great struggle between the temporal and the spiritual power."[28]

The potential power of the Church of Rome was brought home to ordinary Englishmen once more in September 1874 when George Frederick Robinson, the marquess of Ripon, announced his conversion to Catholicism. From the Roman church's point of view, this was no ordinary conversion. Not only had Ripon been born at Ten Downing Street back in 1827 while his father, Viscount Goderich, was prime minister but also he had long been a prominent Liberal statesman. A professed radical, he had defined himself as a Christian Socialist in the 1850s, and he had lectured at workingmen's colleges. An M.P. since 1852 and a peer since 1859, he had joined Palmerston's ministry in that year and had been promoted to the cabinet as secretary of state for war in 1863. In 1866 he had become secretary of state for India and in 1868 Gladstone's lord president of the council. In 1870 Oxford had honored him with a doctor of civil law degree, and the following year, in tribute to his success as chairman of the joint Anglo-American commission to settle the *Alabama* claims, he had been rewarded with a marquessate. In 1870 he had been named grand master of English Freemasons, a post that he resigned on his reception into the Roman Catholic church at Brompton Oratory.[29] That an ornament of the Liberal party, "the party of progress and en-

The marquess of Ripon, the most eminent English convert to Roman Catholicism during the 1870s (from a scrapbook in the University of Illinois Library).

lightenment," and one of England's leading noblemen to boot
should in the prime of life take such a step stirred the often staid
Times to a state of outrage, almost of frenzy. A statesman who
thus renounced his mental and moral freedom, it announced,
"forfeits at once the confidence of the English people. . . . To
become a Roman Catholic and remain a thorough Englishman
are—it cannot be disguised—almost incompatible conditions."
Englishmen who were born Roman Catholics could be excused,

but those who converted betrayed "an irreparable weakness of character," a "fatal demoralization," and "some fatal obliquity of temperament."[30]

Ripon's conversion, the *Globe* agreed, was "a melancholy spectacle." Yet for Conservative papers like the *Globe* and the *Standard*, the step was hardly surprising. Considering how helpful the recent Liberal government had been to Roman Catholic pretensions in Ireland and England, "What is more natural than that in the very bosom of the Liberal Cabinet the Roman Catholic Propagandists should look for conquests?"[31] What a pity, grumbled the *Saturday Review*, that his new church had forced Ripon to resign as grand master of the Masons; in the eyes of his adopted church, Freemasonry, "a harmless trifle," was "a mortal sin."[32] The evangelical *Record* was forced to concede that "the Romanists, always in quest of rich and broad-acred perverts [*sic*]," had landed a major prize in the marquess of Ripon. In the view of most major journals, Ripon had committed political suicide, and only the *Spectator* suggested mildly that he might ultimately be forgiven by his countrymen.[33]

Ripon's conversion was the *cause célèbre* of the season; numerous sermons dealt with the matter, and Queen Victoria could for some time talk of little else. Although Disraeli maliciously suggested that Gladstone was ultimately responsible for Ripon's decision, Gladstone himself was sorely troubled and given new impetus to utilize his pen to enter the pamphlet warfare that the religious concerns of the day were spurring on.[34]

If further reminders were needed in the England of 1874 that, in Disraeli's words, "Europe is more deeply stirred than at any period since the Reformation," such reminders came regularly from Germany.[35] There the *Kulturkampf*—"the struggle for civilization"—was in full swing, and, in the judgment of the *Annual Register*, "the war of Bismarck against the Papacy was the key to all the prominent transactions of the time."[36] Bismarck was fearful that the Roman Catholic states of Europe would unite under papal inspiration to disrupt the newly unified German Empire. He was especially upset by the appearance in the first elected imperial Reichstag of a powerful and predominantly Roman Catholic Center party, whose ultimate allegiance might be bestowed not upon the German emperor but upon Pope Pius IX, a man whom Bismarck denounced as "a peril for all countries and all thrones, a revolutionary, an anarchist."[37] The result was a domestic preventive war whereby the Prussian legislature and, to a lesser degree, the imperial legislature, passed a series of measures designed to undermine clerical independence. In 1872 the Jesuits were expelled from Germany, and in 1873 the civil registration of marriages, births, and deaths was imposed in Prussia, as was the state supervision of religious schools. This step was followed by the so-called May laws whose professed purpose it was to impose state education on all prospective priests and state inspection on all seminaries. The right of the church hierarchy to appoint, to discipline, and to dismiss Roman Catholic priests was subjected to state supervision, and later in the year a special oath of allegiance to the Prussian king was imposed. "The crux of the matter," according to Bismarck, was "the defense of the State; the definition of boundaries between the domain of the Priest and the domain of the King, and this boundary must be so defined as to enable the state to maintain itself." With papal support, an increasing number of bishops and priests defied such laws, and by 1876 every Roman Catholic bishop was either in jail or in exile, and scores of Prussian parishes were bereft of clergy.[38]

The events in Germany distressed the pope and deeply disturbed Archbishop Manning. In December 1873, in *Caesarism and Ultramontanism*, the archbishop launched a fierce attack upon both Bismarck's *Kulturkampf* and upon Englishmen like Earl Russell who had dared to show sympathy toward German anti-Catholic legislation. The German Empire, Manning declared, was suffering from the disease of Caesarism, which was to legitimate civil power "what elephantiasis is to the human frame, or mania to the human mind." Since the acts of the Vatican Council had been "declaratory" rather than "enacting," they could hardly excuse German bigotry. What the German emperor and his chancellor had forgotten was that

> the presence of the Catholic church among the civil powers of the world has changed the whole political order of mankind. It has established upon earth a legislature, a tribunal, and an executive independent of all human authority. It has withdrawn from the reach of human laws the whole domain of faith and conscience. These depend on God alone, and are subjected by Him to His authority, vested in His Church, which is guided by Himself.
>
> This is the solution of the problem, which the world cannot solve. Obedience to the Church is liberty; and it is liberty because the Church cannot err or mislead either men or nations. If the Church were not infallible, obedience to it might be the worst of bondage.

Since the church was infallible, there was no cause for any jurisdictional dispute between the state and the church. Because

the church is "certain with a Divine certainty as to the limits of
its jurisdiction, its voice in such matters is final." The notion of a
"free Church in a free State" was therefore an "impossible
theory."[39]

The *Pall Mall Gazette* found Manning's pamphlet "a remarkable document" even though its assertions had not been supported by proof. *The Times* was equally startled "to hear the
fully-developed Roman theory proclaimed . . . with such vehe-
ment explicitness of iteration." In its Christmas Eve editorial,
The Times countered Manning's assertions in point-blank
fashion: "If there is one thing certain in history, it is that the one
great foe of freedom of conscience, the unscrupulous advocate
of persecutions, the despot of domestic and social life, has been
the Roman Catholic church."[40]

Manning was equally unsuccessful in persuading Earl Russell. In a letter to Sir John Murray, the retired statesman proclaimed that he, for one, would "never exchange my Christian
Liberty for submission to Priestly Supremacy." In the course of
his long political life, he had successfully fought for the political
rights of Roman Catholics, of Protestant Dissenters, and of
Jews, he recalled, but for none of these groups had he sought
more than equal privileges and equal laws. Yet here was Manning proclaiming that the Roman church was separate and
supreme and in sole position to define its proper jurisdiction. To
agree with Manning "is not liberty civil or religious. It is to bow
the knee to a despotic and fallible priesthood." The very same
principles that had caused Russell to work for religious liberty in
England now motivated him to protest against "a conspiracy
which aims at confining the German Empire in chains. . . . I
could no longer call myself a lover of civil and religious liberty all
over the world, if I did not proclaim my adherence to the
Emperor of Germany in the noble struggle in which he is engaged. . . . the cause of the Emperor of Germany is the cause of
liberty, and the cause of the Pope is the cause of slavery."[41]
Russell went on to convoke a London gathering—one of several
in the winter of 1874—which voted its sympathy with the desire
of the Germans to free their empire from papal designs. Bismarck and his emperor were delighted with such firm public
support from a former prime minister, and the Iron Chancellor
warmly thanked "the Nestor of European statesmen" for his
sympathy with "our defensive warfare against the priesthood of
Rome."[42]

It was Disraeli rather than Manning who motivated Gladstone, in the first instance, to embark upon a season of religious

Born in 1792, Lord John Russell, first earl Russell, entered the House of Commons in 1813 and held his first ministerial office in 1830. He twice served as prime minister (from a scrapbook in the University of Illinois Library).

controversy with an article in the October 1874 issue of the *Contemporary Review*. When, during the debate on the Public Worship Bill a few months earlier, Gladstone had sought a precise definition of the "Ritualism" that his political opposite sought to "put down," Disraeli had blandly replied that apparently everyone knew what ritualism was except Gladstone. In "Ritualism and Ritual" the Liberal leader sought to demonstrate that although religious ritual was "a legitimate accompaniment, nay, effect of the religious life," it was neither a religious end in itself nor did it necessarily accompany a specific theology. Scandinavian Lutherans, for example, were deeply ritualistic without therefore desiring a reunion with Rome.

Gladstone was therefore less fearful than were the prime mov-
ers of the Public Worship Bill that particular liturgical practices
within certain Anglican parishes would necessarily result in the
reconversion of England to Roman Catholicism. Such a reconversion, Gladstone declared—in a passage tossed off almost as
an aside—was all the less likely at a time

> when [1] Rome has substituted for the proud boast of *semper eadem*
> a policy of violence and change in faith; when [2] she has refur-
> bished and paraded anew every rusty tool she was fondly thought
> to have disused; when [3] no one can become her convert without
> renouncing his moral and mental freedom, and placing his civil
> loyalty and duty at the mercy of another; and when [4] she has
> equally repudiated modern thought and ancient history.[43]

These words so infuriated a number of Irish journals, who
denounced their erstwhile hero for having irreparably insulted
the religion of most Irishmen, that Gladstone felt compelled to
defend his remarks with a sixty-six-page pamphlet, *The Vatican
Decrees in Their Bearing on Civil Allegiance: A Political Expostulation.* He had no desire, Gladstone explained in his introduction,
to insult his fellow countrymen. They had not, after all, chosen
their ecclesiastical superiors; but those superiors had during the
previous decade created for them a genuine dilemma of conscience by claiming, in effect, full temporal as well as spiritual
authority over their adherents. Gladstone justified the first and
fourth of his propositions by calling attention to the manner in
which the papal encyclicals and decrees of the mid-nineteenth
century had departed from earlier church tradition. He defended his second proposition simply by citing all the propositions condemned in the "Syllabus of Errors": liberty of the
press, liberty of conscience and worship, liberty of speech, and
numerous others. Gladstone devoted the greater portion of his
pamphlet to the third proposition: that the decrees of the Vatican Council in regard to papal infallibility and obedience to
papal fiat undermined the integrity of the civil allegiance that
Roman Catholic citizens owed their nation-state.

It had been argued, Gladstone admitted, that infallibility
applied only when the pope spoke *ex cathedra*. But the pope
could infallibly decree what was *ex cathedra* and what was not. It
had been observed also, Gladstone noted, that the doctrine of
infallibility touched only upon matters of faith and morals.
"Only morals! Will any of the Roman casuists kindly acquaint us
what are the departments and functions of human life which do
not and cannot fall within the domain of morals? . . . I care not
to ask if there be dregs or tatters of human life, such as can

escape from the description and boundary of morals. I submit that Duty is a power which rises with us in the morning, and goes to rest with us at night. It is co-extensive with the action of our intelligence."[44] The third chapter of the Vatican decrees, which demanded universal obedience to the pope, impressed Gladstone as being as all-encompassing as the fourth chapter, which defined the pope's infallibility. As recently as the 1820s, Roman Catholic clergymen had assured a Parliament weighing the desirability of Catholic emancipation that the pope's dictates in no way impaired their temporal allegiance to the monarch. Now the situation had clearly altered, and though Gladstone himself had no desire to turn back the legislative clock, he did maintain that Britons who were Roman Catholics would now have to take special steps to demonstrate their continued civil allegiance.

Although his pamphlet evoked a storm of criticism in Ireland, Gladstone had judiciously left out of his indictment the two cases that would have illustrated his thesis most graphically. Acting on a Galway election petition in 1872, Judge Keogh, himself a Roman Catholic, had found the Roman Catholic bishops and clergy of western Ireland guilty of using intimidation, denunciations from the altar, and even incitements to assassination in order to assist their favored candidate. In a separate incident, Father Robert O'Keefe had been suspended from his position as manager of an Irish national school for favoring mixed (as opposed to denominational) education and for subsequently daring to seek redress in the civil courts. Both cases had been given widespread publicity in press and Parliament alike. The O'Keefe case had indeed caused Newdegate to remind the House of Commons that

> The Emperor of Germany has signed the new laws for the defence of the State of Prussia against the invasion of his rights and those of his subjects. You have it admitted by Cardinal Cullen himself that he acts here under an authority which your courts have declared to be illegal. He has used used that authority to the injury of a British Subject.[45]

Most English and Scottish newspapers welcomed Gladstone's pamphlet. The *Pall Mall Gazette* might wonder whether Gladstone was not, in a sense, seeking to revive political tests against Roman Catholic citizens, and the *Manchester Guardian* failed to see that the pamphlet was serving any practical purpose; but most of the provincial press was jubilant.[46] "So clear and ringing a note of anti-Papal protest has not been sounded in

England for a long time," declared the Liverpool *Daily Post*. For the *Birmingham Morning News*, the pamphlet was one of the most powerful blows ever aimed against ultramontanism, and it relieved all the *Newcastle Daily Chronicle*'s doubts as to the former prime minister's religious integrity. The Conservative London *Morning Post* sang Gladstone's praises, and the weekly *Rock*, a Low Church Anglican weekly, welcomed the return of the prodigal to the fundamental tenets of Protestantism.[47]

Not surprisingly, the Roman Catholic *Universe* found the pamphlet a "disgraceful production," and Dublin's *Freeman's Journal* described its style as "painfully offensive." "We hope we have heard the last of Catholic alliance with the Liberals," thundered the *Catholic Times*.[48] Pope Pius IX himself suggested that Gladstone, "intoxicated by the proceedings of another Minister in another State [Bismarck in Germany], has suddenly come forward like a viper, assailing the barque of St. Peter. . . . The fallen Minister hopes to arrest the luminous triumph of the Church."[49] John Murray, the publisher of the pamphlet, told Gladstone that "the Pope's tirade is the best advertisement." He went on to suggest that the pope had established "his connection with St. Peter the Fisherman by his acquaintance with the language of Billingsgate."[50] Within two months, 145,000 copies of the pamphlet had been sold in England—more than the most popular novel of the day—and Bismarck was distributing a German translation throughout his empire.[51] According to the *York Herald* of 2 December 1874, "the papal controversy shows no sign of abatement. All the newspapers are full of it. No politico-theological movement in modern times ever excited so much attention; or brought out so many contradictory opinions."[52]

The Times wondered about Gladstone's underlying motives for publishing the pamphlet. Was it an accumulation of frustrations hitherto held in check by his prime ministerial position? Had Gladstone found it necessary to repudiate the suspicion that he had personal leanings toward Rome? Or was it a sign of indignation at the manner in which the Irish hierarchy had torpedoed his proposed Irish universities bill the year before?[53] Gladstone conceded in the pamphlet that he had not felt it appropriate to speak publicly as long as he was prime minister and his ministry was engaged in seeking to remedy the ills of Ireland. The measures of 1869 and 1870, the disestablishment of the Church of Ireland and the Land Act, had in large measure eased Ireland's lot. Gladstone's attempt in 1873 also to resolve the question of higher education had, however, met with de-

PUNCH, OR THE LONDON CHARIVARI.—March 19, 1870.

THE IRISH "TEMPEST."

CALIBAN (RORY OF THE HILLS). "THIS ISLAND'S MINE, BY SYCORAX MY MOTHER, WHICH THOU TAK'ST FROM ME."—*Shakspeare.*

William Ewart Gladstone (as Prospero), with his Irish Land Act, protects his daughter Hibernia from the barbarian Roman Catholic rebel (from *Punch*, 19 March 1870, p.111).

feat. The bill had been shot down less by Nonconformists who feared that Gladstone's enlarged University of Dublin would fall under the control of Rome than by Catholic leaders who feared

that it would not. According to Gladstone, the hierarchy therefore "thought fit to procure the rejection of that measure, by the
direct influence which they exercised over a certain number of
Irish Members of Parliament, and by the temptation which they
thus offered . . . to attract the support of the Tory Opposition."[54]
The result had been the fall of the government, and two years
later John Bright, Gladstone's leading Nonconformist supporter, was still angry with the "treacherous" "Irish contingent,
who prostrated themselves before their bishop and destroyed
the best Minister whom England had ever seen." There was no
escape from the domination of domestic and international politics by theological and ecclesiastical questions, Bright observed
to Lord Granville. "When establishments are abolished and the
Pope suppressed, there may perhaps be peace."[55] S. E. de Vere,
an Anglo-Irish convert, privately agreed: "For my part I regard
our Hierarchy as a fatal obstacle to the peace and prosperity of
Ireland and I can hardly blame the Newdegates for the very
natural mistake with which they identify Catholicism with an
overbearing and selfish Hierarchy."[56]

Gladstone had other motives as well, both personal and
political. He had been shocked by Ripon's conversion and yet
more shocked by the excommunication of his old German
friend, the Catholic theologian Dr. Ignaz von Döllinger, whom
he had visited in Munich only a few weeks before.[57] Gladstone
attributed the religious struggle in Germany directly to the
Vatican decrees of 1870, and "when Germany is disquieted,
Europe cannot be at rest." The Liberal leader's underlying public motive was to stop the Roman Catholic ultramontane band-
wagon from continuing "to run its furious course."[58] As he
confided to Lord Granville, his closest political ally, he had a
genuine fear that papal agents were conspiring to bring about a
European war that would enable the pope to regain his temporal
domain. Gladstone desired to do no more than "to put a spoke
in their wheel."[59]

The most immediate repercussions of Gladstone's pamphlet proved to be literary rather than diplomatic. Within two
months, some twenty Roman Catholic writers took their pens in
hand to reply to Gladstone. Three of them—Lord Acton, Lord
Camoys, and Henry Petre—in effect gave Gladstone the assurance that he was seeking. In Petre's words, "The only reply a
loyal subject could possibly make to Mr. Gladstone's appeal
would be 'An Englishman first, a Catholic after.' "[60] Under
Manning's direction, the *Tablet* denounced the three for rank
"apostasy." Three men whose religious position had for years

been looked on with suspicion by their coreligionists had openly
declared themselves at last.[61]

Pamphlets by Bowyer, Bishop Ullathorne, and Manning
himself struck a far sterner tone. Manning's two-hundred-page
exposition was indeed so fervent as to confirm the suspicions of
most non-Catholic readers that Gladstone had been right.[62]
Manning denied that the Vatican decrees had in any fashion
changed the civil allegiance of Catholic Britons, a loyalty limited
only to the degree that "the civil allegiance of all men who
believe in God, or are governed by conscience, is in that sense
divided." Conflicts between church and state, Manning reminded Gladstone, came about only when the state invaded the
spiritual sphere. He charged Gladstone with inviting English
Catholics to rise against the divine authority of the Catholic
church and with "sowing discord and animosities among six
million of his fellow-countrymen. . . . he has been betrayed
into an act for which I can find no adequate excuse." Manning
told his priests that, if any one of them visited Gladstone's
home, he would regard such a step as a personal affront, and,
though Gladstone and Manning had once been close personal
friends, neither ever entered the other's home again.[63] Later that
year, in a piece on "What the Cardinal Did at Oxford," *Punch*
mockingly mused on Manning's thoughts as he revisited his
alma mater.

> He looked with a longing eye at Christ Church Cathedral—and
> indulged in a vision of the day when, the Constitution of England
> re-modelled, the Members of the Legislature converted, the Dis-
> senters exterminated, the Press suppressed, the Middle Classes
> hoodwinked, public opinion stifled, and the Universities restored
> to the happy condition in which they were before the Reforma-
> tion—he should "officiate pontifically" in that misappropriated
> edifice.[64]

In the meantime, one Catholic priest, the Reverend R. O'Keefe,
had assured Gladstone privately that he had made "a great
mistake in writing against the ultramontane party in the R.C.
Church, as if you were writing against the Church itself. . . .
Your language could apply even to such catholics as Dr. Newman and myself . . . whereas I at least believe you only meant it
for such catholics as Dr. Manning . . . whose public utterances
are I will say *offensively* disloyal."[65]

It was John Henry Newman who penned the most elegant
and intellectually acute Catholic reply to Gladstone, *A Letter
Addressed to His Grace the Duke of Norfolk on Occasion of Mr.
Gladstone's Recent Expostulation*. Newman publicly regretted that

Catholics who had spoken wildly, written irresponsibly, and "stretched principles until they were close upon snapping" had "alienated from them so religious a mind" as that of Gladstone.[66] Carefully sidestepping the question of whether a good Catholic was likely also to be an Irishman loyal to the United Kingdom, Newman insisted that all claims to total sovereignty, whether by church or state, had limits—because ultimately the individual conscience was supreme. It did remain possible, therefore, to be at once a good Catholic and a good Englishman. With great care and precision, Newman proceeded to review the history that Gladstone had touched on and to define the implications of the decrees that Gladstone had cited. Many of these documents, Newman suggested, were open to a far more restrictive interpretation than Gladstone had insisted on. "The circumference of State jurisdiction and of Papal are for the most part quite apart from each other," Newman argued; "there are just some few degrees out of the 360 in which they intersect, and Mr. Gladstone, instead of letting these cases of intersection alone, till they occur actually, asks me what I should do, if I found myself placed in the space intersected." Newman proceeded to answer. If the English state by act of Parliament ordered him to attend Protestant services weekly and the pope told him that he would thereby violate his duty to his faith, he would obey the pope and not the law. If, on the other hand, he were a British soldier told to take part in a war that his conscience told him to be just, and the pope suddenly ordered him to desert his post, he would not obey the pope.[67] "I do not think I ever can be sorry for what I have done," Newman privately wrote to Gladstone about his pamphlet rejoinder, "but I never can cease to be sorry for the necessity of doing it."[68]

    In January 1875 Gladstone provided a lengthy anonymous review of "The Speeches of Pope Pius IX," but the cloak of anonymity was soon penetrated; *The Times* dismissed the subjects of the pope's recent speeches as too trivial to warrant such careful attention.[69] A month later, when the duke of Argyll asked the unemotional Granville about the state of Gladstone's health, the earl replied: "He is very well, but neighs like a warhorse at hearing that Newman has issued 110 pages."[70] Gladstone was indeed motivated to answer his critics with another pamphlet, *Vaticanism: An Answer to Replies and Reproofs* (London, 1875), a more diffuse, more careful, and less popular work than its predecessor, and thereafter the controversy began to simmer down. In the meantime, Gladstone had, however, in the opinion of many Englishmen, placed himself squarely in the mainstream of English Protestant thinking. "Messrs. Newdegate and Whalley," wrote *The Times*, "may now boast a triumvirate of good Protestant Champions."[71]

Newdegate, who had always held Gladstone's prowess as both a parliamentarian and a religious controversialist in high regard, was delighted to find himself seeing eye to eye with the Liberal leader and wrote to tell him so; at the same time, he expressed his regret at the news that Gladstone had resigned the leadership of the Liberal party. "I trust that you will not abandon the House, in which you have been for so many years so distinguished. . . . You may, perhaps, be surprised," Newdegate went on, "at these expressions from one, who has humbly but sincerely opposed the policy of which you became the exponent in several important respects. Experience has modified my opinions—But I do not pretend to repent of the course, I have pursued, nor do I regret the personal sacrifice it has entailed; but I beleive [*sic*] that I share with you a desire to preserve the corporate character and self-respect of the House of Commons." Gladstone's reply was equally friendly: "I know the inflexible integrity with which you look at all public questions . . . and it is therefore a great pleasure when I find myself in accord with you. Yet I could wish, very cordially, that the occasion had been different; for the present bias & movement of the Roman Church is a real misfortune to Christendom."[72]

Commonsensical as he may have been in some respects and mentally blinkered and politically isolated as he was in others, Charles Newdigate Newdegate, doughty defender of an idealized Protestant England that never was, felt strangely warmed by the religious and political atmosphere of 1874. Russell, Disraeli, and Gladstone may have failed to aid the specific causes that Newdegate had made particularly his own, but, in their several ways, Britain's most eminent statesmen had testified to the appropriateness of many of his long-held fears and forebodings.

14. Old Soldiers Fade Away

He did not profess to be a prophet, Edward Greene assured the House of Commons in 1876, but unless he were very much mistaken the people of Great Britain were daily growing more and more concerned about the growth of Roman Catholic monasteries and convents.[1] The pages of history are filled with false prophets, and the long-forgotten Greene proved to be one more, because the parliamentary sessions of 1875 and 1876 turned out to be the end of an era for a subject that, according to one Liberal M.P., "had received more discussion in that House since 1853 than almost any other."[2] Like many another cause of popular excitement, the issue subsided gradually to a whimper, and the wider preoccupations with papal pretensions and Roman Catholic power subsided with it. Charles Newdegate, whose political career had been tied up with the issue for more than a decade, was compelled after 1877 to plow his furrows in other, though related, fields.

In 1875 Newdegate was still busily encouraging the Disraeli government to strengthen his verbal arsenal by providing copies of foreign laws and regulations concerning monastic and conventual institutions, and when Prince von Bülow, the German Empire's foreign secretary, replied that each individual German state would have to be consulted, the Conservative ministry shuddered; but eventually it did agree to obtain the information that Newdegate sought from the larger kingdoms and principalities if not from all.[3] At the same time, Newdegate introduced a new bill calling for an official commission of inquiry into the suspect institutions. Again the duke of Norfolk laid the objections of the Catholic laity before Disraeli and offered to lead another deputation to call upon the prime minister. "I know I need not urge our case further upon you," Norfolk concluded, and indeed he did not, for Disraeli had little sympathy for Newdegate's tactics. They would do little for the Conservative political rapprochement with English Catholicism that Gladstone's disappointment with his Irish universities bill and his antipapal pamphlets had indirectly encouraged.[4] Speaking privately of Newdegate's annual anticonvent bill, Disraeli remarked: "For years this man has been a bore; he has now become an institution."[5]

Though ultimately unpersuaded, Gladstone gave Newdegate's proposed measure a far more sympathetic hearing.

I think [Gladstone wrote to Newdegate in April 1875] that, after the sentiments I have published with respect to the relation of the present Papal religion to liberty, it is only just to you that I should give you my opinion on the subject of your Monastic Institutions Bill. . . .

Apart from the question of property, which has been made already the subject of inquiry, we have now to consider whether the law should provide for the inspections of these institutions.

The propriety of such provision depends, in my view, upon the question whether the institutions are so framed and managed as in no respect to impair civil and legal freedom. Of moral and inward freedom our law does not take account.

I cannot say I am convinced in my own mind that civil and legal freedom are in all cases duly respected.

But my suspicions do not warrant my taking part in legislation for which I could allege no other & firmer ground. I do not think that any thing less than facts proving, or powerfully tending to prove, interference with personal freedom, would warrant me, from my political point of view, in supporting measures which, in their aim at securing it, must involve some interference of another kind with the same precious privilege.

I do not at present know that it will be my duty to take any part in the debate or division: but I have seen no allegation in the papers I have read on the behalf of the Bill that such proof as I have mentioned is forthcoming.[6]

Ultimately there was neither a debate nor a division, since Newdegate found it impossible to secure a place on the parliamentary calendar. He had to take whatever comfort he could find in the fact that 1,301 petitions bearing 183,572 signatures were submitted to the House of Commons in support of his proposal, the largest number of petitions presented to Parliament on any subject during that year.[7] He could also take comfort in the fact that, under his inspiration, volume 16 of the year's printed *Parliamentary Papers* was packed with five separate reports on laws and regulations involving convents and monasteries throughout Europe and beyond. He could take no solace at all, however, in the fact that his cousin and fellow Christ Church graduate, Alfred Newdigate, an Anglican vicar, together with his entire family, converted that year to Roman Catholicism.[8]

Before the 1875 session was over, George H. Whalley, Newdegate's onetime Liberal counterpart, decided to stir the religious pot by moving for a select committee "to inquire and report to the House as to the residence in this Country, in contravention of the Act of 10 George 4 [the Catholic Emancipation Act] of any persons being members of the Order of Jesus."

Not even Newdegate was willing to provide a second. Thereupon Whalley accused the entire Disraeli ministry of having become a Jesuit tool. "I do not know how to defend myself,"
replied Disraeli in mock alarm, "but I may say I was reading the
other day a book in which it was stated that one of the most
dangerous of the devices adopted by that malignant society was
to engage some of their lay brethren to go about in disguise
abusing the Order."[9] Disraeli gave Whalley a long and searching
look. Newdegate, long disenchanted with Whalley's political
tactics, was half-persuaded that in this instance his party leader
was right.[10]

In 1876 it was Dr. Thomas Chambers, Newdegate's other
Liberal associate, who took the lead in moving "that it is expedient that an inquiry be undertaken as to the number, rate of
increase, character and present position, in relation to the law,
of Monastic and Conventual Institutions in Great Britain."
Chambers called attention to the enormous increase in the number of monasteries and convents since he had first concerned
himself with the subject back in 1853. Since then, the number of
monasteries had quintupled (from 17 to 99), the number of
convents had grown at a comparable rate (from 53 to 299), and
the number of Roman Catholic colleges had doubled. Chambers
cited a dictum of the Council of Trent to the effect that nuns were
not to be released even if they entered a convent against their
will, and he called attention to two recent incidents demonstrating beyond question that these institutions constituted "an in-
vasion of the liberties of English men and women." A year
before, Chambers asserted, a nun had been seen seeking to
escape over the wall of the convent of the Good Shepherd,
Hammersmith; she had been seized by several men in priestly
robes and forcibly brought back inside. A lady running away
from the convent at Newhall, Essex, had similarly been forced
back. Such incidents were "a scandal to the Church" and raised
anew the question of why Great Britain alone lagged behind the
rest of Europe in regulating such institutions.[11]

William Shaw, one of the Protestant chieftains of the fledgling Irish Nationalist party, took the lead in opposing Chambers's motion. Shaw seemed mentally prepared for Newdegate
rather than Chambers, and he publicly regretted that the question had been snatched out of Newdegate's hands, if only because the Warwickshire M.P. "had a kind of personal property
in it" and had gained thereby a great reputation as a champion
of Protestantism. Shaw recalled that he had once told a Catholic
friend that he looked on Newdegate as an honest man and a

gentleman. "I am very glad to hear of it," said his friend. "I am surprised at that," Shaw had responded, "because I think that if I found a man attacking my Church, I would rather he should be a scamp than an honest man." His friend had demurred: "The reason I am glad of it is this—I am quite sure his mind is working on the subject, and an honest mind never worked on anything connected with our Church without ending in the Church itself."[12]

The real question for Shaw was not whether such institutions had grown but whether they had grown beyond the religious needs of the Roman Catholic church; he thought not. As a Protestant in a Catholic land, he had come to the conclusion that the religious orders were of enormous social as well as religious benefit. The ability to take out a writ of habeas corpus sufficed as a protection against illegal imprisonment "in these days of universal knowledge, when what is whispered in secret is published upon the house-top."[13] Myles William O'Reilly scoffed even more openly at Chambers's charges. If he wanted the number of convents and monasteries, all he had to do was to consult the annual *Catholic Directory;* if he wanted to know the state of the law, all he had to do was to read the report of the select committee of 1870–1871; if he wished to learn more of the character of these institutions, all he had to do was to consult their constitutions and rules in any large library. The cases that Chambers referred to involved quite unsecluded convents whose members either went out regularly to visit the sick or to teach at an attached school; secret imprisonment was impossible in either case. The types of laws that Chambers and Newdegate sought would not kill Catholicism, come what may.

> There was a man who smote Catholicity in these countries with a remorseless and unrelenting fierceness which would have satisfied even the hon. Member for North Warwickshire. I mean Cromwell. In Ireland he struck hard and he struck long; for a monk to be discovered was to meet a speedy death.

And yet the religious orders did not disappear from Ireland. He was confident, O'Reilly concluded, that the House of Commons would "not embark upon an undertaking which centuries of penal laws and a Cromwellian persecution failed to accomplish—the proscription of the religious life, an undertaking which would be equally impolitic and unjust."[14]

O'Reilly was not the last of the resolution's opponents. Dr. William H. O'Leary recalled that, as a convent doctor in Dublin, he had found that the institutions there were more troubled with novices and postulants eager to gain admission than with members seeking to escape.[15] "No doubt, we have read books that profess to be written by liberated nuns," observed Richard Smyth, an Ulster Protestant, but "what does that prove? Why, that the nuns were liberated before they wrote them."[16] Sir George Bowyer called attention to the fact that one of Chambers's cases of presumed oppression turned out to be not "Sister Agnes" of Newhall but a kitchen maid who had stolen some property and had run away. Few of the English orders, Bowyer reminded the house, were very strict. The convents were "in fact female republics. They elect annually their Superior, and all the officers down to portress. They elect those who are admitted."[17]

Before the onslaught of the opposition, Mark Stewart could do little but express the pious hope that "a thoroughly Protestant Government" like Disraeli's would deal with convents, "remnants of the Middle Ages" as they were. Earl Percy lamented that, in the face of a militant Catholicism, Protestants lacked cohesion, while Sir John Kennaway regretted that, even though Newdegate, Cassandra-like, had poured forth his plaint session after session, it had fallen upon unheeding ears. If he were only given full freedom of discussion and the right to address his fellow countrymen, declared Whalley, "he would undertake to drive every Roman Catholic priest out of the country."[18]

To Newdegate was left the opportunity of summing up the case for the supporters of Chambers's motion, and he did his best. It impressed him as disastrous that neither major party dared investigate Roman Catholic convents and monasteries for fear of the largely ultramontane Roman Catholic Irish Home Rulers. Let them beware, Newdegate declared, lest a home-rule movement arose in England and Scotland on this very subject. "What right have you Roman Catholics to plead your susceptibilities, while you make no allowance for the feelings of us Protestants?" Did they think that Protestants welcomed "these robberies of relatives and friends," the manner in which young women were seduced from the warmth of an affectionate family home and thrust into a chill ascetic cloister? Was it truly proper, moreover, that ninety-nine male orders should have been established in Great Britain in defiance of the law, subsisting by no warrant other than the dispensation of the prime minister?[19] Momentous as these questions might be, they failed to persuade the representatives of either the government or the opposition front bench to rise in support of Chambers's motion, and on 31 March 1876, it went down to defeat by a vote of 127 to 87.[20]

For Newdegate, the debate had a highly unpleasant if anti-climactic epilogue. On 6 April he complained to the house that his name had been affixed without permission to a petition from Chatham Dissenters, a petition of whose language Newdegate personally disapproved. The next day Philip Callan observed that Newdegate's signature had apparently also been forged on petitions from Broadstairs, Kensington, and Avebury. All these petitions charged convents with inveigling and corrupting Protestant pupils; asserted that the nuns had "a hell here and a hell hereafter"; declared that conventual institutions "combine in themselves the worst evils of the workhouse, the asylum, the prison, and places of bad repute"; and charged that "nuns were treated most cruelly, and were made the victims of horrors which far surpassed anything that had entered the mind of the most fanatical enemy of the convents." Convent inmates, the petitions concluded, might indeed "be put to death or much worse." Newdegate complained that Callan had associated his name with these additional petitions without warning and before he had completed his investigation of the Chatham petition.[21]

At this point Disraeli intervened to remind members of two Commons rules: that "the language of Petitions should be respectful, decorous, and temperate"—that of the petitions under discussion clearly was not—and that each petition should be authenticated as proper by the signature of the member who presented it.[22] It was not until a month later that Newdegate was given an opportunity to make a public explanation. His private secretary, a highly reliable man who had been in his employ for more than six years, had unwittingly betrayed him by endorsing his name on petitions whose language, he conceded, was both "impolitic and imprudent." This secretary, the only person he had ever authorized to endorse a petition on his behalf, had apologized in a letter that Newdegate proceeded to read.

> Sir,—I beg to inform you that the Petitions from Chatham, Broadstairs, and Leicester came into my hands late in the afternoon of Tuesday, March 28th, just before you were about to present Petitions. I certainly did not give them so much attention as I otherwise should, because I had, by your directions, been in communication with the persons from whom I received them, and had their assurance that the recommendation I had sent them by your orders as to form, according to which these Petitions should be prepared would be attended to.

The secretary had glanced at the first paragraphs and had concluded "too hastily" that Newdegate's recommendations had been observed throughout. Newdegate regretted that he, as a result, "was betrayed into saying that I did not present the Chatham petition. I did present it, but without being aware of its nature." Callan accepted Newdegate's apology, adding ungraciously that, in his judgment, the Warwickshire squire had only himself to blame for the unpleasantness that had resulted from the affair.[23]

In 1877 Newdegate, Chambers, and James M. Holt introduced a new bill seeking an investigation of convents and monasteries, but it was dropped without ever being discussed, and in 1878 the subject was not even mentioned within the walls of Parliament. During the latter year Pope Pius IX died after a contentious thirty-two-year reign. He was succeeded by Leo XIII, a man with a quite different personality, who saw little point in either amending or in reiterating the all-encompassing doctrinal claims of his immediate predecessor. When the Roman Catholic hierarchy was formally restored that same year to Scotland as it had been reestablished in 1850 in England, the change caused relatively little controversy.[24]

In 1874, when Gladstone first published *The Vatican Decrees*, the Liberal *Daily News* had reminded the former prime minister that it was quite possible that Roman Catholics, like other human beings, failed to push their philosophical beliefs to their logical consequences.[25] In 1878, when Gladstone included his original *Contemporary Review* article in volume 6 of his collected *Gleanings of Past Years*, he added a footnote acknowledging this very point: "some at least who have joined the Latin Church since the great change effected by the Vatican Council would, upon occasion given, whether with logical warrant or not, adhere under all circumstances to their civil loyalty and duty."[26] In 1880 Gladstone gave practical confirmation to this admission by appointing Lord Ripon as viceroy of India. Years later Gladstone was to go still further, conceding that Ripon's conversion had coincided with the awakening of the latter's religious life. "When I looked around the Cabinet to see to whom I could look as a man whose life and heart were given to God, it was to Ripon I turned. I say not that the others were not so—but I knew it of Ripon."[27]

Ripon had, in the meantime, become—after the duke of Norfolk—the most eminent Catholic layman in England, and he staunchly resisted the pronounced tendency of Catholic noblemen and squires during the 1870s to become Tories. That tendency applied to the still youthful duke of Norfolk whose wedding at Brompton Oratory Disraeli attended in 1877. "I have always thought that I should some day join the Conservative Party," Norfolk wrote to the prime minister a year later. In 1879 he did join, and his brother became a candidate for Parliament in the Conservative interest.[28]

Problems of religion continued to concern Newdegate during the later 1870s. Thus in 1876 he expressed to Archibald Campbell Tait, the archbishop of Canterbury, his fear that the government's new education bill had neglected the Bible. "You will forgive my still wishing," he wrote Tait, "that the right of parents to claim Scriptural education for their children in the elementary schools, to which they are by law compelled to send them, had been by law asserted."[29] A year later he sought the aid of Lord Dartmouth in discouraging a particular man from being elected to the House of Commons. He had no influence in either Blackheath or Greenwich, Dartmouth responded, "so that I fear I can in no way aid in the desirable object of keeping the Jew Candidate for that borough out of Parliament."[30]

Yet other issues ranked still higher—not least of all the subject of agricultural protection. In the midst of the agricultural depression of the later 1870s, Newdegate was able to point, in a mildly "I told you so" spirit, to the unfortunate long-range consequences of the repeal of the Corn Laws back in 1846.[31] He was also prepared to scoff at those of his colleagues who were prepared to ease the rigorous compulsory cattle-destruction acts with which British governments sought to keep the hoof-and-mouth disorder on the other side of the Channel. "Unless prepared to support free trade in disease," Newdegate observed in 1878, "the House is bound to exercise its functions for the limitations of this disease."[32] Newdegate's Tory paternalism showed itself as well in his support for a bill designed to combat river pollution and for another designed to give cities like Birmingham the right to collect sufficient water from outlying areas for the needs of their citizens. He was a firm supporter of compulsory vaccination against smallpox, a policy that many mid- and late Victorian Radicals attacked on the ground that it interfered unduly with individual liberty. Analogously, he firmly supported an 1873 measure to raise the age of consent for girls from twelve to fourteen; he could see no excuse whatever "for the seduction of these children."[33] Newdegate was also a firm opponent of the manner in which many Victorian schools, originally endowed for the purpose of educating the poor, were applying their funds to the education of the wealthy. Parliament had sanctioned this misuse, and he protested against such disgraceful "class legislation," which involved "a policy of con-

fiscation of the property of the labouring classes." He also
sympathized with a new agricultural holdings bill that gave
farm tenants the legal right to compensations for improvements
they had made in the land they leased.[34] At the same time,
Newdegate remained as suspicious as ever of all measures that
diluted the authority of local justices of the peace, and he firmly
opposed the "confiscatory character" and "centralizing tendency" of an 1876 measure to reform the management of
prisons.[35]

The general election of 1880 proved to be an unhappy one
for Disraeli—now Lord Beaconsfield—who lost his final duel
with Gladstone, but it brought a surprisingly easy triumph for
Newdegate and William Bromley-Davenport, his Conservative
associate. The Liberals failed to put up any opposition whatever, and so for the ninth time—the fourth without opposition—Charles Newdegate was returned to Parliament by the
electors of North Warwickshire. The second Gladstone ministry
unexpectedly provided Newdegate with an opportunity for a
last crusade, not in this case against Roman Catholicism, but
against atheism.

Atheism, republicanism, and voluntary contraception (a
doctrine associated by most Victorians with prostitutes rather
than with respectable married women) were all three embodied
in the person of Charles Bradlaugh, the newly elected Liberal
M.P. for Northampton. Bradlaugh preferred to take his seat by
means of affirmation rather than by means of an oath ending
with the words "So help me God," but a select committee
decided by a single vote that, unlike Quakers, Bradlaugh was
ineligible to affirm. The maverick Victorian then announced
that, although the oath included "words of idle and meaning-
less character," he was fully prepared to take that oath in the
same spirit in which he would have been pleased to take the
affirmation. An irate House of Commons majority, made up of
Conservatives, Irish Home Rulers, and some forty Liberals,
denied him that opportunity by a vote of 275 to 230. Bradlaugh
was prepared to challenge in the streets and at the bar of the
House of Commons a decision that, in effect, overturned the
verdict of the electors of Northampton. Gladstone, after several
days of consultation, came up with a compromise solution, a
compromise in some ways reminiscent of the manner in which
he had dealt with Newdegate's successful motion for an inquiry
into convents and monasteries ten years earlier. The resolution
asked "that every person returned as a Member of this House,
who may claim to be 'a person for the time being by Law

permitted to make a solemn Affirmation or Declaration, instead of taking an Oath', shall henceforth . . . be permitted without question to make and subscribe a solemn Affirmation . . . subject to any liability by statute."

After the resolution had been approved by the House of Commons by a vote of 303 to 249 and after Bradlaugh had been duly admitted on 2 July to that august assembly under its provisions, most of his new colleagues assumed that the temporary *cause célèbre* was at an end. Newdegate felt otherwise, however.[36] Scarcely had Bradlaugh affirmed his allegiance than one Henry Clarke, at Newdegate's behest, sued Bradlaugh for sitting in Parliament without having taken the required oath. Newdegate personally served the writ on Bradlaugh. Eight months later Clarke's claim that Bradlaugh was ineligible to make a parliamentary affirmation was upheld. It was upheld once more on appeal, and as of 30 March 1881, Bradlaugh was again excluded from the House of Commons and was held liable to pay five hundred pounds for having voted illegally. Three reelections in Northampton, numerous popular demonstrations, and several attempts at legislation all failed to return him to the pinnacle from which Newdegate's legal initiative had toppled him.

Over the years Bradlaugh did gain two satisfactions, however, in his rivalry with Newdegate. In April 1883 he persuaded Britain's highest judicial tribunal, the House of Lords, that Clarke, "a common informer," had not been eligible to sue him; any legal suit should have been brought by the crown in the person of the attorney general. The judgment freed Bradlaugh from the liability of the five-hundred-pound fine and imposed the costs of Bradlaugh's appeal on Clarke. Bradlaugh also charged Newdegate, who had admitted formally pledging to indemnify the obscure Clarke against all legal costs and expenses, with the ancient crime of "maintenance," of maliciously hiding behind and financially supporting another man in a legal case. Newdegate's lawyer replied that his client's sole purpose had been to help determine "a question of great public interest" and that he had utilized Clarke only because he had mistakenly assumed that as a member of Parliament he was ineligible to sue in this instance. In 1883 the Court of the Queen's Bench, in the person of Lord Chief Justice John Duke Coleridge, ruled that Newdegate was indeed guilty of maintenance and therefore liable to pay all of Bradlaugh's legal costs. "I think that Mr. Bradlaugh is entitled to an indemnity for every loss which Mr. Newdegate's maintenance has caused him."[37]

Although by most criteria, Newdegate was a wealthy man, he sorely felt the costs of serving as the doughty warrior who drove the heathen barbarian from the walls of the Christian (or at least theistic) castle. A Newdegate Testimonial Fund had been begun in August 1881 to assist the veteran M.P. in the actions he had taken "to vindicate the Christian character of Parliament." The fund had raised over fourteen hundred pounds, but that sum was exhausted by 1883. In April of that year Newdegate appealed to the marquess of Salisbury, by then the Conservative leader in the House of Lords, for more support. Salisbury contributed one hundred pounds to what became a two-thousand-pound fund. Yet, as Newdegate felt compelled to remind Salisbury in August 1883, even that fund had fallen thirteen hundred pounds short of meeting the legal expenses that Newdegate had incurred. "I have never considered this a mere party contest," he reminded Salisbury; "it is much more—but it has afforded the Conservative party their only permanent and effective success, since 1880. In fact, it has reunited the Conservative party with public opinion."[38]

Lord Harlech, with Salisbury's blessing, headed a third drive on Newdegate's behalf, provided that the Warwickshire squire made no attempt to appeal Coleridge's decision and that he ceased to sponsor the *English Churchman and St. James's Chronicle*. Newdegate reluctantly agreed to these conditions, but a year later he reminded Salisbury, by then the de facto leader of the Conservative party, that not all the promised funds had arrived. He urged Salisbury not to heed "certain busybodies with little knowledge of the facts [who] are spreading misrepresentations."[39] Newdegate's political career had hardly been noted for its pattern of unsullied victories, and the Bradlaugh case constituted no exception.

For Newdegate, the struggle against Britain's premier atheist had one other unexpected result. Inasmuch as among religious leaders Cardinal Manning proved to be Newdegate's most faithful ally in his anti-Bradlaugh campaign and inasmuch as members of the largely Roman Catholic Irish Home Rule party proved to be among the keenest of Bradlaugh's political opponents, the House of Commons began to be aware of some very strange bedfellows indeed. The Home Rulers occasionally expressed an affectionate regard for the, to them, mildly eccentric Tory codger,[40] and he in turn candidly reciprocated their regard. Thus on 20 August 1883 Newdegate declared that the action of Irish M.P.s in joining English Conservatives successfully to bar avowed atheism from the House of Commons "has formed a bond of union between myself and the Roman Catholic members of this House." In order to promote that bond, Newdegate declared, he had deliberately not revived any of those subjects—like the regulation of convents and monasteries—that he had raised during earlier sessions and that Roman Catholics had found so distasteful.[41]

While Newdegate kept alight the flame of religious feeling in the Parliament of 1880–1885, his health gradually deteriorated. Although he was rumored to be a candidate for the speakership as late as 1880, he had suffered a stroke shortly before his reelection to Parliament that year, and in 1882 he was seized with a fit while riding with the Atherstone hunt at Arbury Park. He fell from his horse, but, announcing that "Charles Newdegate shall not be beaten," he remounted his horse and pursued the fox as though nothing unfortunate had occurred.[42] The hunt and the shooting party were ever Newdegate's favorite avocations, and in the 1880s the apocryphal story went the rounds that at "Newdy's" shooting parties the cover fire was so hot and careless that it resembled a battle in a thick wood. According to one participant, "the man who was sheriff of Warwickshire, the man who is sheriff, and the man who will be sheriff are all of them one-eyed, and all lost their other eye in one of Newdy's shooting parties."[43] The *Warwick Advertiser* was to recall Newdegate as among "the keenest of Midland sportsmen," and "one of the boldest riders to hounds in Warwickshire. . . . He never showed to greater advantage than when in the field."[44]

Not that Newdegate lacked all other interests. He served as deputy lieutenant for Warwickshire, and he remained an intermittently active justice of the peace both in Warwick and in Middlesex. He contributed three hundred pounds a year to primary schools at Chilvers Coton and at Astley, and at the end of each summer he would invite the children to a picnic at Arbury Hall. He also provided weekly allowances for several old people unable to work.[45] He paid for most of the cost of restoring the Astley church. As a consequence of the agricultural depression of the 1870s, he reduced rents, and in 1882 he finally sold the estate collieries, which had been losing money for several years.

By 1885 it had become clear that he was no longer physically able to remain a truly active member of Parliament. He looked haggard, and quite frequently he would fall asleep over a book in his study; his servants would discover him there when they opened the shutters the next morning. The passage of the Reform Act of 1884 and, even more important, the accompanying Redistribution Act, which altered significantly the boundaries of Newdegate's constituency, gave him additional reasons for not seeking reelection. In October 1885, with the dissolution of the Parliament elected five and a half years before, Newdegate's forty-two-year-long parliamentary career came to an end. Only a handful of men in the history of the English Parliament could claim to have served the same constituency for a longer period.

Though ailing, Newdegate survived long enough to gain the recognition of a new Conservative prime minister; in 1886, on Lord Salisbury's recommendation, Newdegate was named a member of the Privy Council, a distinction that would have been his automatically if he had accepted office at the hands of Lord Derby three decades before. It gave him the opportunity henceforth to be addressed as "the Right Honourable Charles Newdegate." In December 1886 a special gathering of Newdegate's constituents met at Coventry to present the veteran M.P. with an illuminated address and a check for £547. Lord Leigh, the Liberal lord lieutenant for the county of Warwick, presided, and numerous M.P.s were present. It was a distinctly nonpartisan affair, though it paid due heed to Newdegate's principles— "Protectionist, Protestant, Church of England, and National." In reply to the testimonial, Newdegate conceded that his principles were said to be old-fashioned, but they were, he reminded his hearers, "the principles of the English Constitution and of the English Common Law, which were derived from the Bible."[46]

The Bible was much in Newdegate's thoughts during his later years. He remained an active supporter of both the Scripture Readers' Society and the Church Missionary Society, and one of the last of the letters preserved in his files deplored the decline of Bible reading in the schools: "I consider," he wrote, "this loss of scriptural study and knowledge, while other elements of instruction are enormously advanced, both spiritually and nationally dangerous—not merely politically dangerous, but socially and morally dangerous. . . . I am convinced that the more I beleive [sic] in the Bible the better for me now and hereafter."[47]

The hereafter began for Charles Newdegate on 9 April 1887, Easter Sunday. His health had failed rapidly that year, and even the London specialist called in by his regular Nuneaton doctor could not help. "The cause of his death," it was agreed, "was no doubt a complete breakdown of the system, due to overwork of the brain."[48] On the day of his funeral, church bells tolled in

Nuneaton and elsewhere in the county, flags waved at half-mast, and shops were closed. The tenant farmers, laborers, and gardeners at Arbury Hall served as bearers of the coffin and as pallbearers. In Newdegate, the Reverend S. T. Taylor Taswell declared, "all have lost a warm friend, a just landlord, a kind master. . . . He realised the highest type of the true English gentleman, a devoted servant of the Queen, a humble yet earnest believer in Christ Jesus the Deliverer, he realised in modern time the ideal of that medieval chivalry which was 'without fear and without reproach' father to the fatherless, friend to the widow." Newdegate's life, Taylor concluded, "was one of absolute purity, pitched in the bright key of a lofty sense of duty—spotless, adorned with a singular mixture of courtly grace and urbanity of manner, a warm and gracious heart, and an absolute love and tenacity of truth."[49] The newspapers were somewhat less high-flown in their expression of obituary sentiment. *The Times* described his career as one "which never rose to be eminent, but which was long conspicuous, and always honourable."[50] "Such a man," decided the *Standard*, "may not be fitted for the times in which we live now; but there was at all events an earnestness, a simplicity, and a patriotism in such a creed which we cannot but honour."[51] "He was a true English gentleman of the old school," agreed the *Warwick Advertiser*, while the *Dundee Advertiser* added, "When the Pope was not in his mind, he was one of the most pleasant of men."[52]

After the initial funeral ceremony at Arbury Hall, the body was transported to Harefield, Middlesex, the site of Newdegate's other manor. There he was formally laid to rest in the village parish church next to the remains of his ancestors.

15. Victorian Anti-Catholicism: A Reappraisal

It has been the underlying thesis of this work that the phenomenon of mid-Victorian anti-Catholicism ought to be viewed not merely as testimony to "the enduring sensitivity of the Roman nerve"[1] in English history but also as an episode in the history of popular religion with specifically nineteenth-century roots, an episode in which Catholics were active participants rather than passive victims. Both in the United Kingdom and within the wider European world, the more justifiable context is one of Protestant–Catholic rivalry rather than anti-Catholicism.

The roots of the Victorian hostility toward Catholicism admittedly lie in the eighteenth-century evangelical revival, that movement of religious renewal that manifested itself both within and outside the Anglican church in an absorption with individual conversion, with Bible study, and with active lay involvement in matters spiritual. Evangelicals reawakened a distrust of the Roman Catholic creed on points of doctrine (such as the priestly caste and the papacy), on political principles (as a threat to both individual and national liberty), and on "moral" grounds (distrust of clerical celibacy, of auricular confession, and of the priest as rival father).[2] In the early decades of the nineteenth century, evangelicalism appeared to be the dominant religious mood, but by the 1830s and 1840s, the evangelicals had come to see themselves as defending their tenets and practices against a yet newer spirit, the ritualistic Oxford movement, with its emphasis upon liturgy, hierarchy, and the apostolic succession. For the evangelicals, this countertendency, which held such extraordinary appeal for many of England's most educated and eminent young men, represented a proto-Catholicism, a "mass in masquerade." The specter of mid-Victorian Catholicism loomed larger for such evangelicals than it might have, had they not seen their "own" Church of England undermined from within by a theological fifth column. In the later eighteenth century, and even in the early nineteenth, it had come to seem a waste of time for Anglican clergymen to preach on the evils of popery or to enter into theological controversy with Catholic prelates.[3] The Oxford movement and the Catholic revival quickly altered the situation. The mid-Victorian "ultra-Protestant" was far more likely to be fearful than confident, far more likely to suspect than to exalt the religious integrity of his clerical and political leaders.

During the 1860s the Victorian religious revival was given a new lease on life with what has been called "the Second Evangelical Awakening."[4] But as John Stuart Mill observed at the time, "What is boasted of at the present time as the revival of religion, is always, in narrow and uncultivated minds, at least as much the revival of bigotry."[5] Mill's contemporary, Matthew Arnold, wrote balefully of members of that same "philistine" middle class, after a stultifying day at the office and an unappetizing meal at home, going out in the evening "for a great treat, [to] a lecture on teetotalism or nunneries."[6] *On Liberty* and *On the Origin of Species* were both published in 1859, but the 1860s were far less obviously a secular decade than one absorbed with religion; and the major political controversies of the day were almost all in some sense religious.[7] On the propriety of the link between politics and religion, Newdegate and Manning would have concurred. For Manning, it was a figment of the imagination to separate the two; politics, after all, was "a part of morals, and they cannot be separated, morals are a part of religion, and they are indissoluble."[8]

Sensitized as they were to the proto-Catholicism of the Oxford movement and its inheritors, evangelically minded Anglicans were all the more likely to take at face value the projections of Nicholas Wiseman as to the manner in which a new generation of converts would restore "Catholic England" to "its orbit in the ecclesiastical firmament." They were equally prepared to take to heart the assurance of Wiseman's successor as archbishop of Westminster, Henry Edward Manning, that he had devoted his life to "working for the Irish occupation in England." The religious revival of the 1860s did, after all, overlap the first two decades of large-scale Irish immigration to England. For many lower-class Englishmen, the Irish settlements that dotted Lancashire and the Midlands clearly constituted a disturbing religious as well as socioeconomic threat.

"In all ecclesiastical matters Englishmen have favoured a policy of conservatism combined with concession." So wrote Albert Venn Dicey in his classic *Law and Public Opinion in England during the Nineteenth Century.*[9] The assessment may be accurate enough, but one of its consequences has been neglected by historians: the nineteenth-century parliamentary calendar involved not one Roman Catholic Emancipation Act—that of 1829—but hundreds. At least one bill involving the abolition of special Catholic oaths, or Catholic property rights, or Catholic schools, or the rights of Catholic chaplains in the army, in the workhouse, and in the prison was likely to be encountered by

members of Parliament during every legislative session.
"Catholic emancipation" for Low Church Protestant M.P.s involved not a single tidal wave that had washed away old constitutional landmarks but a leaky faucet that, drip by drip, but with
equal inexorability, sought still one more concession, yet one
further impairment of the Protestant character of the English
nation. This very gradualness kept alive old fears and aroused
new suspicions.

These fears were accentuated by the obvious spirit of militancy with which Wiseman and the generation of converts
spearheaded by Manning (though excluding Newman) set
about promoting the reconversion of England and upholding
the most all-encompassing of papal claims. The Roman Catholic
church, the Liberal *Daily Telegraph* acknowledged in 1871,
"overawes by her antiquity, by the vastness of her empire, and
by the tremendous character of her pretensions." Even though
the British Empire constituted the stronghold of Protestantism,
it housed no fewer than 114 Roman Catholic archbishops and
bishops. "When we go beyond the limits of the British Empire
we gain an even more vivid idea of the strength which still
resides in Rome."[10] A specter that seemed to haunt even the
"blood and iron" chancellor, Prince Otto von Bismarck, could
hardly be dismissed out of hand by the average Englishman.

It was under this conflux of influences that a keen sense of
Catholic–Protestant rivalry affected, and at times dominated,
the socioreligious life of mid-Victorian England. Antipopery
cemented a common spirit of nationalism, and it provided a
broad if temporary umbrella for prime minister and lowly labor-
er, for churchman and Dissenter, for Tory and Radical.[11] Antipopery reached a high point with the papal bull of 1850 that
reestablished the Catholic hierarchy in England. It ebbed somewhat in the later 1850s and the early 1860s only to revive and to
reach a second high point with the Vatican Council of 1869–1870
and such related parliamentary eddies as Newdegate's successful motion to investigate English convents.

Many of the causal factors that came into conjunction in
midcentury were indeed novel rather than historic, but it is fair
to concede that numerous mid-Victorians possessed a highly
vivid sense of medieval history. There was but a narrow mental
gap between the Victorian Gothic and the true Gothic. Just as
the new Roman Catholic converts found satisfaction in observing that the great Anglican cathedrals had once been "theirs,"
so could Bismarck declare that, unlike the eleventh-century
emperor Henry IV, he would not seek peace with the papacy at

Canossa, and so could Newdegate speak of Thomas Becket and of Henry Edward Manning with an equal sense of immediacy.

Yet from the mid–1870s on, this atmosphere of Protestant–Catholic hostility began to subside, and the champions of ultra-Protestantism found their audiences significantly less responsive during the century's final quarter. Why? One reason clearly is that the Roman church became less militant. Leo XIII, who was enthroned as pope in 1878, differed sharply from Pius IX. His condemnation of the Anglican orders in 1897 did give rise briefly to "intense and sometimes acrimonious discussion,"[12] but the fever pitch of the early 1870s did not return. One of Newman's biographers has contrasted the social liabilities suffered by a convert to Catholicism in the 1840s and 1850s unfavorably with those experienced by a convert to communism in the 1940s and 1950s.[13] Yet, except for brief intervals, Newman's prestige among educated Englishmen remained remarkably high. Newman, in turn, in his *Apologia Pro Vita Sua* (1864), found it possible to display a generosity to the friends and thoughts of his Anglican past that was rarely matched by his fellow converts. By elevating him to the rank of cardinal in 1879, his adopted church gave its stamp of approval to judicious moderation just as the elevation of Manning to the same rank four years earlier had represented an imprimatur upon doctrinal militancy. By 1880 it was clear also that the pope was likely to remain a "prisoner of the Vatican" rather than an independent temporal ruler and that no general European war was ever likely to be fought on his behalf. Even Newdegate was forced to concede that, in consequence, people were becoming less conscious of the iniquities for which popes had been responsible. "The world has lost much useful warning from the emancipation of Italy and Rome from Papal government. Mankind have no longer before their eyes that great example of misgovernment."[14]

At least as important in mitigating the late Victorian sense of Catholic–Protestant rivalry as a tempering of Catholic militancy was a gradual realization that the immigration of Irishmen was abating rather than increasing and that the promised (or threatened) conversion of England had not taken place. When Dr. Thomas Chambers reminded the House of Commons in 1876 how rapidly the number of convents had grown in mid-Victorian England, a fellow M.P. reminded him that back in 1854 Chambers had warned that within twenty years the land would be dotted with 3,000 to 4,000 such institutions; in truth there were but 299.[15] By 1900 there were indeed to be 600 separate communities of religious women, but the average convent contained no more than twelve members.[16] The male orders also continued to increase at a similar pace, though their absolute number remained smaller, and Cardinal Manning attained a status that allowed his name to appear in the court circular above that of Anglican bishops and immediately beneath that of the Prince of Wales.[17] In the 1890s the flow of converts continued at a rate of ten thousand a year,[18] and yet the spirit of overweening confidence of 1850 would not be recaptured. "The rush of converts forty, thirty, and twenty years ago," wrote Gladstone in 1878, "was such as to raise a fair presumption that so many teachers would surely be followed by a corresponding multitude of the taught."[19] That presumption was not fulfilled, however, and Gladstone himself had called attention to a fascinating statistic: in 1854, 4.89 percent of all English marriages had been performed by a Roman Catholic priest; in 1871, only 4.02 percent were performed under such auspices.[20]

What had happened, Edward Lucas suggested in 1885, was that in the course of a little more than four decades, 750,000 to 1,000,000 Roman Catholics had fallen from the faith. Manning himself once conceded that the lack of an effective Catholic temperance organization had cost the church some 100,000 members in mid-Victorian London alone.[21] In his meticulous investigation of late Victorian London, Charles Booth was much impressed by the manner in which Roman Catholicism constituted a single force bridging social classes; he was equally impressed by the influence of the priests and by the piety and loyalty of the faithful. At the same time, Booth noted that only one Londoner in twenty—some 200,000 in all—was a Roman Catholic. "Even in the aggregate," he concluded, "the numbers involved are not large, and, if we exclude the Irish and those of foreign blood, are surprisingly small."[22]

The average English workingman seemed blind to the appeal of Catholicism; thus, despite the efforts of numerous priests, the converts came almost exclusively "from the leisured class or the leisured members of a busy class." As one Catholic witness confided to Booth, "We gain in position socially, but we do not increase in number."[23] Henry Winterbotham, the Liberal M.P. for Stroud, had observed back in 1870: "How many doctors, lawyers, merchants, mechanics, or artisans are ever heard of as becoming Roman Catholics? The converts are women, parsons, and peers." And the House of Commons, Winterbotham added tartly, could hardly complain about the conversion of women until "we give to women a higher, and I will add, a more manly education—until we open to them larger spheres of usefulness and activity."[24] Sir George Mivart, writing in the *Dublin Review* in 1884, attributed the failure to realize the hopes of the previous generation to the widespread falling away from the faith of many Irish immigrants, to a general world movement hostile to religion, to the reaction evoked by Continental ultramontanes, and to the revival of a rich and reverent liturgical life within the Church of England.[25] Whatever the explanation, it seems clear that, for Roman Catholics in England, what had been hailed as "a second spring" had turned into a drab and cheerless summer.

Just as the failure of large-scale conversion helps to account for the mellowing of Protestant–Catholic relations in the England of the 1880s and 1890s, so does the virtual cessation of the piecemeal legislative relief efforts that, under Whig or Liberal auspices, had been a feature of the parliamentary scene since 1829. The reason for such legislative hesitation was clear to William Shaw, the Protestant Irish Nationalist. "The very moment that the Government stirred in it," he observed in 1876, "the whole subject would be agitated, and religious strife would be aroused all over the country."[26] To end the last of the anti-Catholic penal laws would raise a Protestant storm; to enforce them would precipitate a Catholic counterstorm. As in the case of the select committee report of 1871, Conservative and Liberal governments preferred therefore to take the easy way out— neither to repeal nor to enforce. And though G. F. A. Best describes the Catholic Emancipation Act of 1829 as "innocent of all but a few insignificant face-saving securities,"[27] the statute book, if literally interpreted, suggested otherwise. Section 26 of the act forbade any Roman Catholic ecclesiastic to conduct any religious service or to wear any habit except within a Roman Catholic place of worship or a private home; a fine of fifty pounds was set for each offense. Sections 28, 29, 30, 31, 32, and 33 outlawed the Jesuit order on English soil except on special personal license by the secretary of state. Sections 34, 35, and 36 banished Roman Catholic monks from the kingdom in a similar manner.[28] Though left in abeyance, these prohibitions remained very much a part of the statute book for two generations more, and not until 1926 was a determined effort made to revise the law.[29]

Echoes of earlier hostilities could admittedly still be heard. Writing in 1892, the Reverend Edward Thurston, S.J., told of the Anglican clergyman then touring the country with an illustrated magic-lantern lecture entitled "Convents Romish and Anglican" designed for Young Men's Christian Associations and

Sunday schools. Slide number 30 pictured the walling up of a nun and slide number 31 pictured the skeleton of an immured nun.[30] The home-rule controversy of 1886 necessarily reawakened religious passions, for was not home rule all too likely to turn into Rome rule? Home rule was opposed by major Nonconformist clergymen like the Reverend C. H. Spurgeon who feared that an autonomous Ireland would establish Roman Catholicism and who therefore described any supporter of the scheme as a "madman."[31] In Belfast and Liverpool, a sense of Protestant–Catholic rivalry remained keen, and as late as 1910 a parliamentary election was fought on the issue of whether King George V should amend the coronation oath in order to make it less offensive to Roman Catholics. As one contemporary doggerel phrased it:

> Vote for Kyffin-Taylor
> Let the Oath remain
> Keep the Empire Protestant
> We don't want Rome again![32]

Kyffin-Taylor won, but the oath was altered anyway. Denunciations of the doctrine of transubstantiation and of the idolatry implicit in the invocation of the Virgin Mary were replaced by a simple declaration that the new sovereign was "a faithful Protestant."

Roman Catholicism never became simply one more Christian denomination, and even apathetic working-class parents, who were willing to send their children to whichever Sunday school was closest to home, drew the line against a Catholic school.[33] Yet whatever the case might be in Ireland, in England proper the new century brought a high degree of tranquillity to Protestant–Catholic relations. Looking back upon the troubled history of his fellow religionists in 1901, Percy Fitzgerald could take comfort in the fact that in Edwardian England "all the attempts to 'get up' fanatical ferments seem to fall quite flat, as though religious excitement were too trivial a thing to indulge in."[34]

By then, admittedly, several other changes had been made in the law. An act of 1888 had ended the limitations on Roman Catholic bequests imposed by the Charitable Uses Act of 1735, and an act of 1890 had ended remaining legal limitations on Roman Catholic religious and educational societies.[35] In the decision of *Bourne* v. *Keane* (1919), the House of Lords ruled that a Catholic gift for the saying of masses for the dead was not, after all, "void as a gift to superstitious uses."[36]

In 1926, with the cooperation of a number of non-Catholic M.P.s, F. N. Blundell introduced a Roman Catholic relief bill whose purpose was, in Denis Herbert's words, "to do away . . . with certain relics of religious strife and bitterness which are entirely out of place in our laws at present."[37]When one considered the patriotism that Roman Catholic men had demonstrated during the Great War, it seemed anomalous that Roman Catholic priests should yet be barred from wearing their cassocks in public and that bequests to Roman Catholic orders might not be reported as charitable gifts. The bill was given a second reading without division on 15 March 1926 and committed to a standing committee for detailed appraisal.

The debate occasioned by the bill reported to the Commons six weeks later by the committee demonstrated that all the old fires had not yet died. A request for the formal repeal of a statute of Edward VI's Parliament seeking the destruction of church images and Catholic prayer books caused one M.P. to wonder whether "we are beginning to be a little ashamed of the Reformation." Was it really sensible, suggested another, to authorize outdoor religious processions that might arouse public hostility? Malcolm MacNaghten, the M.P. for Londonderry (Northern Ireland), reminded the house that monastic orders were "the members of a corporation formed under a foreign law." Frederick George Penny, the M.P. for Kingston-upon-Thames, was equally upset by the decision of Stanley Baldwin's government, "at a time like the present, when we want peace and good will in the country, [to] give facilities to a private Member's Bill of such a contentious nature. . . . We have to remember that this is a Protestant country."[38]

Despite these grumbles, when it came time for the veteran T. P. O'Connor, the onetime Irish radical who had become "Father of the House," to move "that the question be now put," no one agreed to serve as a teller for the no votes. The House of Lords also passed the measure without dissent after Viscount Fitzalan made a plea for the spirit of religious toleration that it represented and after the archbishop of Canterbury spoke in its support. Earl Russell, the elder brother of the philosopher, commended Fitzalan for his speech and expressed the hope that Fitzalan's coreligionists would show similar toleration when questions involving divorce and birth control came before Parliament. On 15 December 1926, the measure received the royal assent.[39]

The measure did not apply to Northern Ireland, whose constitution, the Home Rule (Government of Ireland) Act of

1920, had already outlawed "any existing enactment by which
any penalty, disadvantage or disability is imposed on account of
religious belief on any member of any religious order."[40]
Attempts to exempt Scotland from its provisions were decisively defeated. Thus in 1926 a whole bevy of restrictions dating
back to the age of George III, George IV, and William IV were at
last stricken from the statute book. All that remained was the
seventeenth-century ban against Roman Catholics serving as
monarchs of England (or as their spouses), as lords chancellor,
and as high commissioners of the Church of Scotland. It also
remained a statutory offense to maintain or to defend within the
United Kingdom the ecclesiastical or spiritual authority of any
foreign prince or prelate. In characteristic English fashion, the
clause specifying the penalty for this offense had been repealed,
but the clause defining the offense had been kept.[41]

Just as pre-Victorian and Victorian statutes lingered on in
the twentieth-century statute book, so did Newdegates linger
on at Arbury Hall. The estate was inherited in 1887 by a second
cousin, Lt. Gen. Sir Edward Newdigate-Newdegate. When he
died childless in 1902, he was followed by the son of another
second cousin, Sir Francis Alexander Newdigate Newdegate.
Sir Francis, a member of Parliament from 1892 to 1906 and again
from 1909 to 1917, was one of the last of the Tory squires who
had for so many decades constituted the backbone of Britain's
Conservative party. He died in 1936, and despite the intervening perils of war and confiscatory death duties, Arbury Hall in
the 1980s remains in the possession of Sir Francis's grandson.[42]

The controversy over the propriety of convents as institutions and of the manner in which they ought to be treated by the
laws of England was central to the Protestant–Catholic hostility
of the mid-Victorian years, and Charles Newdegate became for
many years the most notable champion of the investigation and
ultimately of the inspection of organizations whose apparently
steady growth he both regretted and feared. The technical illegality of Roman Catholic orders for men was blatant, whereas
the legal title of the female orders was only clouded; but there is
little question that the all-male Victorian House of Commons
found the lives of nuns a far more intriguing subject for debate
than the lives of monks; in analogous fashion, it had been far
more concerned two decades earlier with the working lives of
female miners than of their far more numerous male counterparts. The Victorians, like ourselves, often pondered the proper
role of women, and they were deeply disturbed by the large
surplus of women over men that the census of 1871 confirmed.[43]

A society most of whose members looked upon the female of the species as designed by God and nature to preside over the home found this disparity—in part the result of selective emigration— a significantly uncomfortable one. Lower-class spinsters could serve as domestic servants, but how many middle-class governesses could the land absorb?

One plausible division of sexual roles had been proclaimed by a character in Alfred Lord Tennyson's "The Princess."

> Man for the field and woman for the hearth,
> Man for the sword and for the needle she;
> Man with the head, and woman with the heart;
> Man to command, and woman to obey. All else
>   confusion.

Neither Newdegate nor most of his Roman Catholic adversaries would have felt cause to differ sharply with that assessment of the proper role of women. Roman Catholics had been taught to believe that it was desirable for a select number of young women to seclude themselves from the world in order to pray and to render service to the poor, the ill, and the homeless. Both Newdegate and his Catholic opponents saw themselves as champions of such ultimately helpless women against the selfish schemes of other men. Newdegate, the census disparity notwithstanding, perceived designing priests cajoling innocent young Englishwomen from the bosom of affectionate Anglican families and inducing them to enter a cloistered life of misery and evil from which iron bars and foolish vows prevented escape. Newdegate wanted protection for such women, but he in no sense sought political equality for them. He had no desire to create "among women that system of self-dependence which would lead them to ignore the distinctions of nature, the relations of the family, and to discard all those safeguards which they legitimately draw from the feeling, which the Creator has implanted in the breast of every man worthy of the name, that the comparative weakness of woman establishes on her part a claim to considerate protection and to privileges which he would refuse to his fellow man."[44] The irony of Newdegate, a convinced bachelor, seeking to call wayward nuns back to joys of English family life was one that even political enemies considerately failed to mention.

For the Roman Catholic M.P.s, nuns were equally deserving of protection. They were devout relations who had dedicated their lives to the service of God and of fellow human beings in distress, and they needed to be guarded against the inspectors, the investigators, and the nosy snoops with which

Newdegate wished to pester them. Only in convents, insisted the Catholic *Weekly Register*, could a life be led that was truly "in keeping with the modesty of the feminine character—a matter all the more requisite now in these days of fastness and female forwardness."[45] "In this age of idolatry and materialism," declared T. M. Sullivan in 1876, let us not "blot out from among us this element of purity and self-sacrifice."[46] Women required protection not from the perils of the cloister but from the perils of the outside world.

Although numerous Victorian publications, including the 1871 report of the select committee, made it clear that only a small minority of the Roman Catholic convents of the day were contemplative and secluded and that the great majority involved members who left the convent enclosure daily to teach or to tend the sick, the Protestant opponents of the conventual system almost always spoke as if the women who had taken their vows were unlikely ever to see the English sun again. The Roman Catholic defenders of the institutions, though occasionally correcting this impression, did so less often than might be expected—perhaps because, for them, the contemplative and secluded orders were the truly holy, the authentically medieval.[47]

It may be argued that, even if nunneries had not awed and at times aroused sexual fantasies among Victorian parliamentarians, the latter might still have found just cause to inspect and regulate them, just as the House of Commons had set into motion the inspection and regulation of lunatic asylums, factories, and schools. What was lacking, as many a Roman Catholic M.P. had observed—and as Gladstone reiterated in his 1875 letter to Newdegate—was any obvious example of abuse, a single clear case of illegal imprisonment. However much it may have disturbed *The Times*, the case of *Saurin* v. *Star* did not quite fit the bill. It had shown convent life to be dreary and petty, but neither illegal nor immoral. And, as Florence Nightingale commented privately, "I have known a good deal of convents and of the petty, grinding tyrannies supposed to be exercised there, but I know nothing like the petty, grinding tyranny of the good English family."[48] Neither Newdegate nor his Catholic opponents took comfort in the thought that some Victorian women might find liberation from masculine authority within convent walls. In any event, it seemed clear that, even in the absence of a new statute, no convent could resist a writ of habeas corpus. And, however many suspicious tales they might investigate, Newdegate and his allies failed to uncover the single incident or witness who might have clinched the case for convent inspection. Thus, in the case of convents as of other manifestations of Roman Catholicism, Newdegate was forced to make do with the evidence in hand.

For some Victorians, he became a figure of fun. The papers of Sir Hardinge Giffard, the Conservative M.P. and, as Earl Halsbury, future lord chancellor, contain a sketch by Giffard of a soldier and a nurse wheeling a pram. The sketch is accompanied by a mock question: "Mr. Newdegate will ask the Secretary for the War Department whether it is true that a soldier of the 1st Life Guards has been seen wheeling a child with an unmistakably Papal cast of countenance in the Park."[49] Yet was Newdegate altogether an odd man out? In his biography of Disraeli, Robert Blake suggests "that toleration of Rome at this time, like reform of the homosexuality laws in our own day, was a matter on which most intelligent politicians agreed, but defiance of the bigotry of the masses involved political dangers which they were loath to risk."[50] The analogy may be apt, but it is useful to remember how closely the prestigious *Times* echoed Newdegate in 1870, far more closely than its editorial writers cared to recall twenty years later. "A deep-rooted suspicion of the whole [conventual] system is instinctive with all classes of Englishmen," *The Times* had then declared.[51] Disraeli and Gladstone, though their outlook was hardly identical to Newdegate's, both found cause in the course of their political careers to concede the reality of Roman Catholic power and to express their distrust of Roman Catholic influence. That some of his fellow Englishmen saw him as a Don Quixote, Newdegate conceded, but they also admitted his courage and his integrity, and like Don Quixote's fellow Spaniards, they developed a high degree of affection for him— and surprisingly often they suspected that he might, after all, be right. Newdegate's public life and his personal life became largely one; if he was not a hero, neither was he a hypocrite.

In many respects, Newdegate was a champion of lost causes, yet, as the late Sir Herbert Butterfield reminded us in *The Whig Interpretation of History*, the present is determined not merely by the winners of past conflicts but by the interaction of winners and losers. Abstract ideas, we would also do well to remember, cannot readily be divorced from the individuals whose lives either embody or contradict them. Thus the actions of Lord Ripon the human being ultimately defused Gladstone's fears as to the philosophical implications of the Vatican decrees. Just so did the prejudices—and the ideals—of a Charles Newdegate help to produce that blend of religious and irreligious pluralism that, in Great Britain if not in Northern Ireland, emerged from decades of vigorous controversy among Victorians for whom religion was a preoccupation at once central and absorbing.

Notes

Notes to Chapter 1

1. G. F. A. Best, "Popular Protestantism in Victorian Britain," in *Ideas and Institutions of Victorian Britain*, ed. Robert Robson (London, 1967), pp. 115–42.

2. E. R. Norman, *Anti-Catholicism in Victorian England* (New York, 1968).

3. Giovanni Costigan, *Makers of Modern England* (New York, 1967), p. 51. Henry Matthews served as home secretary from 1886 to 1892; the second marquess of Ripon served as viceroy from 1880 to 1885.

4. Kenneth Scott Latourette, *A History of the Expansion of Christianity* (New York, 1941), 4:123.

5. Josef L. Altholz, "The Political Behavior of English Catholics, 1850–1867," *Journal of British Studies* 4, no. 1 (November 1964): 93.

6. George Kitson Clark, *The Making of Victorian England* (London, 1961), p. 20.

7. See, for example, Spencer Walpole, *A History of England from the Conclusion of the Great War in 1815*, new impression (London, 1912), 5:251.

8. S. C. Carpenter, *Church and People, 1789–1889* (London, 1933), p. 151.

9. Best, "Popular Protestantism," pp. 118, 122, 135–36.

10. W.S. Holdsworth, *A History of English Law* (London, 1922–1938), 8:412.

11. See, for example, Asa Briggs, "Thomas Atwood and the Economic Background of the Birmingham Political Union," *Cambridge Historical Journal* 9 (1948): 212–16; D. C. Moore, "The Other Face of Reform," *Victorian Studies* 5 (September 1961): 7–34.

12. John Morley, *Life of Gladstone* (London, 1903), 1:53–54, 72.

13. G. F. A. Best, "The Protestant Constitution and Its Supporters, 1800–1829," *Transactions of the Royal Historical Society*, 5th ser. 8 (1958):105–28.

14. Cited in Briggs, "Thomas Atwood," p. 216. The origins of the Protestant Association are discussed by G. I. T. Machin in *Politics and the Churches in Great Britain, 1832 to 1868* (Oxford, 1977), pp. 94–99.

15. R. L. Hill, *Toryism and the People, 1832–1846* (London, 1929), p. 59.

16. *Hansard's Parliamentary Debates* (hereafter cited as *Hansard*), 3d ser., vol. 118 (1851), col. 1115.

17. Best, "Protestant Constitution," p. 120.

18. *Statutes of the Realm*, 3d rev. ed. (London, 1950), 3:312–13.

19. Cited in David Douglas, gen. ed., *English Historical Documents* (London, 1953–), 12 (pt.1):367–68.

20. Norman, *Anti-Catholicism*, pp. 23–51, provides an incisive account of the controversy.

21. Benjamin Disraeli, *Lord George Bentinck: A Political Biography* (London, 1852), p. 134.

22. See Norman, *Anti-Catholicism*, pp. 52–79. The best brief account of the background of the crisis may be found in Walter Ralls, "The Papal Aggression of 1850: A Study in Victorian Anti-Catholicism," *Church History* 43, no. 2 (June y974):242–56.

23. Costigan, *Makers*, p. 139.

24. Robert Rhodes James, "Britain: Soldiers and Biographers," *Journal of Contemporary History* 3 (1968): 95.

Notes to Chapter 2

1. George Kitson Clark, *The Making of Victorian England* (London, 1961), p. 45.

2. *The Victoria History of the County of Warwick* (London, 1908), 2:226–27.

3. Gordon Nares, *Arbury Hall, Warwickshire* (Country Life, Ltd., 1964), pp. 4–18; also see the articles on Sir Richard Newdigate and Sir Roger Newdigate in the *Dictionary of National Biography* (London, 1882–1900) and the article on Sir Roger Newdigate in Sir Lewis B. Namier and John Brooke, *The House of Commons, 1754–1790* (New York, 1964), 3:196–99.

4. The Papers of Henry Richard Harpur, Lord of the Manor of Coton Hall, Nuneaton, f. 437, Northamptonshire Record Office. Nares, *Arbury Hall*; John Burke, *A Genealogical and Heraldic History of the Extinct and Dormant Baronetcies of England, Ireland, and Scotland*, 2d ed. (London, 1844), p. 383.

5. See *Coventry Herald and Free Press*, 15 April 1887, p. 5.

6. Charles Newdigate Newdegate Papers, CR 136/B4417–19; Warwickshire Record Office; also unnumbered documents including the will of Charles Parker Newdegate.

7. Cited in J. I. Brash, "Disraeli's Visit to Arniston House, October 1867," *Newsletter: The Disraeli Project, Queen's University* 5, no. 1 (Spring 1980): 10.

8. Edward Stanford, ed., *Stanford's Parliamentary County Atlas* (London, 1885), pp. 256–61.

9. England, Local Government Board, *England and Wales: Return of Owners of Land, 1873* (London, 1875), 1:12; 2:83.

10. *Dictionary of National Biography*, 15:239.

11. Newdegate Papers, B31.

12. Dennis Milburn, *Nuneaton: The Growth of a Town* (Nuneaton, 1963), p. 35 (mimeographed).

13. Ibid., pp. 58, 107.

14. Harpur Papers, ff. 438, 456, 510; *Hansard*, 3d ser., vol. 221 (1874), col. 215.

15. Harpur Papers, f. 449.

16. The Papers of Archibald Campbell Tait, Archbishop of Canterbury, vol. 145, f. 376, Lambeth Palace Library, London. Also Newdegate Papers, CR 136/B4347; *Vanity Fair* 3 (13 August 1870):69.

17. Harpur Papers, f. 454; Newdegate refers to his role as a justice of the peace in *Hansard*, 3d ser., vol. 198 (1869), cols. 593, 601; see also *Midland Counties Herald*, 18 February 1886 (clipping in Newdegate Papers, B52).

18. Namier and Brooke, *House of Commons*, 3:196–99.

19. *Hansard*, vol. 195 (1869), col. 860; *The English Churchman*, 21 April 1887, p. 200.

20. Newdegate Papers, CR 136/B4421; *Victoria History: Warwick*, 2:466.

21. Harpur Papers, 21 February 1843, f. 427.

22. Harpur Papers, undated, f. 568.

23. *Hansard*, 3d ser., vol. 228 (1876), col. 1696; Charles N. Newdegate, *The Speech of C. N. Newdegate, M.P., at the Annual Meeting of the Rugby and Dunchurch Agricultural Association, November 26th, 1858* (London, 1859), p. 10.

24. See Norman McCord, "Cobden and Bright in Politics, 1846–1857," in *Ideas and Institutions of Victorian Britain*, ed. Robert Robson (London, 1967), p. 106.

25. *The Times*, 27 February 1843, p. 5; 28 February 1843, p. 5; 1 March 1843, p. 5; 10 March 1843, p. 8; 11 March 1843, p. 7.

26. According to H. J. Hanham, 407 of 670 M.P.s in 1868 came from families owning more than two thousand acres of land; *Elections and Party Management: Politics in the Time of Disraeli and Gladstone* (London, 1959), p. xv.

27. John Bateman, *The Great Landowners of Great Britain and Ireland*, 4th ed. (London, 1883), pp. xxi, 331.

28. *Hansard*, 3d ser., vol. 79 (1845), col. 712; Benjamin Disraeli, *Lord George Bentinck: A Political Biography* (London, 1852), p. 300.

29. *Hansard*, 3d ser., vol. 76 (1844), col. 65; R. L. Hill, *Toryism and the People, 1832–1846* (London, 1929), pp. 165–66.

30. *Hansard*, 3d ser., vol. 74 (1844), col. 1414.

31. E. R. Norman, *Anti-Catholicism in Victorian England* (New York, 1968), chap. 2.

32. *Hansard*, 3d ser., vol. 79 (1845), cols. 717–18.

33. Norman Gash, *Sir Robert Peel* (London, 1972), pp. 471, 574.

34. Harpur Papers, f. 432; Mary Lawson-Tancred, "The Anti-League and the Corn Law Crisis of 1846," *Historical Journal* 3, no. 2 (1960): 174.

35. *Hansard*, 3d ser., vol. 83 (1846), col. 1283; Hill, *Toryism*, p. 174.

36. *Hansard*, 3d ser., vol. 83 (1846), col. 1295.

37. Wilbur Devereux Jones and Arvel B. Erickson, *The Peelites,1846–1857* (Columbus, Ohio, 1972), p. 53.

38. See, for example, the Papers of the Fourteenth Earl of Derby, 148/1, utilized at Christ Church, Oxford.

39. Newdegate to Stanley, 21 October 1846, Derby Papers; J. B. Conacher, *The Peelites and the Party System, 1846–1852* (Newton Abbot, Devon, 1972), p. 21.

40. Newdegate Papers, CR 136/B6623.

41. Newdegate Papers, CR 1841/36; diary entries for 17 May 1846, 12 March 1851, and passim.

42. Newdegate Papers, CR 1841/35. Stanley is referred to in diary entries for 6 May 1846, 25 June 1846, and 1 April 1851; Bentinck in entries for 26 April 1846, 24 June 1846, and 31 March 1847; Disraeli in the entry for 26 April 1846 and passim.

43. Newdegate Papers, CR 1841/36; diary entry for [December ?] 1846.

44. Newdegate Papers, CR 136/B6329.

45. The Papers of Benjamin Disraeli, First Earl of Beaconsfield, B/XXI/N/86, Hughenden Manor, High Wycombe.

46. *The Times*, 9 August 1847, p. 3; 11 August 1847, p. 4; 16 August 1847, p. 4; 17 August 1847, p. 4.

47. Newdegate to Henry Richard Harpur, 15 April 1849, Harpur Papers, f. 438.

48. *The Times*, 23 October 1847, p. 5.

Notes to Chapter 3

1. See W. L. Burn, *The Age of Equipoise* (London, 1964); and George Kitson Clark, *The Making of Victorian England* (London, 1961).

2. *Hansard*, 3d ser., vol. 95 (1857), col. 1370.

3. See Charles Whibley, *Lord John Manners and His Friends* (London, 1925), 1:285–86.

4. Robert Blake, *Disraeli* (London, 1966), pp. 247–48; Benjamin Disraeli, *Lord George Bentinck: A Political Biography* (London, 1852), pp. 485–512.

5. Cited in Whibley, *Lord John Manners*, 1:282.

6. *Hansard*, 3d ser., vol. 95 (1857), cols. 1365–71. In a subsequent debate, Newdegate insisted that Jewish oaths were not to be trusted because the annual Day of Atonement excused Jews from adhering to all formal vows. This accusation, and others that were furnished to Newdegate by an unnamed informant,

led to a newspaper debate with Morris Jacob Raphall, the rabbi who served as headmaster of the Hebrew National School in Birmingham. Though Raphall would appear to have come out ahead in the exchange of letters, the correspondence was printed, at Newdegate's instigation, as *Jewish Dogmas: A Correspondence between Dṛ. Raphall, M.A., and C.N. Newdegate, M.P.* (London, 1849). I am grateful to Abraham Gilam for making a copy of the pamphlet available to me.

7. Cited in Whibley, *Lord John Manners*, 2:292.

8. Stanley to Granby, 6 January 1849, the Papers of the Fourteenth Earl of Derby, 178/1, utilized at Christ Church, Oxford. See also Robert Stewart, *The Politics of Protection: Lord Derby and the Protectionist Party, 1841–1852* (Cambridge, 1971), pp. 122–26.

9. W. F. Monypenny and G. E. Buckle, *The Life of Benjamin Disraeli, Earl of Beaconsfield*, 6 vols. (London, 1910–1920), 3:110.

10. Stanley to Beresford, 10 December 1848, Derby Papers, 178/1; Newdegate to Stanley, 19 December 1848, Derby Papers, 148/1; Blake, *Disraeli*, pp. 252–54.

11. Newdegate to Stanley, 22 January 1849, Derby Papers, 148/1; the letter is misdated 22 January 1848.

12. Whibley, *Lord John Manners*, 1:309; Blake, *Disraeli*, pp. 254–57.

13. The Papers of Benjamin Disraeli, First Earl of Beaconsfield, B/XXI/N/88, 89, Hughenden Manor, High Wycombe.

14. Charles Newdigate Newdegate Papers, CR 1841/34, CR 136/B6330, B6631, Warwickshire Record Office.

15. Blake, *Disraeli*, p. 232.

16. *Quarterly Review* 86 (December 1849): 175–76. A similar series of letters to J. W. Henley, Labouchere's successor, followed in 1852; Newdegate Papers, CR 1841/34; diary entries for 1 and 7 April 1851.

17. *Hansard*, 3d ser., vol. 97 (1848), col. 181; vol. 105 (1849), col. 953; vol. 109 (1850), col. 1008.

18. *Hansard*, 3d ser., vol. 119 (1852), col. 1120; vol. 123 (1852), cols. 517–18.

19. *Hansard*, 3d ser., vol. 119 (1852), col. 1120; vol. 90 (1847), col. 171; vol. 111 (1850), cols. 1264–65.

20. *Hansard*, 3d ser., vol. 126 (1853), col. 1111.

21. *Hansard*, 3d ser., vol. 93 (1847), col. 729.

22. Newdegate to Derby, Good Friday, 1848, Derby Papers, 148/1.

23. See David Roberts, *Victorian Origins of the British Welfare State* (New Haven, Conn., 1960).

24. *Hansard*, 3d ser., vol. 110 (1850), col. 154.

25. Newdegate Papers, CR 1841/34; diary entries for 26 April 1846, 6 March 1851, and 22 February 1852.

26. Newdegate Papers, CR 1841/34; diary entry for 26 February 1851.

27. Newdegate Papers, CR 1841/37; diary entries for 22 and 24 February 1852.

28. Newdegate Papers, CR 1841/37; diary entry for 24 February 1852.

29. Newdegate to Derby, 24 February 1852, Newdegate Papers, CR 136/B6427.

30. Newdegate Papers, CR 1847/37; diary entry for 25 February 1852.

31. *Hansard*, 3d ser., vol. 105 (1849), col. 1197; Charles N. Newdegate, *The Speech of C. N. Newdegate, M.P., at the Annual Meeting of the Rugby and Dunchurch Agricultural Association, November 26th, 1858* (London, 1859), p. 7.

32. *The Times*, 16 April 1852, p. 8; *Spectator* 25 (27 March 1852):296.

33. Newdegate to Henry Richard Harpur, 11 February 1851 and 18 June 1852, the Papers of Henry Richard Harpur, Lord of the Manor of Coton Hall, Nuneaton, ff. 446, 457, Northamptonshire Record Office.

34. Harpur Papers, ff. 464, 471.

35. *The Times,* 29 June 1852, p. 5; 10 July 1852, p. 4; 13 July 1852, p. 4; 20 July 1852, p. 5. *Spectator* 25 (17 July 1852): 674; Newdegate Papers, D3 (election poster).

36. Harpur Papers, ff. 457, 472, 475, 483.

37. Edward Michael Whitty, *The Governing Classes of Great Britain* (London, 1854), p. 193.

38. Newdegate Papers, B51.

39. Ibid.

40. Newdegate Papers, CR 136/B6333.

41. Newdegate Papers, B6557.

42. Newdegate Papers, B6346.

43. *The Times,* 4 April 1857, p. 8; *Hansard,* 3d ser., vol. 203 (1870), col. 1773; Newdegate to Disraeli, 23 January 1856 (draft), Newdegate Papers, B51, B4474.

44. *Hansard,* 3d ser., vol. 117 (1851), col. 912; vol. 128, col. 310; Frederick Boase, *Modern English Biography* (Truro, 1892–1901), 3:691.

45. *The Times,* 17 March 1857, p. 5; 4 April 1857, p. 8.

46. Newdegate Papers, B52.

47. Monypenny and Buckle, *Life of Disraeli,* 4:183.

48. Newdegate Papers, B6641, B6642. See also George Stone, "The Reform Bill of 1859" (Ph.D. diss., University of Illinois–Urbana, 1975), and Newdegate, *Speech at Rugby and Dunchurch,* p. 5.

49. *The Times,* 8 April 1859, p. 5; 11 April 1859, p. 11; 3 May 1859, p. 1.

50. Newdegate Papers, CR 136/B6641.

51. Newdegate Papers, B6636, B6637; *Vanity Fair* 3 (13 August 1870): 65.

52. Walter Bagehot, "Parliamentary Reform," in *The Works and Life of Walter Bagehot,* ed. Mrs. Russell Barrington (London, 1915), 3:161–62; William White, *The Inner Life of the House of Commons* (London, 1897), 2:166; T. H. S. Escott, *Gentlemen of the House of Commons* (London, 1902), 1:315.

53. Newdegate Papers, B4423.

54. Harpur Papers, f. 489.

55. Harpur Papers, f. 527; *Hansard,* 3d ser., vol. 214 (1873), cols. 482, 483.

56. Harpur Papers, f. 514. The general context is provided by Hugh S. Cunningham, *The Volunteer Force: A Social and Political History, 1859–1908* (Hamden, Conn., 1975).

57. Obituary of Newdegate, *Nuneaton Chronicle,* 15 April 1887, p. 5.

58. Newdegate Papers, CR 136/B4424; Harpur Papers, ff. 489, 558.

59. Letter from Derby's secretary, Newdegate Papers, B52; letter from Lord Exeter, 220 October 1859, Newdegate Papers, B51; clipping in D3.

60. *English Churchman,* 21 April 1887, p. 200.

61. Newdegate Papers, CR136/B6565.

62. See *Vanity Fair* 3 (13 August 1870): 65.

Notes to Chapter 4

1. See, for example, Josef L. Altholz, "The Political Behavior of English Catholics, 1850–1867," *Journal of British Studies* 4, no. 1 (November 1964): 93. See also chapter 1 of E. R. Norman, *Anti-Catholicism in Victorian England* (New York, 1968). A significant recent exception to this historiographic tendency is J. Derek Holmes, *More Roman than Rome: English Catholicism in the Nineteenth Century* (London, 1978).

2. *Punch* 20 (1851): 46. The cartoon admittedly also alludes to the relative

physical statures of Russell and Wiseman. One of Wiseman's Irish servants once inadvertently referred to the cardinal as "His Immense."

3. Henry Edward Manning cited in Edmund Sheridan Purcell, *The Life of Cardinal Manning* (London, 1895), 2:80–81.

4. The bishop of Exeter had refused to install the Reverend G. C. Gorham as a parish priest in his diocese. He found abhorrent to Anglican doctrine Gorham's view that infant baptism did not wash away the taint of original sin and did no more than express the pious hope that salvation might be granted by a God whose ultimate will was not knowable by man. Gorham appealed the decision to the Judicial Committee of the Privy Council, thereby raising the overriding question: Was the Church of England primarily a church, that is, an autonomous spiritual body dispensing doctrine and law, or was it a body dependent on the state, and destined always to alter its message in accordance with the changing pressures of national policy or popular opinion? The Privy Council, with the assent of the archbishops of Canterbury and York, ultimately ruled in Gorham's favor. In the eyes of Gorham's defenders, the council thus saved a Protestant nation from sacerdotal oppression; in the eyes of his opponents, it thus acted as the quasi-pagan enemy of the true faith. The Gorham case confirmed the fear of those who became converts to Rome that the Church of England was ultimately an arm of the state and not part of a universal Christian communion. The philosophical implications are cogently explored in A. O. J. Cockshut *Anglican Attitudes: A Study of Victorian Religious Controversies* (London, 1959), pp. 39–61. The chronology of the affair is carefully summarized in Owen Chadwick, *The Victorian Church* (London, 1966–1970), 1:250–63.

5. According to a German observer of mid-Victorian England, most Britons continued to believe, as did the Roman Catholics, in holding fast to the principle *nulla salus extra ecclesiam catholicam* ("no safety outside the Catholic church") with regard to the Church of England. See Walter L. Arnstein, ed., "A German View of English Society," *Victorian Studies* 16, no. 2 (December 1972): 202.

6. Alphons Bellesheim, *A History of the Catholic Church of Scotland*, trans. D. Oswald Hunter Blair (Edinburgh, 1890), 4:291.

7. W. Gordon-Gorman, *Converts to Rome*, 4th ed. (London, 1899), pp. xi and passim.

8. Roger Fulford, ed., *Your Dear Letter: Private Correspondence of Queen Victoria and the Crown Princess of Prussia, 1865–1871* (New York, 1971), p. 160; see also p. 149.

9. Charles Whibley, *Lord John Manners and His Friends* (London, 1925), 1:73.

10. Cited in Gordon-Gorman, *Converts to Rome*, p. vi.

11. See Henry Edward Manning, *Sermons on Ecclesiastical Subjects* (Dublin, 1863), 1:119; and Wilfrid Ward, *The Life and Times of Cardinal Wiseman*, new ed. (London, 1912), 2:218–20.

12. *Church Opinion*, 5 March 1870, p. 14.

13. Cited in David Mathew, *Lord Acton and His Times* (London, 1968), p. 53.

14. Ambrose de Lisle, a convert, foresaw the conversion of the entire Anglican clergy; Brian Fothergill, *Nicholas Wiseman* (Garden City, N.Y., 1963), p. 112. When it was suggested to Manning in his old age that "it was only the converts who were enterprising," he replied, "Yes, but it would never do for us to say so"; Shane Leslie, "Mrs. Crawford, Sir Charles Dilke, and Cardinal Manning," *Dublin Review* 241 (Autumn 1967): 196.

15. See the first volume of W. Ward, *Cardinal Wiseman*, and the first three chapters of Fothergill, *Nicholas Wiseman*.

16. Cited in Fothergill, *Nicholas Wiseman*, p. 99. The *Dublin Review*, despite its title, was published in London.

17. Cited in Fothergill, *Nicholas Wiseman*, p. 126.

18. Cited in E. E. Y. Hales, *Pio Nono* (New York, 1954), p. 141. Technically, the papal document reestablishing the hierarchy was a "rescript" rather than a "bull"; the use of the latter term, however, has become customary.

19. *The Times*, 14 October 1850, p. 4. See also Gordon Albion, "The Restoration of the Hierarchy," in *The English Catholics, 1850–1950*, ed. George A. Beck (London, 1950), pp. 86–116.

20. Cited respectively in Fothergill, *Nicholas Wiseman*, pp. 293–97, and in Francis Warre Cornish, *The English Church in the Nineteenth Century* (London, 1910), 1:344.

21. Cited in Norman, *Anti-Catholicism*, pp. 159–61.

22. *Punch* 19 (1850): 190.

23. W. Ward, *Cardinal Wiseman*, 2:6–7; Cornish, *English Church*, 1:343.

24. Fothergill, *Nicholas Wiseman*, pp. 72–73.

25. *The Times*, 21 November 1850, p. 4.

26. Fothergill, *Nicholas Wiseman*, pp. 180, 223; Richard John Schiefen, "The Organisation and Administration of Roman Catholic Dioceses in England and Wales in the Mid-Nineteenth Century" (Ph.D. diss., University of London, 1970), pp. 96, 106, 361.

27. Fothergill, *Nicholas Wiseman*, p. 180; Francesca M. Steele, *The Convents of Great Britain* (London, 1902), p. 1.

28. Cited in "Letters of Cardinal Wiseman," *Dublin Review* 164 (1919): 17.

29. *Spectator* 25 (19 June 1852): 581; W. Ward, *Cardinal Wiseman*, 2:26. "The Derby Ministry's Proclamation," Newdegate assured a friend, "appears to give general satisfaction except to the Papists and their allies"; The Papers of Richard Henry Harpur, Lord of the Manor of Coton Hall, Nuneaton, f. 456, Northamptonshire Record Office.

30. Cited in J. J. Dwyer, "The Catholic Press, 1850–1950," in Beck, ed., *English Catholics*, p. 483.

31. Manning, *Sermons*, 1:76.

32. See J. M. Capes, "The Jesuits in England," *Contemporary Review* 21 (December 1872): 37.

33. See Mathew, *Acton*, p. 172.

34. *The Times*, 24 February 1865, p. 5; John Archer Jackson, *The Irish in Britain* (London, 1963), p. 155.

35. John Bossy, *The English Catholic Community, 1570–1850* (London, 1975), pp. 295–300, 331–37, 395–99, 427, and passim.

36. Jackson, *The Irish*, pp. 7, 138; Ernst Georg Ravenstein, *Denominational Statistics of England and Wales* (London, 1870).

37. *The Times*, 12 February 1851, p. 5, cited in Sheridan Gilley, "Protestant London, No Popery, and the Irish Poor: II (1850–1860)," *Recusant History* 11, no. 1 (January 1971): 24. Tertullian was the Christian convert of the second century A.D. who predicted the Christian conquest of the Roman Empire.

38. Jackson, *The Irish*, pp. 75–90.

39. "The English Protestant Marriage Law," *Dublin Review*, n.s. 14 (January 1870): 77.

40. Cited in Gilley, "Protestant London: II," p. 26.

41. Cited in Jackson, *The Irish*, pp. 49–50.

42. W. G. Lumley, "The Statistics of Roman Catholics in England and Wales," *Journal of the Statistical Society* 27 (September 1864): 320.

43. *Saturday Review* cited in *Public Opinion*, 30 January 1869, p. 123. L. P. Curtis, Jr., provides a revealing pen-portrait of the stereotyped Victorian Irishman in chapter 4 of *Anglo-Saxons and Celts: A Study of Anti-Irish Prejudice in*

Victorian England (Bridgeport, Conn., 1968).

44. Gilley, "Protestant London: II," p. 26; Evelyn Garratt, *Life and Personal Recollections of Samuel Garratt* (London, 1908), pp. 236–37; Chadwick, *The Victorian Church*, 2:403.

45. Cited in Gilley, "Protestant London: II," p. 30.

46. Ibid., p. 37.

47. Garratt, *Samuel Garratt*, pp. 39–40; Gilley, "Protestant London: II," pp. 25, 34; Sheridan Gilley, "Protestant London, No Popery, and the Irish Poor: I (1830–1850)," *Recusant History* 10, no. 1 (January 1970): 227; Jackson, *The Irish*, p. 145. Not all Irish settlers attended mass faithfully, but as Lynn Hollen Lees has confirmed in *Exiles of Erin: Irish Migrants in Victorian London* (Ithaca, N.Y., 1979), the Irish maintained remarkably close-knit residential and economic communities within the metropolis.

48. Cited in Purcell, *Manning*, 2:677. Also see Dennis Gwynn, "The Irish Immigrants," in Beck, ed., *English Catholics*, p. 279.

49. Cited in W. Ward, *Cardinal Wiseman*, 2:5.

50. Jackson, *The Irish*, p. 7.

51. See Gilley, "Protestant London: I," p. 212; W. M. Walker, "Irish Immigrants in Scotland: Their Priests, Politics, and Parochial Life," *The Historical Journal* 15, no. 4 (1972): 649–68.

52. James Edmund Handley, *The Irish in Modern Scotland* (Cork, 1947), pp. 93–96, 112–17, and passim; George Scott-Moncrieff, *The Mirror and the Cross: Scotland and the Catholic Faith* (London, 1960), p. 144.

53. Cited in Emmet Larkin, "The Devotional Revolution in Ireland, 1850–1875," *American Historical Review* 77, no. 3 (June 1972): 626n.

54. "The Maynooth Commission," *Edinburgh Review* 102 (July 1855): 179.

55. R. D. Edwards and T. D. Williams, eds., *The Great Famine: Studies in Irish History, 1845–1852* (New York, 1957), pp. v, 388.

56. Cited in Desmond Bowen, *Souperism: Myth or Reality?* (Cork, 1970), p. 144; see also pp. 78, 101, 148, and passim. Bowen's book provides a judicious examination of the thesis that converts to Protestantism were attracted by food (that is, soup) rather than by faith. A comprehensive assessment of Protestant missionary efforts in nineteenth-century Ireland is provided by the same author in *The Protestant Crusade in Ireland, 1800–1870* (London, 1978).

57. Larkin, "Devotional Revolution," pp. 625–52.

58. See also Emmet Larkin, "Church, State, and Nation in Modern Ireland," *American Historical Review* 80, no. 1 (December 1975): 1254–58; and *Catholic Historical Review* 65 (October 1979): 648–50.

59. T. H. Whyte, *The Independent Irish Party, 1850–1859* (Oxford, 1958), p. 24.

60. Ibid., pp. 63–76.

61. Donald H. Akenson, *The Irish Education Experiment* (London, 1970), pp. 2–3.

62. Cited in Emmet Larkin, *The Making of the Roman Catholic Church in Ireland, 1850–1860* (Chapel Hill, N.C., 1980), p. 35. Larkin's study is the first systematic account of the inner history of the Irish Roman Catholic hierarchy and of the manner in which Archbishop Cullen established his dominance.

63. Walter Ralls, "The Papal Aggression of 1850: A Study in Victorian Anti-Catholicism," *Church History* 43, no. 2 (June 1974): 252.

64. Larkin, "Church, State, and Nation," pp. 1254–56; "The Maynooth Commission," p. 182 and passim; Frederick Boase, *Modern English Biography* (Truro, 1892–1901), 3:691. The annual grant was ended in 1871 as part of a general disestablishment of the Church of Ireland. It was replaced, however, by a permanent endowment.

65. Cited in E. R. Norman, *The Catholic Church and Ireland in the Age of Rebellion, 1859–1873* (Ithaca, N.Y., 1965), p. 12.

66. Ibid., pp. 22–24, chap. 2.

67. Cited in ibid., pp. 1, 5.

68. See Ray Allen Billington, *The Protestant Crusade, 1800–1860: A Study of the Origins of American Nativism* (New York, 1938), pp. 180, 290–91, 303, 387, and passim.

69. *The Times*, 25 February 1869, p. 9.

70. *Annual Register for 1855* (London, 1856), p. 279.

71. See "The Feast of Conception," *Quarterly Review* 87 (June 1855): 148. See also Hales, *Pio Nono*, chap. 4.

72. "Feast of Conception," pp. 181 and passim.

73. Charles Stephen Dessain, *John Henry Newman* (London, 1966), p. 124.

74. For example, Mathew, *Acton*, pp. 160–66.

75. The Papers of Lord John (First Earl) Russell, PRO 30/22/150, f. 671, Public Record Office, London.

76. *Burns's Standard Reading Books* (London, n.d.), 5:143.

77. Ibid., 2:8, 81–82.

78. Ibid., 3:25 and passim.

79. Ibid., 4:84.

80. Ibid., 5:32, 192–93.

81. Ibid., 5:39, 195.

82. Ibid., 5:119, 134, 157–64.

83. Purcell, *Manning*, 2:72, 75, 92, and passim.

84. Cited in ibid., 2:152.

85. Manning, *Sermons*, 1:123, 131, 142.

86. Ibid., p. 166.

87. Ibid., p. 164; Purcell, *Manning*, 2:140.

88. Manning, *Sermons*, 1:65–66.

89. Ibid., pp. 35, 60, 143.

90. Richard John Schiefen, " 'Anglo-Gallicanism' in Nineteenth-Century England," *Catholic Historical Review* 63, no. 1 (January 1977).

91. Josef L. Altholz, *The Liberal Catholic Movement in England* (London, 1962), pp. 219–44; Dessain, *Newman*, pp. 129–31; *Westminster Gazette* cited in *The Bulwark*, 1 January 1868, p. 181.

92. Manning, *Sermons*, 1:143; Talbot cited in Purcell, *Manning*, 2:318.

93. Russell Papers, PRO 30/22/15D, ff. 707, 709, 729.

94. Purcell, *Manning*, 2: chap. 10.

Notes to Chapter 5

1. For example, in 1849, Newdegate and his colleague Richard Spooner had introduced a "Protection of Women" bill to punish persons procuring or inducing the prostitution of women. Lord John Russell's government opposed the bill as unnecessary, and it did not become law; *Hansard*, 3d ser., vol. 106 (1849), col. 1028.

2. *Hansard*, 3d ser., vol. 210 (1872), col. 1689; vol. 216 (1873), col. 1665.

3. Introduction by Father Herbert Thurston, S.J., to Francesca M. Steele, *The Convents of Great Britain* (London, 1902).

4. *Hansard*, 3d ser., vol. 219 (1874), cols. 1507–9, 1517.

5. A Protestant, *Nunneries* (London, [1852]), p. 7.

6. *Hansard*, 3d ser., vol. 116 (1851), cols. 948–89; vol. 127 (1853), col. 96; vol.

128 (1853), cols. 548–85; vol. 129 (1853), cols. 1463–69. See also Bishop [William Bernard] Ullathorne, *A Plea for the Rights and Liberties of Religious Women with Reference to the Bill Proposed by Mr. Lacy* (London, 1851). In chapter 7 of his novel *The Warden* (1855), Anthony Trollope was motivated to invent a 137-clause "Convent Custody Bill," "the purport of which was to enable any Protestant clergyman over fifty years of age to search any nun whom he suspected of being in possession of treasonable papers or jesuitical symbols."

7. Juliana Wadham, *The Case of Cornelia Connelly* (London, 1956), cited in Owen Chadwick, *The Victorian Church* (London, 1966–1970), 1:509.

8. Chadwick, *Victorian Church*, 1:509.

9. Ibid. Also William Bernard [Archbishop] Ullathorne, *Autobiography, with Selections from His Letters* (London, 1891–1892), 2:48.

10. Cited by Sheridan Gilley, "Protestant London, No Popery, and the Irish Poor: II (1850–1860)," *Recusant History* 11, no. 1 (January 1971):35.

11. *Hansard*, 3d ser., vol. 174 (1864), cols. 633–42, 656; vol. 198 (1869), col. 595.

12. *Hansard*, 3d ser., vol. 174 (1864), cols. 647–61; *The Times*, 11 April 1864, pp. 8–9. The electoral analysis in this as in future instances is based on the division lists in the light of the party preference expressed in *Dod's Parliamentary Companion* (annual).

13. Charles Newdigate Newdegate Papers, CR 764/177, Warwickshire Record Office.

14. *Hansard*, 3d ser., vol. 177 (1865), cols. 1045–56.

15. *Hansard*, 3d ser., vol. 177 (1865), col. 1058. The home secretary, Sir George Grey, had inquired into the case. The British consul and minister in Belgium had visited the asylum, had found it well conducted, and had concluded that Mary Ryan truly was insane. A member of the British Lunacy Commission had reached the same conclusion. Although the Belgian authorities had expressed their willingness to return the lady to English soil, the British government decided not to make such a request. Nor did it prosecute those who had taken her to Belgium. The commission did suggest that Roman Catholics might find it useful to set up their own insane asylum within the United Kingdom. See *Hansard*, 3d ser., vol. 177 (1865), cols. 1078, 1646–51; G. F. A. Best, "Popular Protestantism in Victorian Britain," in *Ideas and Institutions of Victorian Britain*, ed. Robert Robson (London, 1967), pp. 127–32.

16. *Hansard*, 3d ser., vol. 177 (1865), cols. 1058–64.

17. *Hansard*, 3d ser., vol. 177 (1865), col. 1046.

18. E. R. Norman, *Anti-Catholicism in Victorian England* (New York, 1968), p. 2; Frederick Boase, *Modern English Biography* (Truro, 1892–1901), 3:1293.

19. *Hansard*, 3d ser., vol. 177 (1865), cols. 1064–69, 1086.

20. T. E. Kebbel, *Lord Beaconsfield and Other Tory Memories* (London, 1907), p. 29; Robert Blake, *Disraeli* (London, 1966), p. 429. Disraeli observed later in 1865 that post–1850 fears of "papal aggression" had been happily disappointed, that most Roman Catholics sought merely the free exercise of their religion, and that most Protestants were prepared to grant this. He acknowledged the existence of Protestant and Catholic extremists; fortunately, their violence and asperity were being softened and mitigated by "the Gulf Stream of Common-sense"; *Hansard*, 3d ser., vol. 180 (1865), cols. 52–64.

21. *Hansard*, 3d ser., vol. 177 (1865), cols. 1077–85.

22. The parliamentary vote is usually reported without counting that of the two tellers (or counters) on each side. With the tellers included, the ayes and the nays each increase by two.

23. Cited in Edmund Sheridan Purcell, *The Life of Cardinal Manning* (London, 1895), 1:684.

24. Cited in Charles N. Newdegate, *Monastic and Conventual Institutions* (Edinburgh, 1866), pp. 37–48.

25. Cited in ibid., pp. 45–46.

26. Charles P. Mander, the justice of the peace who had interviewed her in her new convent, conceded that she did not wish to leave. "What could I do if I left?" she asked Mander. "All my relations and friends are Roman Catholics, and they would turn their backs upon me, and what do I know of life?"; letter to *The Times*, 14 April 1870, p. 5.

27. Maria Monk's pseudonymous *Awful Disclosures of the Hotel Dieu Nunnery of Montreal* (New York, 1836) told of illicit relations with priests, the strangling of babies, secret passages, attempts by nuns to escape, their harrowing lives as fugitives, and so on. Three hundred thousand copies of the book were sold in the United States between 1836 and 1861. The work served as the *"Uncle Tom's Cabin* of Know-Nothingism" and as a leading inspiration of mid-nineteenth-century American anti-Catholicism. See Ray Allen Billington, *The Protestant Crusade, 1800–1860: A Study of the Origins of American Nativism* (New York, 1938), pp. 99–108.

28. Newdegate, *Monastic and Conventual Institutions* (1866), pp. 47–48; Dom Cuthbert Butler, *The Life and Times of Bishop Ullathorne, 1806–1889* (London, 1926), 2:162–63.

29. Newdegate, *Monastic and Conventual Institutions* (1866), pp. 50–53.

30. Percy Fitzgerald, *Fifty Years of Catholic Life* (London, 1901), 1:124–26; Purcell, *Manning*, 1:685; Wilfrid Ward, *The Life and Times of Cardinal Wiseman*, new ed. (London, 1912), 2:73.

31. Cited in Newdegate, *Monastic and Conventual Institutions* (1866), pp. 56–61.

32. Ibid., pp. 62–64.

33. Ibid., p. 66.

34. Ibid., pp. i–ii; James Edward Handley, *The Irish in Modern Scotland* (Cork, 1947), p. 99; Norman, *Anti-Catholicism*, p. 65.

Notes to Chapter 6

1. Owen Chadwick, *The Victorian Church* (London, 1966–1970), 1:491.

2. *The Times*, 18 April 1864, p. 8.

3. See Margaret M. Maison, *The Victorian Vision: Studies in the Religious Novel* (New York, 1961), pp. 55–57, 97.

4. *Fraser's Magazine* 54 (July 1856):41.

5. *Annual Register for 1867*, pt. 2, p. 139. Also see Alan M. Stephenson, *The First Lambeth Conference: 1867* (London, 1967).

6. Charles N. Newdegate, *Speech of C. N. Newdegate, M.P., at the Annual Meeting of the Rugby and Dunchurch Agricultural Association, November 26th, 1858* (London, 1859), p. 7; *Hansard*, 3d ser., vol. 201 (1870), cols. 1379–80.

7. *Hansard*, 3d ser., vol. 179 (1865), col. 1064; also vol. 178 (1865), col. 33; vol. 179 (1865), cols. 1052, 1064; vol. 180 (1865), cols. 83, 328.

8. Charles Newdigate Newdegate Papers, B6565, Warwickshire Record Office.

9. *Dod's Parliamentary Companion for 1865* (London, 1865), p. 153.

10. *Dod's Parliamentary Companion for 1868* (London, 1868), p. 270.

11. In the House of Commons, Newdegate had indeed denounced "the outrage which has been committed by [the] Prussian Government upon inoffen-

sive Denmark, our neighbor across the channel"; *Hansard*, 3d ser., vol. 174 (1864), col. 645.

12. *The Times*, 18 July 1865, p. 7.

13. Cited in Charles N. Newdegate, *Monastic and Conventual Institutions* (Edinburgh, 1866), pp.65–66.

14. Ibid., pp. 67–71.

15. *The Times*, 25 July 1865, p. 6.

16. *Dod's for 1865*, pp. 135, 143, 263, 213.

17. Ibid., pp. 269, 220.

18. *Harper's Magazine* 31 (November 1865): 740.

19. Josef L. Altholz, "The Political Behavior of English Catholics, 1850–1867," *Journal of British Studies* 4, no. 1 (November 1964): 93–98; Robert Blake, *Disraeli* (London, 1966), p. 435; T. E. Kebbel, *Lord Beaconsfield and Other Tory Memories* (London, 1907), p. 29.

20. Cited in Edmund Sheridan Purcell, *The Life of Cardinal Manning* (London, 1896), 2:165–66.

21. *Hansard*, 3d ser., vol. 181 (1866), cols. 456, 1728, 1732.

22. *Hansard*, 3d ser., vol. 181 (1866), col. 1713.

23. For example, *Hansard*, 3d ser., vol. 182 (1866), cols. 516–17.

24. *Hansard*, 3d ser., vol. 178 (1865), col. 570.

25. *Hansard*, 3d ser., vol. 179 (1865), col. 1060; vol. 181 (1866), col. 459. See also K. S. Inglis, *Churches and the Working Classes in Victorian England* (London, 1963), p. 126.

26. *Hansard*, 3d ser., vol. 186 (1867), col. 368.

27. *Hansard*, 3d ser., vol. 184 (1866), col. 87; vol. 185 (1867), col. 1092; vol. 186 (1867), col. 1414.

28. *Hansard*, 3d ser., vol. 185 (1867), cols. 112–16, 1092–94, 1102–9.

29. *Hansard*, 3d ser., vol. 187 (1867), col. 568; vol. 186 (1867), col. 1442; Disraeli to Cairns, 13 and 16 March 1868, the Papers of Sir Hugh (First Earl) Cairns, 30/51/1, ff. 4, 5, Public Record Office, London.

30. Newdegate Papers, C136/6337A; *Hansard*, 3d ser., vol. 185 (1867), cols. 933–35.

31. [Charles N. Newdegate], *A Glimpse of the Great Secret Society*, 2d ed. (London, 1868), pp. xii, xv, xxviii. A third edition of the work was published in 1872 and a fourth in 1880. The work is attributed to Newdegate by the National Union Catalog though not by the British Library. Although there is no reference to the work in the Newdegate Papers, a rather haphazard collection, the obituary of Newdegate in the *English Churchman* (21 April 1887, p. 200) confirms Newdegate's involvement: "The first edition of this [1761] report [about the Jesuits] is rare and was in Mr. Newdegate's possession. The "Glimpse," as he called it, has passed through several editions and he frequently acknowledged its authorship."

32. A tract in the British Library, vol. 4406.g.2.

33. *Church Association Lectures* (London, 1869).

34. *The Bulwark*, 2 July 1866, p. 18; 1 January 1869, pp. 194–95.

35. *The Bulwark*, 1 October 1868, p. 85.

36. Protestant Educational Institute, *Transactions of the Protestant Educational Institute* (London, 1872), p. 61.

37. See, for example, *Hansard*, 3d ser., vol. 224 (1875), col. 1170.

38. Newdegate Papers, CR 136/B51.

39. *Hansard*, 3d ser., vol. 188 (1867), cols. 1594–95. *The Bulwark* took comfort in the thought that a reformed Parliament could hardly be less heedless of the danger from Rome than an unreformed one and that "the great mass of the

working classes are not only Protestants, but being drawn, as they are, into constant contact, with the Irish Papists, they have much better means of knowing what they are than the higher classes, who have hitherto monopolised the power of legislation. There is no love of Popery amongst the honest tradesmen"; *The Bulwark*, 2 September 1867, p. 57.

40. *The Times*, 2 November 1868, p. 8.

41. *The Times*, 24 October 1868, p. 5; 11 November 1868, p. 8.

42. *The Times*, 11 November 1868, p. 8; 16 October 1868, p. 7; 27 October 1868, p. 5; 2 November 1868, p. 8.

43. *The Times*, 16 October 1868, p. 7; 6 November 1868, p. 7; 23 October 1868, p. 6.

44. *The Times*, 31 October 1868, p. 8. *Warwick Advertiser*, 24 October 1868; 31 October 1868; 21 November 1868.

45. *The Times*, 19 November 1868, p. 5; 23 November 1868, p. 6. *Warwick Advertiser*, 28 November 1868.

46. *Hansard*, 3d ser., vol. 186 (1867), col. 1396; vol. 189 (1867), col. 1622.

Notes to Chapter 7

1. The only "biography" of William Murphy is a brief, incomplete memoir prepared by Robert Steele and printed serially in the *Monthly Record of the Protestant Evangelical Mission and Electoral Union* 8 (1878): 3–5, 21–24, 33–37, 61–64, 76–80, 106–10, and 123–26 (hereafter cited as *Monthly Record*). This has been supplemented by Murphy's own slightly different account printed in the *Bacup Times*, 25 April 1868, which may be found in the Public Record Office/ Home Office File 45, o. s. 7991, f. 39 (hereafter cited as H. O. Papers). H. J. Hanham provides a brief account of the impact of the Murphy riots on Lancashire politics in 1868 in *Elections and Party Management: Politics in the Time of Disraeli and Gladstone* (London, 1959), pp. 303–8.

2. H. O. Papers, ff. 3, 62; *Monthly Record* 8 (1878): 36–37; *The Conspirators' Schemes* (London, 1871), pp. 14–15.

3. H. O. Papers, f. 62.

4. Liguori's justification of equivocation troubled Englishmen more eminent than the obscure compiler of *The Confessional Unmasked*. The subject was a key to the attack by Charles Kingsley that evoked John Henry Newman's *Apologia Pro Vita Sua* (London, 1864). See Josef L. Altholz, "Truth and Equivocation: Liguori's Moral Theology and Newman's Apologia," *Church History* 44, no. 1 (March 1975): 1–12.

5. *Monthly Record* 1 (1871): 147; 8 (1878): 24, 123. H. O. Papers, f. 39.

6. H. O. Papers, f. 3.

7. Dom Cuthbert Butler, *The Life and Times of Bishop Ullathorne, 1806–1889* (London, 1926), 2:164.

8. H. O. Papers, ff. 1, 3, 4, 6.

9. H. O. Papers, f. 5.

10. *The Times*, 17 June 1867, p. 6; 18 June 1867, p. 14; 20 June 1867, p. 7. See also John Alfred Langford, *Modern Birmingham and Its Institutions* (Birmingham, 1877), 2:299–300.

11. The Chartist disturbance of July 1839 appears to have done less damage; see F. C. Mather, *Public Order in the Age of the Chartists* (Manchester, 1959), p. 13.

12. *The Times*, 18 June 1867, p. 14; 19 June 1867, p. 12. *Birmingham Daily Post*, 18 June 1867, p. 4. H. O. Papers, ff. 8–10.

13. *The Times*, 18 June 1867, p. 14; 19 June 1867, p. 12; 20 June 1867, p. 7.

Birmingham Daily Post, 18 June 1867, p. 4. Butler, *Ullathorne*, 2:166.

14. *The Times*, 20 June 1867, pp. 7, 10; *Annual Register for 1867*, pt. 2, p. 79. For a study of religious rivalry and public disorder in Victorian Belfast, see Sybil E. Baker, "Orange and Green," in *The Victorian City*, ed. H. J. Dyos and Michael Wolff (London, 1973), 2:789–814.

15. *Annual Register for 1867*, pt. 2, p. 79. *The Times*, 20 June 1867, p. 7; 21 June 1867, p. 12.

16. Richard Hofstadter, *The Paranoid Style in American Politics* (New York, 1965), p. 21; *The Times*, 22 June 1867, p. 12; H. O. Papers, f. 11. "A Latin folio which no one is likely to see or hear of unless he has special motives for looking into it is one thing," the Catholic *Weekly Register* observed, "and a six-penny pamphlet in broad English hawked about the streets is quite another. . . . What would he think of a Roman Catholic, who, in order to show the practical immoralities of Protestant populations and to found thereon an argument in favour of the confessional, sent special reporters to every brothel in London, . . . and published in a cheap form faithful accounts of every infamous practice which he witnessed?"; *Weekly Register*, 13 July 1867, p. 24.

17. *Birmingham Daily Post*, 18 July 1867, p. 4; letter to *The Bulwark*, 1 November 1867, p. 139; Charles Maurice Davies's *Philip Paternoster, a Tractarian Love Story*, 2 vols. (London, 1858), cited in Margaret M. Maison, *The Victorian Vision: Studies in the Religious Novel* (New York, 1961), p. 76.

18. H. O. Papers, f. 19.

19. H. O. Papers, f. 17.

20. H. O. Papers, ff. 37, 23, 24.

21. H. O. Papers, f. 26.

22. H. O. Papers, ff. 29, 30, 39.

23. *The Times*, 13 April 1870, p. 9; *Monthly Record* 1 (1871): 75–76.

24. H. O. Papers, ff. 34–40.

25. *Hansard*, 3d ser., vol. 192 (1868), cols. 818–21.

26. *Hansard*, 3d ser., vol. 192 (1868), cols. 822–25.

27. *Hansard*, 3d ser., vol. 192 (1868), col. 346.

28. *Hansard*, 3d ser., vol. 192 (1868), cols. 828, 830–32. In its issue of 20 July 1867, the Catholic *Weekly Register* had urged the Roman Catholic laity to take *The Confessional Unmasked* to court. "We must cast aside our apathy, and combine to punish those who have insulted us, and without delay" (p. 40). A Wolverhampton Watch Committee obtained a warrant against a local book dealer for selling the volume and was upheld in the magistrate's court. The judgment was overturned in Quarter Sessions but was reaffirmed on 29 April 1868 by Lord Chief Justice Alexander Cockburn and four associates in the Queen's Bench on the ground that, whatever the motives of its publishers, the work was likely to "deprave and corrupt the minds of those into whose hands the book might fall." Although the Protestant Evangelical Mission and Electoral Union could take muted satisfaction from the fact that, by implication, Roman Catholic teaching had thus been legally condemned, it attempted in 1869 to put out a revised edition that removed "some of the most filthy and abominable passages." One of the society's lecturers, George Mackey, was, however, found guilty by Hampshire Quarter Sessions in January 1871 of selling the new edition, and he ultimately spent fifteen months in Winchester jail. When Richard Steele, the union's secretary, put out yet another edition as part of a *Report on the Trial of George Mackey*, the copies were seized by the metropolitan police, whose actions were ultimately upheld by the Court of Common Pleas on 30 April 1872. Chief Justice Bovill condemned the trial report as a subterfuge for reprinting the condemned pamphlet and reaffirmed the Cockburn decision: "Whilst the lib-

erty of free discussion is preserved, discussion must not run into obscenity"; *Monthly Record* 1 (1871): 21, 39, 84; 2 (1872): 29, 63, 84–113. Although Gathorne Hardy had found the Cockburn decision surprising (H. O. Papers, f. 26), his Liberal successor as home secretary, Henry Austin Bruce, did not: since the pamphlet was "one of the most obscene, beastly, and disgusting pamphlets that can be imagined," anyone who published it or sold it "committed a crime against society"; cited in *Monthly Record* 1 (1871): 168. The Liberal attorney general, Sir Henry James, agreed that Cockburn had handed down "an excellent decision"; *Monthly Record* 2 (1872): 110.

29. H. O. Papers, ff. 48, 58, 59.

30. H. O. Papers, f. 60. *The Times*, 5 September 1868, p. 10; 17 November 1868, p. 5; 19 November 1868, p. 4. *Manchester Guardian*, 5 September 1868, and *Manchester City News*, 19 September 1868, cited in Hanham, *Elections and Party Management*, p. 307. *Warwick Advertiser*, 10 October 1868, p. 3.

31. Hanham, *Elections and Party Management*, pp. 303–8; *The Times*, 23 November 1868, p. 7; *Dublin Review*, n.s. 14 (1870): 278. See also J. C. Lowe, "The Tory Triumph of 1868 in Blackburn and Lancashire," *Historical Journal* 16 (1973): 738–43.

32. H. O. Papers, ff. 60a–62; *Hansard*, 3d ser., vol. 195 (1869), col. 760; vol. 198 (1869), col. 614.

33. *Daily News*, 2 March 1870, p. 5.

34. *Hansard*, 3d ser., vol. 198 (1869), cols. 594–97. For Roebuck's career as a Radical M.P., see Asa Briggs, *Victorian People* (Chicago, 1955), chap. 3.

35. *Hansard*, 3d ser., vol. 198 (1869), cols. 596, 601, 610. Newdegate was consistent on such matters. Less than two weeks later, when Bruce defended his habitual-criminals bill, Newdegate took strong exception to the clause permitting a police officer to arrest without warrant any ex-convict whom he "had reason to believe" was securing a livelihood by dishonest means. Newdegate deplored the unconstitutional manner in which the measure "would deprive these criminals of the primary right of every Englishman that he should be held to be innocent until he had been proved guilty" (col. 1267). The measure, slightly amended, passed all the same. See W. L. Burn, *The Age of Equipoise* (London, 1964), pp. 191–94.

36. *Hansard*, 3d ser., vol. 198 (1869), cols. 626–27.

37. *Hansard*, 3d ser., vol. 198 (1869), cols. 613–18, 630–32.

38. Matthew Arnold, *Culture and Anarchy*, ed. J. Dover Wilson (Cambridge, 1960), p. 79.

39. *The Times*, 20 June 1867, p. 10; *Daily News*, 2 March 1870, p. 5.

40. *The Times*, 24 October 1868, p. 5.

41. Donald Richter makes a persuasive case for that thesis in "The Struggle for Hyde Park in the 1860's," *Research Studies* 42 (1974): 246–56.

42. In the words of William Temple, archbishop of Canterbury (1942–1944), "Order is to be valued on the basis of freedom; only in a well ordered society are the members of society really free"; *Christianity and the Social Order* (London, 1942), p. 60.

43. H. O. Papers, f. 64. *The Times*, 7 April 1870, p. 5; 8 April 1870, p. 12; 11 April 1870, p. 10; 19 April 1870, p. 10.

44. *Pall Mall Gazette*, 13 April 1870, p. 3.

45. *Monthly Record* 1 (1871): 67–69, 87, 90, 126, 189; 2 (1872): 49–52.

46. George Mackey's *In Memoriam* goes on for forty-four lines more; *Monthly Record* 2 (1872): 79.

47. *The Irishman*, 21 October 1871, cited in *Monthly Record* 1 (1871): 180; Timothy Michael Healy, *Letters and Leaders of My Day* (London, 1928), 1:24.

48. *Daily News,* 14 March 1872, p. 5.

49. Letter of 2 April 1872 printed in *Monthly Record* 2 (1872): 67.

Notes to Chapter 8

1. *The Great Convent Case: Saurin v. Star and Kennedy,* with a preface by James Grant (London, 1869), pp. 10, 22; *The Times,* 4 February 1869, p. 10.

2. *Great Convent Case,* pp. 26, 94, 151, 157; *The Times,* 4 February 1869, p. 10; *Illustrated Weekly News,* 2 February 1869, p. 964. The "Duke" in Coleridge's name was a middle name rather than a title.

3. *The Times,* 16 February 1869, p. 10.

4. *Great Convent Case,* p. 12.

5. Ibid., pp. 21, 29.

6. *The Times,* 4 February 1869, p. 10.

7. *Great Convent Case,* pp. 6–10, 14, 16, 19–20.

8. *The Times,* 22 February 1869, p. 10; *Great Convent Case,* p. 121.

9. *The Times,* 4 February 1869, p. 10; *Great Convent Case,* p. 68.

10. *The Times,* 10 February 1869, p. 7.

11. *The Times,* 11 February 1869, p. 10.

12. *Great Convent Case,* pp. 46–47.

13. Ibid., pp. 48–50. The "Mrs." in the names of Mrs. Star and Mrs. Kennedy was a token of social, rather than marital, status. Neither had ever been married.

14. Ibid., pp. 53, 84.

15. Ibid., p. 112.

16. Ibid., pp. 16, 42, 63; *The Times,* 12 February 1869, p. 10.

17. *Great Convent Case,* pp. 87, 101, 113; *The Times,* 11 February 1869, p. 10; 9 February 1869, p. 10; 17 February 1869, p. 11.

18. *The Times,* 11 February 1869, p. 10; 17 February 1869, p. 11.

19. *Great Convent Case,* pp. 60, 71, 53, 55; *The Times,* 11 February 1869, p. 10.

20. *Great Convent Case,* pp. 20, 85; *The Times,* 13 February 1869, p. 10.

21. *The Times,* 16 February 1869, p. 10.

22. *Great Convent Case,* p. 115; *The Times,* 16 February 1869, p. 10.

23. *Great Convent Case,* p. 119.

24. *The Times,* 22 February 1869, p. 10; 9 February 1869, p. 11; *Great Convent Case,* pp. 121–27.

25. *The Times,* 23 February 1869, p. 11.

26. *The Times,* 22 February 1869, pp. 10–11; 18 February 1869, p. 11.

27. *Great Convent Case,* pp. 137–46.

28. Ibid., pp. 147–56.

29. Ibid., pp. 157–66.

30. Ibid., pp. 167–70.

31. Ibid., pp. 170–71.

32. Cited in *Public Opinion,* 6 March 1869, p. 287.

33. *The Times,* 27 February 1869, p. 9. When one considers that the total legal cost of Miss Saurin's case was twelve thousand pounds, the five-hundred-pound award was indeed "prosaic"; *Public Opinion,* 27 March 1869, p. 390.

34. Cited in *Public Opinion,* 6 March 1869, p. 284.

35. *Punch,* 20 February 1869, p. 70.

36. *Punch,* 6 March 1869, p. 94.

37. *Great Convent Case,* pp. 1–2.

Notes to Chapter 9

1. The story is told in authoritative detail in P. M. H. Bell, *Disestablishment in Ireland and Wales* (London, 1969).

2. *Hansard*, 3d ser., vol. 196 (1869), col. 284.

3. *Hansard*, 3d ser., vol. 195 (1869), cols. 1117–18, 1596; vol. 196 (1869), col. 763; vol. 198 (1869), col. 624.

4. *Hansard*, 3d ser., vol. 195 (1869), col. 848.

5. W. F. Monypenny and G. E. Buckle, *The Life of Benjamin Disraeli, Earl of Beaconsfield*, 6 vols. (London, 1910–1920), 5:105; *Osservatore Romano* cited in *Public Opinion*, 12 June 1869, p. 750.

6. *Hansard*, 3d ser., vol. 195 (1869), col. 866.

7. *Hansard*, 3d ser., vol. 196 (1869), cols. 109, 118; William Jeans, *Parliamentary Reminiscences* (London, 1912), p. 92; [Henry W. Lucy], *Men and Manners in Parliament* (London, 1874), p. 204.

8. *Nuneaton Chronicle*, 15 April 1887. Newdegate's promise is cited in his mother's diary (entry for 26 April 1846) in Charles Newdigate Newdegate Papers, CR 1841/36, Warwickshire Record Office.

9. *Spectator* cited in *Public Opinion*, 8 May 1869, p. 570; Newdegate Papers, CR 136/B51.

10. *Hansard*, 3d ser., vol. 196 (1869), cols. 118–20. In 1875, when the House of Commons debated the suggestion that it appoint official parliamentary reporters, Disraeli agreed that men like Newdegate sought "a Speech Preservation Act"; Henry W. Lucy, *A Diary of Two Parliaments*, 2 vols. (London, 1885), 1:88. The Catholic *Weekly Register* of 19 June 1869 took pride in the fact that "there is not in London a single newspaper of which some of the leading reporters, and one or more of the chief persons on its staff are not Catholics." The Protestant Educational Institute offered courses in shorthand as well as Protestant theology in order to provide journalistic competition. See *Transactions of the Protestant Educational Institute* (London, 1872), p. 65.

11. *Hansard*, 3d ser., vol. 181 (1866), col. 1730; vol. 183 (1866), col. 625; vol. 192 (1868), col. 1808.

12. Newdegate Papers, box B32.

13. *Hansard*, 3d ser., vol. 194 (1869), cols. 384–99.

14. *Hansard*, 3d ser., vol. 198 (1869), cols. 1014, 1032.

15. *Hansard*, 3d ser., vol. 200 (1870), col. 872.

16. *Hansard*, 3d ser., vol. 200 (1870), cols. 872–94.

17. See "The Convent Committee," *Dublin Review*, n.s. 15 (October 1870):274.

18. Ernest Hartley Coleridge, *Life and Correspondence of John Duke Lord Coleridge*, 2 vols. (London, 1904), 2:147–48; *The Times*, 30 March 1870, p. 9.

19. *Hansard*, 3d ser., vol. 200 (1870), cols. 895–98.

20. *Hansard*, 3d ser., vol. 200 (1870), cols. 898–901.

21. Dom Edward Cruise, "The Development of the Religious Orders," in *The English Catholics, 1850–1950*, ed. George A. Beck (London, 1950), p. 446.

22. *Hansard*, 3d ser., vol. 200 (1870), cols. 905–6.

23. *Report of the Select Committee on Parliamentary Petitions, 1865–1875*, British Library State Paper Room: (1865), p. 716, appendix, p. 3; (1868–1869), p. 1098, appendix, pp. 129, 225, 580, 686, 779; (1870), p. 1152, appendix, p. 292. (Hereafter cited as *Select Committee on Petitions* with year.)

24. The party affiliation figures are derived from a comparison of the names cited in the *Division Lists* with the party preferences expressed in *Dod's Par-*

liamentary Companion for 1869 (London, 1869).

25. *The Times*, 30 March 1870, p. 10; *Spectator* cited in *Dublin Review*, n.s. 15 (October 1870):277.

26. The subject is explored by Susan P. Casteras in "Virgin Vows: The Early Victorian Artists' Portrayal of Nuns and Novices," *Victorian Studies* 24, no. 2 (Winter 1981): 157–84.

27. John Nicholas Murphy, *Terra Incognita: The Convents of the United Kingdom* (London, 1873), p. 2.

28. Rev. Herbert Thurston, S. J., *The Immuring of Nuns*, vol. 5 of *Historical Papers*, ed. the Reverend John Morris, S. J. (London, 1892), pp. 1–7. The references are to Sir Walter Scott's *Marmion*, canto 2, and to Elizabeth Barrett Browning's *Lay of the Brown Rosary*.

29. See, for example, *The Times*, 30 March 1870, p. 9; *Daily Telegraph*, 31 March 1870, p. 4.

30. Cited in *Public Opinion*, 7 August 1869, p. 175; 28 August 1869, p. 270.

31. J. R. Digby Beste, *Now-a-days; or, Courts and Courtiers at Home and Abroad* (London, 1870), cited in *Annual Register for 1870*, pt. 2, pp. 322–23.

32. William Hogan, *Auricular Confession and Nunneries* (London, 1869), pp. 9–13.

33. J. Mordaunt Crook cited in David Cannadine, "Aristocratic Indebtedness in the Nineteenth Century: The Case Re-opened," *Economic History Review* 30, no. 4 (November 1977): 640.

34. The most detailed account and the quotations from Bute and from the *Daily News* may be found in Sir David Hunter Blair, *John Patrick, 3rd Marquess of Bute, K.T., a Memoir* (New York, 1921), pp. 40, 80, and passim. *The Times* is cited in *Public Opinion*, 16 January 1869, p. 79; the *Tablet* is cited in George Scott-Moncrieff, *The Mirror and the Cross: Scotland and the Catholic Faith* (London, 1960), p. 146.

35. Monypenny and Buckle, *Life of Disraeli*, 5:5–10, 151–52; Margaret M. Maison, *The Victorian Vision: Studies in the Religious Novel* (New York, 1961), pp. 63–64; John P. Rossi, "Lord Ripon's Resumption of Political Activity, 1878–1880," *Recusant History* 11, no. 2 (April 1971): 63.

36. So argues Nils Clausson in "English Catholics and Roman Catholicism in Disraeli's Novels," *Nineteenth-Century Fiction* 33 (March 1979): 454–74. The earlier quotations are derived from E. L. Woodward, *The Age of Reform* (Oxford, 1938), p. 184, and from *Public Opinion*, 7 May 1870, pp. 569, 570 (citing the *Morning Post* and the *Daily Telegraph*). See *Annual Register for 1870*, pt. 2, p. 348, and David Painting, "Disraeli and the Roman Catholic Church," *Quarterly Review* 304 (January 1966): 17–25.

37. *Spectator* cited in *Dublin Review* n.s. 15 (October 1870): 289; M. D. Stephen, "Liberty, Church and State: Gladstone's Relations with Manning and Acton, 1832–1870," *Journal of Religious History* 1, no. 4 (December 1961): 218. The most complete account in English is Dom Cuthbert Butler, *The Vatican Council*, 2 vols. (London, 1930). In *Pius IX and the Politics of Persuasion* (New York, 1981), August Bernhard Hasler employs hitherto inaccessible Vatican archives to demonstrate how fiercely the opponents of the doctrine of infallibility fought their battle and how grimly determined Pius IX was to secure the assent of the assembled bishops.

38. The Papers of Lord John (First Earl) Russell, PRO 30/22/16F, f. 1959 (January 1869), Public Record Office, London. Much of Odo Russell's correspondence has been reprinted in Noel Blakiston, ed., *The Roman Question: Extracts from the Despatches of Odo Russell from Rome, 1858–1870* (London, 1962).

39. *Spectator* cited in *Public Opinion*, 23 July 1870, p. 87; *The Times*, 18 April 1871, p. 9.

40. *The Times*, 15 November 1869, p. 7. See also Stephen, "Liberty, Church and State," p. 218. In *The English Bishops and the First Vatican Council* (Louvain, 1971), Frederick J. Cwiekowski has demonstrated that Manning successfully concealed a considerable divergence of attitudes among the English bishops.

41. *The Times*, 7 February 1870, p. 9; the Papers of Archibald Campbell Tait, Archbishop of Canterbury, vol. 167, item 49; vol. 171, item 069, Lambeth Palace Library, London. The archbishop ultimately limited himself to a "Discourse on Papal Infallibility."

42. *Hansard*, 3d ser., vol. 195 (1869), col. 862.

43. Lord Edmond Fitzmaurice, *The Life of Granville George Leveson Gower Second Earl Granville*, 2 vols. (London, 1905), 2:17.

44. William Ewart Gladstone Papers, Add Mss. no. 44426, f. 7, British Library.

45. Cited in *Public Opinion*, 25 March 1871, p. 349.

46. Gladstone Papers, Add Mss. no. 44426, f. 178.

47. Gladstone Papers, Add Mss. no. 44426, f. 51. Gladstone's letter to Manning is reprinted in John Morley, *Life of Gladstone*, 3 vols. (London, 1903), 2:509; Edmund Sheridan Purcell, *The Life of Cardinal Manning*, 2 vols. (London, 1896), 2:442, 472; Arthur Wollaston Hutton, *Cardinal Manning* (London, 1892), pp. 135–43; Sir John Leslie, *Henry Edward Manning* (London, 1921), p. 224.

48. Henry Austin Bruce, *Letters of the Rt. Hon. Henry Austin Bruce, G.C.B., Lord Aberdare of Duffryn*, 2 vols. (Oxford, 1902), 1:278; Roger Fulford, ed., *Your Dear Letter: Private Correspondence of Queen Victoria and the Crown Princess of Prussia, 1865–1871* (New York, 1971), pp. 147–48, 241, 246, 247.

49. Cited in *Public Opinion*, 21 August 1869, p. 239.

50. *The Times*, 11 April 1864, pp. 8–9; 30 March 1870, p. 10; 11 April 1870, p. 9.

51. *Daily News*, 30 March 1870, p. 5; 21 April 1870, p. 4.

52. *Daily Telegraph* cited in *Public Opinion*, 13 February 1869, p. 194; 31 March 1870, p. 4.

53. Cited in *Church Opinion*, 2 April 1870, p. 318; *Daily Telegraph*, 9 February 1869, cited in *Public Opinion*, 13 February 1869, p. 194.

54. Cited in *Dublin Review*, n.s. 15 (October 1870): 279.

Notes to Chapter 10

1. William Ewart Gladstone Papers, Add Mss. no. 44426, f. 152, British Library.

2. *The Times*, 11 April 1870, p. 11.

3. *The Times*, 6 April 1870, p. 5.

4. *Daily News*, 20 April 1870, p. 2.

5. *The Times*, 12 April 1870, p. 12.

6. See, for example, Dom Cuthbert Butler, *The Life and Times of Bishop Ullathorne, 1806–1889*, 2 vols. (London, 1926), 2:173.

7. *Dublin Review*, n.s. 15 (October 1870): 275, 280, 285–86.

8. Father M. Gavin, S.J., *Memoirs of Father P. Gallwey, S.J.* (London, 1913), pp. 15, 59, 151, 198, 231, and passim; Percy Fitzgerald, *Fifty Years of Catholic Life*, 2 vols. (London, 1901), 2:10, 12, 16.

9. Father [Peter] Gallwey, S.J., *The Committee on Convents—The Nun's Choice: Newgate or Newdegate* (London, 1870).

10. Gavin, *Gallwey*, pp. 16, 198.

11. Odo Russell to Gladstone, 15 May 1870, and Manning to Russell, 15 May 1870, Gladstone Papers, Add Mss. no. 44426, ff. 222, 224.

12. *The Times*, 9 April 1870, p. 12; *Hansard*, 3d ser., vol. 200 (1870), cols. 2027–28.

13. *The Times*, 11 April 1870, p. 9; *Select Committee on Petitions* (1870), pp. 297–305, 1152, appendix, pp. liv, 51.

14. The estimate is Manning's; Gladstone Papers, Add Mss. no. 44426, f. 226.

15. *Select Committee on Petitions* (1870), pp. 336, 379–80, 420–43, 1152, appendix, pp. liv, 188.

16. *The Times*, 12 April 1870, p. 12.

17. Cited in *Church Opinion*, 12 April 1870, p. 343.

18. *Morning Post*, 11 April 1870, p. 4.

19. *Standard*, 11 April 1870, p. 4. *The Times*, 11 April 1870, p. 9; 13 April 1870, p. 9.

20. *Daily News*, 21 April 1870, p. 4; *Pall Mall Gazette* cited in *Church Opinion*, 30 April 1870, p. 116; *Standard* cited in *Pall Mall Gazette*, 12 April 1870, p. 5.

21. *Illustrated Times* 16 (7 May 1870): 294.

22. *Hansard*, 3d ser., vol. 200 (1870), cols. 1588, 2026.

23. *Hansard*, 3d ser., vol. 200 (1870), cols. 1588–95.

24. *Hansard*, 3d ser., vol. 200 (1870), cols. 1596–98.

25. *Hansard*, 3d ser., vol. 200 (1870), cols. 2025–33.

26. Gladstone Papers, Add Mss. no. 44426, ff. 84–86.

27. Gladstone Papers, Add Mss. no. 44426, ff. 92, 197.

28. Gladstone Papers, Add Mss. no. 44426, f. 152.

29. *The Times*, 11 April 1870, p. 9.

30. Gladstone Papers, Add Mss. no. 44426, ff. 43–44, 123–26, 188.

31. *Hansard*, 3d ser., vol. 201 (1870), cols. 66–73, 76–80; *Dublin Review*, n.s. 15 (October 1870): 273.

32. *Hansard*, 3d ser., vol. 201 (1870), cols. 80–83.

33. *The Times*, 3 May 1870, p. 9. *Church Opinion*, 7 May 1870, p. 136; 14 May 1870, p. 145. *Record* cited in *Public Opinion*, 7 May 1870, p. 573.

34. *Illustrated Times*, 16 (7 May 1870): 294.

35. *Hansard*, 3d ser., vol. 201 (1870), col. 529; *Dod's Parliamentary Companion for 1869* (London, 1869).

36. H. Leonards to Newdegate, 10 August 1870, in Charles Newdigate Newdegate Papers, CR 136/B51, Warwickshire Record Office; *Vanity Fair* 3 (13 August 1870): 65.

Notes to Chapter 11

1. *Hansard*, 3d ser., vol. 205 (1871), col. 198; see also vol. 216 (1873), col. 1669, and vol. 228 (1876), col. 985.

2. *Hansard*, 3d ser., vol. 216 (1873), col. 1679.

3. *Parliamentary Papers* (1870), 7:iv–x.

4. Ibid., pp. 15–19, 26; W. S. Holdsworth, *A History of English Law* (London, 1924–1958), 8:412–13.

5. *Parliamentary Papers* (1870), 7:13–26, 193.

6. Ibid., pp. 26–30, 45–48.

7. Ibid., pp. 33–42.

8. Ibid., pp. 71–77.

9. Ibid., pp. 80–91.

10. Ibid., pp. 84–85.

11. Ibid., pp. 93–95, 174.

12. According to John Nicholas Murphy, the Sisters of Notre Dame were especially concerned with the education of poor girls, the Ursulines with the training of young ladies, the Sisters of Charity of Saint Vincent de Paul with hospital work, and the nuns of the Good Shepherd with the reclamation of fallen women; *Terra Incognita: The Convents of the United Kingdom* (London, 1873). For several centuries the Catholic church had formally prohibited noncontemplative female religious orders; only in the early nineteenth century did they become canonical. See Anthony Fahey, "Female Asceticism in the Catholic Church: A Case Study of Nuns in Ireland in the Nineteenth Century" (Ph.D. diss., University of Illinois at Urbana–Champaign, 1982), chap. 3.

13. *Parliamentary Papers* (1870), 7:55, 64; "The Convent Committee," *Dublin Review*, n.s. 15 (October 1870): 283.

14. Owen Chadwick, *The Victorian Church* (London, 1966–1970), 1:505–6.

15. *Parliamentary Papers* (1870), 7:64; *Illustrated Times* 16 (30 April 1870): 274; *Dublin Review*, n.s. 15 (October 1870): 297. According to Murphy (*Terra Incognita*, p. 391), a lady who became a nun was expected to bring a dower of at least six hundred pounds. At 5 percent interest, this sum would yield an income of thirty pounds a year, a sum deemed adequate to pay for her food, clothing, and other requisites.

16. *Parliamentary Papers* (1870), 7:52–55, 58–68.

17. Ibid., p. 132.

18. Ibid., pp. 192–96.

19. Ibid., pp. 6–10, 158–68.

20. Ibid., pp. 117–27.

21. Ibid., pp. 134–37, 149.

22. *Hansard*, 3d ser., vol. 205 (1871), col. 200.

23. *Dublin Review*, n.s. 15 (October 1870): 294.

24. See *The Conspirators' Schemes* (London, 1870), pp. 8–9.

25. *Parliamentary Papers* (1870), 7:viii; A. M. Allchin, *The Silent Rebellion: Anglican Religious Communities, 1845–1900* (London, 1958), pp. 176–80. All the Anglican communities are enumerated in Peter F. Anson, *The Call of the Cloister* (London, 1955).

26. *Parliamentary Papers* (1870), 7:183–86, 191, 201–6; Chadwick, *Victorian Church*, 1:507, 510.

27. *Hansard*, 3d ser., vol. 201 (1870), col. 1244.

28. Cited in *Public Opinion*, 22 October 1870, p. 526.

29. Cited in *Church Opinion*, 4 March 1871, p. 21.

30. *Hansard*, 3d ser., vol. 204 (1871), cols. 646–54.

31. *Standard* (London) cited in *Public Opinion*, 28 January 1871, p. 93; *Hansard*, 3d ser., vol. 210 (1872), col. 812; vol. 213 (1872), cols. 538–41, 425–38; vol. 214 (1873), col. 447.

32. William Ewart Gladstone, *Gleanings of Past Years*, 7 vols. (London, 1879), 3:217.

33. *Hansard*, 3d ser., vol. 204 (1871), cols. 274, 798–808; vol. 202 (1870), col. 1472; *Weekly Register*, 15 July 1871, p. 24.

34. *Hansard*, 3d ser., vol. 205 (1871), cols. 179–96.

35. *Hansard*, 3d ser., vol. 205 (1871), cols. 197–203, 259; vol. 206 (1871), col. 2044; *Parliamentary Papers* (1871), 7:ii.

36. *Hansard*, 3d ser., vol. 210 (1872), col. 1702.

37. *Parliamentary Papers* (1871), 7:ii, ix.

38. *Hansard*, 3d ser., vol. 204 (1871), col. 788.

39. See, for example, *Hansard*, vol. 205 (1871), col. 199; vol. 216 (1873), col. 1670.

40. *Parliamentary Papers* (1871), 7:iii–xv.

41. *The Times*, 29 June 1871, p. 9.

42. *Saturday Review*, 1 July 1871, p. 9.

43. *Globe*, 3 May 1870, cited in *Public Opinion*, 7 May 1870, p. 573; *St. James's Chronicle* cited in *Church Opinion*, 8 July 1871, p. 309.

44. Cited in *Catholic Opinion*, 8 April 1871, p. 26.

45. Murphy, *Terra Incognita*, p. 384; *Law Quarterly Review* 63 (October 1947): 424; *Weekly Register*, 29 July 1871, p. 59.

Notes to Chapter 12

1. *Hansard*, 3d ser., vol. 200 (1870), col. 1408.

2. *The Times*, 11 April 1887, p. 7.

3. Cited in *English Churchman and St. James's Chronicle*, 21 April 1887 (clipping in Charles Newdigate Newdegate Papers, box D3, Warwickshire Record Office). See also *The Times*, 11 April 1887, p. 7.

4. *Spectator*, 12 March 1870, p. 320.

5. *Daily News* cited in *Coventry Herald and Free Press*, 15 April 1887, p. 7.

6. Cited in Henry W. Lucy, *A Diary of Two Parliaments*, 2 vols. (London, 1885), 1:17.

7. *Hansard*, 3d ser., vol. 212 (1872), col. 1271.

8. William White, *The Inner Life of the House of Commons*, 2 vols. (London, 1897), 2:113; Newdegate to Granville, 1869 (copy), Newdegate Papers, B6366.

9. *Vanity Fair* 3 (13 August 1870): 65.

10. Lucy, *Diary*, 1:79, 409. See also [Henry W. Lucy], *Men and Manners in Parliament* (London, 1874), pp. 202–3; *Coventry Herald and Free Press*, 15 April 1887, p. 7.

11. Sir John Robinson, *Fifty Years of Fleet Street* (London, 1904), p. 90; Lucy, *Diary*, 1:186, 409–10.

12. *Midland Counties Herald*, 18 February 1886 (clipping in Newdegate Papers, B52).

13. *Hansard*, 3d ser., vol. 220 (1874), col. 1657; see also vol. 221 (1874), col. 1050.

14. *Hansard*, 3d ser., vol. 186 (1867), col. 260; see also vol. 208 (1871), col. 257.

15. *Hansard*, vol. 223 (1875), cols. 1400–1402; vol. 215 (1873), col. 211. The resolution of the church-rate controversy is recounted in G. I. T. Machin, *Politics and the Churches in Great Britain, 1832–1868* (Oxford, 1977), pp. 343–55.

16. *Hansard*, 3d ser., vol. 215 (1873), col. 208.

17. *Hansard*, 3d ser., vol. 215 (1873), col. 210.

18. Protestant Educational Institute, *Transactions of the Protestant Educational Institute* (London, 1872), pp. 3–6, 29–30.

19. *Hansard*, 3d ser., vol. 216 (1873), col. 1531; vol. 218 (1874), cols. 125, 130; Newdegate Papers, B6611.

20. *Hansard*, 3d ser., vol. 228 (1876), cols. 1696–1700, 1739. For the wider context, see Constance Rover, *Women's Suffrage and Party Politics in Britain, 1866–1914* (London, 1967), and Walter L. Arnstein, "Votes for Women: Myths and Reality," *History Today* 18, no. 8 (August 1968): 531–39.

21. *Hansard*, 3d ser., vol. 206 (1871), col. 118; VOL. 219 (1874), col. 224; Justin McCarthy, *A History of Our Own Times*, 3 vols.(London, 1880), 3:369.

22. *The Reverend Dr. Manning and Mr. Newdegate, M.P.* (London, 1873); see

also *The Times*, 30 October 1873, p. 7; Newdegate Papers, box 54.

23. *Hansard*, 3d ser., vol. 210 (1872), cols. 1760–67.

24. *Hansard*, 3d ser., vol. 210 (1872), col. 1780.

25. *Hansard*, 3d ser., vol. 210 (1872), cols. 1768–72.

26. *Hansard*, 3d ser., vol. 210 (1872), col. 1776.

27. *Hansard*, 3d ser., vol. 210 (1872), cols. 1786–90.

28. *Hansard*, 3d ser., vol. 210 (1872), cols. 1793–96; Henry Austin Bruce, *Letters of the Rt. Hon. Henry Austin Bruce, G.C.B., Lord Aberdare of Duffryn*, 2 vols. (Oxford, 1902), 1:341.

29. *Hansard*, 3d ser., vol. 211 (1872), cols. 281, 288.

30. *Hansard*, 3d ser., vol. 210 (1872), cols. 1690–1701; *Select Committee on Petitions* (1872), p. 1469.

31. *Hansard*, 3d ser., vol. 210 (1872), cols. 1708–9.

32. *Hansard*, 3d ser., vol. 210 (1872), cols. 1704–9.

33. [Charles N. Newdegate], *Public Meeting in the Kinnaird Hall, Dundee, on Thursday, 28th November 1872* (London, 1872).

34. *Hansard*, 3d ser., vol. 214 (1873), col. 526; vol. 216 (1873), cols. 1650–68.

35. *Hansard*, 3d ser., vol. 216 (1873), cols. 1668–76, 1679–80, 1684.

36. *Hansard*, 3d ser., vol. 216 (1873), cols. 1677–78, 1681–82.

37. *Hansard*, 3d ser., vol. 216 (1873), cols. 1684–85.

38. *The Times*, 3 July 1873, p. 11.

Notes to Chapter 13

1. J. M. Capes, "The Jesuits in England," *Contemporary Review* 21 (December 1872): 27–28.

2. G. E. Buckle, ed., *The Letters of Queen Victoria*, 2d ser., 2 vols. (London, 1926–1928), 2:290.

3. Geoffrey F. A. Best, "Popular Protestantism in Victorian Britain," in *Ideas and Institutions of Victorian Britain*, ed. Robert Robson (London, 1967), p. 137.

4. *Hansard*, 3d ser., vol. 216 (1873), col. 1683.

5. *Monthly Record*, March 1872, cited in H. J. Hanham, *Elections and Party Management: Politics in the Time of Disraeli and Gladstone* (London, 1959), p. 305.

6. *Warwick Advertiser*, 7 February 1874.

7. Henry W. Lucy, *A Diary of Two Parliaments*, 2 vols. (London, 1885), 1:3.

8. Cited in Lord Edmond Fitzmaurice, *The Life of Granville George Leveson Gower Second Earl Granville*, 2 vols. (London, 1905), 2:134.

9. *Hansard*, 3d ser., vol. 218 (1874), col. 288; the Papers of Benjamin Disraeli, First Earl of Beaconsfield, B/XXI/N/154, Hughenden Manor, High Wycombe.

10. *Hansard*, 3d ser., vol. 219 (1874), cols. 1298–1301.

11. *Punch*, 20 June 1874, pp. 256–57.

12. *Hansard*, 3d ser., vol 219 (1874), cols. 1498–1519.

13. *Hansard*, 3d ser., vol 219 (1874), cols. 1519–20.

14. *Select Committee on Petitions* (1874), p. 990.

15. *Hansard*, 3d ser., vol. 219 (1874), col. 1512.

16. *Public Opinion*, 18 July 1874, p. 70.

17. *Public Opinion*, 11 July 1874, pp. 38–39.

18. *Public Opinion*, 25 July 1874, p. 103; 18 July 1874, p. 71.

19. *Hansard*, 3d ser, vol. 221 (1874) col. 832.

20. Cited in *Annual Register for 1874*, pt. 1, p. 67.

21. Cited in *Public Opinion*, 1 August 1874, p. 142.

22. Buckle, ed., *Letters of Victoria*, 2:291, 351.

23. Ibid., p. 309. Peter T. Marsh discusses the subject with admirable clarity in *The Victorian Church in Decline: Archbishop Tait and the Church of England, 1868–1882* (London, 1969), pp. 158–92. It is taken up in even greater detail in James Bentley, *Ritualism and Politics in Victorian Britain: The Attempt to Legislate for Belief* (London, 1978).

24. *Annual Register for 1874*, pt. 1, pp. 79–89. The phrase "to put down ritualism" afterward did Disraeli considerable political damage. See T. E. Kebbel, *Lord Beaconsfield and Other Tory Memories* (London, 1907), p. 51, and Richard Assheton Cross, *A Political History* (London, 1903), p. 30.

25. *Annual Register for 1874*, pt. 1, p. 88.

26. *Hansard*, 3d ser., vol. 221 (1874), col. 1168; Lucy, *Diary*, 1:33.

27. Buckle, ed., *Letters of Victoria*, 2:348.

28. Cited in *Public Opinion*, 3 October 1874, p. 430; 25 July 1874, p. 90.

29. Lucien Wolf, *Life of the First Marquess of Ripon*, 2 vols. (London, 1921), vol. 1, and entry for Ripon in *Dictionary of National Biography, Supplement, 1901–1910* (London, 1912), 3:216–21.

30. *The Times*, 5 September 1874, p. 9.

31. Cited in *Public Opinion*, 12 September 1874, p. 314.

32. Cited in *Public Opinion*, 19 September 1874, p. 353.

33. Cited in *Public Opinion*, 12 September 1874, p. 314; 19 September 1874, p. 353.

34. John P. Rossi, "Lord Ripon's Resumption of Political Activity, 1878–1880," *Recusant History* 11, no. 2 (April 1971): 62 and passim; Wolf, *Ripon*, pp. 286–93.

35. Cited in *Annual Register for 1874*, pt. 1, p. 6.

36. Cited in ibid., p. 207.

37. Cited in Francis B. Arlinghaus, "The Kulturkampf and European Diplomacy, 1871–1875," *Catholic Historical Review* 28 (October 1942): 354.

38. Bismarck cited in Johannes Hohlfeld, ed., *Documente der deutschen Politik von 1848 bis zur Gegenwart* (Berlin, 1951), 1:336. See also *New Cambridge Modern History* (Cambridge, 1962), 11:288; *Annual Register for 1873*, pt. 1, pp. 186, 198; *Annual Register for 1874*, pt. 1, pp. 213–14.

39. Henry Edward [Manning], *Caesarism and Ultramontanism* (London, 1873), pp. 56, 24, 35, 44, and passim.

40. *Pall Mall Gazette*, 26 December 1873, cited in *Public Opinion*, 3 January 1874, p. 2. *The Times*, 24 December 1873, p. 9.

41. The Papers of Lord John (First Earl) Russell, PRO 30/22/17a, ff. 256–60, Public Record Office, London.

42. Russell Papers, ff. 267–71; Spencer Walpole, *The Life of Lord John Russell*, 2 vols. (London, 1889), 2:446–49.

43. *Contemporary Review* 24 (October 1874): 674. The article is reprinted in William Ewart Gladstone, *Gleanings of Past Years*, 7 vols. (London, 1879), 6:108–42.

44. William Ewart Gladstone, *The Vatican Decrees in Their Bearing on Civil Allegiance: A Political Expostulation* (London, 1874), pp. 36–37.

45. See Hilary Jenkins, "The Irish Dimension of the British *Kulturkampf*: Vaticanism and Civil Allegiance, 1870–1875," *Journal of Ecclesiastical History* 30, no. 3 (July 1979): 353–77; *Hansard*, 3d ser., vol. 215 (1873), col. 2053.

46. *Pall Mall Gazette*, 14 November 1874, cited in *Public Opinion*, 21 November 1874, p. 634; *Guardian*, 9 November 1874, cited in *Public Opinion*, 14 November 1874, p. 603.

47. Cited, respectively, in *Public Opinion*, 14 November 1874, pp. 603, 602; 21 November 1874, p. 635.

48. Cited in *Public Opinion*, 14 November 1874, p. 603; 21 November 1874, p. 635.

49. Cited in *Public Opinion*, 14 November 1874, p. 606.

50. A. Tilney Bassett, ed., *Gladstone to His Wife* (London, 1936), p. 206.

51. Ibid.; John Morley, *Life of Gladstone*, 3 vols. (London, 1903), 2:516.

52. Cited in *Public Opinion*, 5 December 1874, p. 701.

53. *The Times*, 9 November 1874, p. 9.

54. Gladstone, *Vatican Decrees*, p. 60.

55. Cited in Fitzmaurice, *Granville*, 2:141, 143.

56. Cited in Jenkins, "The Irish Dimension of the British *Kulturkampf*," pp. 364ff.

57. Owen Chadwick, *The Victorian Church*, 2 vols. (London, 1966–1970), 2:418–19; Morley, *Gladstone*, 2:513; Stephen Tonsor, *Victorian Studies* 7, no. 2 (December 1963): 198. Almost two decades earlier, in an anonymous contribution to the *Quarterly Review*, Gladstone had warned both of papal provocation and of "a band of proselytes, bred in the Church of England, [who] have passed within the Papal borders, and seem to have carried with them a flame of ultramontane fanaticism" that was undermining the political loyalty of English Roman Catholics; "The Declining Efficiency of Parliament" 99 (September 1856): 568–70.

58. Gladstone, *Vatican Decrees*, p. 55, cited in Wolf, *Ripon*, 1:296.

59. Agatha Ramm, ed., *The Political Correspondence of Mr. Gladstone and Lord Granville, 1868–1876*, 2 vols. (London, 1952), 2:458. This motive is emphasized by Josef L. Altholz, "Gladstone and the Vatican Decrees," *The Historian* 25 (May 1963): 312–24. In January 1874 Manning had predicted that Europe would soon be involved in a general war that would result in the restoration of the pope's temporal power (p. 315). See also Josef L. Altholz, "The Vatican Decrees Controversy, 1874–1875," *Catholic Historical Review* 57 (1972): 598–99.

60. Cited in *Annual Register for 1874*, pt. 1, p. 105.

61. Cited in *Public Opinion*, 28 November 1874, p. 673.

62. Chadwick, *Victorian Church*, 2:419; *The Times*, 30 January 1875, p. 9.

63. Henry Edward Manning, *The Vatican Decrees in Their Bearing on Civil Allegiance* (London, 1875), pp. v, 3, 5, 177, and passim; Edmund Sheridan Purcell, *The Life of Cardinal Manning*, 2 vols. (London, 1896), 2:477–83, 487, 490.

64. *Punch*, 4 December 1875, p. 236.

65. William Ewart Gladstone Papers, Add Mss. no. 44446, f. 86, British Library.

66. Alvan Ryan, ed., *Newman and Gladstone: The Vatican Decrees* (South Bend, Ind., 1962), p. 76.

67. Ibid., pp. 123–24.

68. Gladstone Papers, Add Mss. no. 44446, f. 62. Both the introduction and many of the letters included in vol. 27 of *The Letters and Diaries of John Henry Newman*, ed. Charles Stephen Dessain and Thomas Gornall, S.J. (Oxford, 1975), deal with the controversy spawned by Gladstone's *Vatican Decrees*.

69. *The Times*, 18 January 1875, p. 9; Bassett, ed., *Gladstone to His Wife*, p. 209.

70. Cited in Fitzmaurice, *Granville*, 2:141.

71. *The Times*, 9 November 1874, p. 9.

72. Charles Newdigate Newdegate Papers, B6350, Warwickshire Record Office; Gladstone Papers, Add Mss. no. 44446, f. 146.

Notes to Chapter 14

1. *Hansard*, 3d ser., vol. 228 (1876), col. 1009.

2. *Hansard*, 3d ser., vol. 228 (1876), col. 998.

3. *Hansard*, 3d ser., vol. 223 (1875), cols. 78, 79, 1450.

4. The Papers of Benjamin Disraeli, First Earl of Beaconsfield, B/XXI/N/155, Hughenden Manor, High Wycombe.

5. Cited in Wilfrid Meynell, *Benjamin Disraeli: An Unconventional Biography* (New York, 1903), p. 141.

6. Gladstone to Newdegate, 27 April 1875, Charles Newdigate Newdegate Papers, CR 136/B51, Warwickshire Record Office.

7. *Select Committee on Petitions* (1875), p. 1129; *Hansard*, 3d ser., vol. 228 (1876), col. 999.

8. W. Gordon-Gorman, *Converts to Rome*, 4th ed. (London, 1899), p. 161.

9. *Hansard*, 3d ser., vol. 225 (1875), col. 1666; Justin McCarthy, *Portraits of the Sixties* (London, 1903), pp. 150–51.

10. *Hansard*, 3d ser., vol. 225 (1875), col. 1423.

11. *Hansard*, 3d ser., vol. 228 (1876), cols. 970–78.

12. *Hansard*, 3d ser., vol. 228 (1876), cols. 979–80.

13. *Hansard*, 3d ser., vol. 228 (1876), cols. 981–82.

14. *Hansard*, 3d ser., vol. 228 (1876), cols. 985–93, 1001.

15. *Hansard*, 3d ser., vol. 228 (1876), cols. 1003–4.

16. *Hansard*, 3d ser., vol. 228 (1876), col. 1008.

17. *Hansard*, 3d ser., vol. 228 (1876), cols. 1012–13.

18. *Hansard*, 3d ser., vol. 228 (1876), cols. 999, 996, 984, 1016.

19. *Hansard*, 3d ser., vol. 228 (1876), cols. 1017–27.

20. *Hansard*, 3d ser., vol. 228 (1876), col. 1035.

21. *Hansard*, 3d ser., vol. 228 (1876), cols. 1317, 1395–96, 1400.

22. *Hansard*, 3d ser., vol. 228 (1876), col. 1402.

23. *Hansard*, 3d ser., vol. 229 (1876), cols. 583–86.

24. Alphons Bellesheim, *A History of the Catholic Church of Scotland*, trans. D. Oswald Hunter Blair (Edinburgh, 1890), 4:312–13.

25. Cited in *Public Opinion*, 14 November 1874, p. 601.

26. Cited in Lucien Wolf, *Life of the First Marquess of Ripon*, 2 vols. (London, 1921), 1:311.

27. Cited in J. B. Conacher, ed., "A Visit to the Gladstones in 1894," *Victorian Studies* 2 (December 1958): 159.

28. Wolf, *Ripon*, 1:313; Disraeli Papers, B/XXI/N/156, 157, 62.

29. The Papers of Archibald Campbell Tait, Archbishop of Canterbury, vol. 96, f. 184, Lambeth Palace Library, London.

30. Newdegate Papers, B6410.

31. *Hansard*, 3d ser., vol. 247 (1879), col. 1539.

32. *Hansard*, 3d ser., vol. 241 (1878), col. 371.

33. *Hansard*, 3d ser., vol. 230 (1876), col. 1878; vol. 224 (1875), col. 877; vol. 221 (1874), col. 836; vol. 215 (1873), col. 474.

34. *Hansard*, 3d ser. vol. 221 (1874), col. 632; vol. 225 (1875), col. 505.

35. *Hansard*, vol. 230 (1876), col. 313.

36. The events of May and June 1880 are described in detail in Walter L. Arnstein, *The Bradlaugh Case* (Oxford, 1965), pp. 40–52, 72–82, and passim.

37. Ibid., pp. 92–95, 238–45.

38. Newdegate to Salisbury, 5 April and 22 August 1883, in Salisbury Papers, cited in ibid.. pp. 245–46.

39. Ibid., pp. 246–47.

40. See, for example, T. P. O'Connor, *Memoirs of an Old Parliamentarian*, 2 vols. (London, 1929), 1:70–71.

41. *Hansard*, 3d ser., vol. 278 (1883), cols. 1737–38.

42. *Truth*, 11 March 1880, p. 326. *Warwick Advertiser*, 2 April 1880, p. 3; 16 April 1887, p. 7.

43. *Warwick Advertiser*, 29 January 1887, p. 5.

44. *Warwick Advertiser*, 16 April 1887, p. 7.

45. *Coventry Herald and Free Press*, 15 April 1887, p. 7; *Warwick Advertiser*, 16 April 1887, p. 7.

46. *Warwick Advertiser*, 16 April 1887, p. 7; Newdegate Papers, D3.

47. Newdegate Papers, B33, B52.

48. *Warwick Advertiser*, 16 April 1887, p. 7.

49. *Warwick Advertiser*, 16 April 1887, p. 7; 23 April 1887, p. 7.

50. *The Times*, 11 April 1887, p. 7.

51. *Warwick Advertiser*,16 April 1887, p. 7.

52. *Dundee Advertiser* cited in *Coventry Herald and Free Press*, 15 April 1887, p. 7.

Notes to Chapter 15

1. G. M. Young and W. D. Hancock, eds., *English Historical Documents* (London, 1956), 12 (pt. 1): 333.

2. The theme is well stated in the three articles by Geoffrey F. A. Best cited in Chapter 1 and listed in the bibliography.

3. See S. C. Carpenter, *Church and People, 1789–1889* (London, 1933), p. 151.

4. Edwin Orr, *The Second Evangelical Awakening in Great Britain* (London, 1949).

5. John Stuart Mill, *On Liberty*, chap. 2. The passage may be found on p. 282 of Max Lerner, ed., *The Essential Works of John Stuart Mill* (New York, 1961).

6. Matthew Arnold, *Friendship's Garland* (London, 1871), p. 143.

7. See Walter L. Arnstein, "The Religious Issue in Mid-Victorian Politics: A Note on a Neglected Source," *Albion* 6, no. 2 (Summer 1974): 134–43.

8. Cited in *Church Opinion*, 21 January 1871, p. 325.

9. Albert Venn Dicey, *Law and Public Opinion in England during the Nineteenth Century* (London, 1905), p. 316.

10. Cited in *Catholic Opinion*, 7 January 1871, pp. 235, 247.

11. Gilbert A. Cahill noted two decades ago to how significant a degree the spirit of British nationalism during the 1830s and 1840s was based on anti-Catholicism and to how important an extent that spirit promoted the social stability of early Victorian England; "Irish Catholicism and English Toryism," *Review of Politics* 19 (January 1957): 62–76.

12. J. J. Dwyer, "The Catholic Press," in *The English Catholics, 1850–1950*, ed. George A. Beck (London, 1950), p. 499.

13. Charles Stephen Dessain, *John Henry Newman* (London, 1966), p. 79.

14. *Hansard*, 3d ser., vol. 219 (1874), col. 1501.

15. *Hansard*, 3d ser., vol. 228 (1876), col. 996.

16. Francesca M. Steele, *The Convents of Great Britain*(London, 1902), pp. x–xi.

17. Dom Edward Cruise, "Development of the Religious Orders," in Beck, ed., *English Catholics*, pp. 453–54.

18. W. Gordon-Gorman, *Converts to Rome*, 4th ed. (London, 1899), p. ix.

19. William Ewart Gladstone, *Gleanings of Past Years*, 7 vols. (London, 1879), 3:221.

20. William Ewart Gladstone, *The Vatican Decrees in Their Bearing on Civil Allegiance: A Political Expostulation* (London, 1874), p. 28.

21. K. S. Inglis, *Churches and the Working Classes in Victorian England* (London, 1963), pp. 122, 127.

22. Charles Booth, *The Life and Labour of the People of London*, 3d ser.: "Religious Influences" (London, 1903), 7:242–51.

23. Ibid., p. 258.

24. *Hansard*, 3d ser., vol. 201 (1870), col. 63.

25. "The Conversion of England," *Dublin Review*, 3d ser. 12 (July–October 1884): 65–86.

26. *Hansard*, 3d ser., vol. 228 (1876), col. 981.

27. Geoffrey F. A. Best, "The Protestant Constitution and Its Supporters, 1800–1829," *Transactions of the Royal Historical Society*, 5th ser. 8 (1958): 120.

28. *Statutes of the Realm*, 3d rev. ed. (London, 1950), 3:312–15.

29. An appeal by a private citizen in 1890 to have a magistrate expel a Jesuit from the country was denied by the judge; his discretionary power to deny the request was upheld by the Court of the Queen's Bench. See *Hansard*, 5th ser., vol. 200 (1926), cols. 1621–22.

30. Rev. Herbert Thurston, S. J., *The Immuring of Nuns*, vol. 5 of *Historical Papers*, ed. the Reverend John Morris, S. J. (London, 1892), p. 2.

31. *The Times*, 3 June 1886, cited in Thomas William Heyck, *The Dimensions of British Radicalism* (Urbana, Ill., 1974), p. 296.

32. Cited in Sir Charles Petrie, *The Victorians* (London, 1961), p. 97.

33. Henry Pelling, *Popular Politics and Society in Late Victorian Britain* (London, 1968), p. 30; see also Booth, *Life and Labour*, 7:252.

34. Percy Fitzgerald, *Fifty Years of Catholic Life*, 2 vols. (London, 1901), 2:389.

35. *Halsbury's Laws of England*, 3d ed. (London, 1955), 13:524; 53–54 Vict. c. 19; 51–52 Vict. c. 4.

36. *Law Quarterly Review* 36 (January 1920): 53–57.

37. *Hansard*, 5th ser., vol. 192 (1926), col. 2305.

38. *Hansard*, 5th ser., vol. 200 (1926), cols. 1602, 1619, 1622, 1630.

39. *Hansard* (Lords), 5th ser., vol. 65 (1926), cols. 1487, 1491, 1638–39.

40. *Hansard*, 5th ser., vol. 200 (1926), col. 1573.

41. *Statutes Revised*, 19:176–77; *Halsbury's Laws*, 13:40.

42. Gorden Nares, *Arbury Hall, Warwickshire* (Country Life, Ltd., 1964), pp. 16–17 and passim; James Cornford, "The Parliamentary Foundations of the Hotel Cecil," in *Ideas and Institutions of Victorian Britain*, ed. Robert Robson (London, 1967), p. 282. Newdegate had entailed the estate upon the fourth son of his first cousin Francis Newdegate, and, if the latter had no heirs, upon his eldest brother, and matters had so worked out. "But if any person who may be entitled as tenant for life or in tail," Newdegate's will went on, "shall profess or be converted to the Roman Catholic faith or religion, the devise in his favour is revoked"; *English Churchman*, 16 June 1887, p. 328.

43. See *Spectator*, 24 June 1871, pp. 761–62.

44. *Hansard*, 3d ser., vol. 240 (1878), col. 1868.

45. *Weekly Register*, 1 July 1871, p. 6.

46. *Hansard*, 3d ser., vol. 228 (1876), col. 1028.

47. See Steele, *Convents of Great Britain*, pp. 5–11 and passim.

48. Cited in Stella Margetson, *Leisure and Pleasure in the Nineteenth Century* (New York, 1969), p. 104.

49. The Papers of the First Earl of Halsbury, envelope 32, in private custody.

50. Robert Blake, *Disraeli* (London, 1966), p. 320.

51. *The Times*, 11 April 1870, p. 9.

Bibliography

Manuscript Collections

The Papers of Benjamin Disraeli, Earl of Beaconsfield. Hughenden Manor, High Wycombe.

The Papers of Sir Hugh (First Earl) Cairns. Public Record Office, London.

The Papers of the Fourteenth Earl of Derby. Utilized at Christ Church, Oxford, through the courtesy of Lord Blake.

The Papers of the First Earl of Halsbury. In private custody. The papers of Sir Hardinge Giffard, Conservative M.P., through the courtesy of the third earl of Halsbury.

The Papers of Henry Richard Harpur, Lord of the Manor of Coton Hall, Nuneaton. Northamptonshire Record Office.

William Ewart Gladstone Papers. British Library, London.

The Papers of Charles Newdigate Newdegate and related Newdegate family papers. Warwickshire Record Office, through the courtesy of F. H. M. FitzRoy Newdegate.

The Papers of Lord John (First Earl) Russell. Public Record Office, London.

The Papers of the Third Marquess of Salisbury. Utilized at Christ Church Library, Oxford, through the courtesy of the fifth marquess of Salisbury.

The Papers of Archibald Campbell Tait, Archbishop of Canterbury. Lambeth Palace Library, London.

Public Documents

England. Local Government Board. *England and Wales: Return of Owners of Land, 1873*. London, 1875.

Hansard's Parliamentary Debates 3d series. 1843–1885.

————. 5th series. 1926.

Parliamentary Papers

"Report from the Select Committee on the Law Respecting Conventual and Monastic Institutions." Vol. 7, 1870.

"Report from the Select Committee on the Law Respecting Conventual and Monastic Institutions." Vol. 7, 1871.

Home Office Papers File. Public Record Office, London.

Report of the Select Committee on Parliamentary Petitions, 1865–1875. British Library State Paper Room, London.

Statutes of the Realm. 3d rev. ed. London, 1950.

Printed Primary Sources

Anderson, David. *"Scenes" in the Commons*. London, 1884.
Arnold, Matthew. *Culture and Anarchy*. London, 1869.
————. *Friendship's Garland*. London, 1871.
Arnstein, Walter L., ed. "A German View of English Society: 1851."
    Victorian Studies 16 (December 1972): 183–204.
B., C. [Bryce, David?], ed. and trans. *The Confessional Unmasked*.
    London, 1867.
Bagehot, Walter. *The Works and Life of Walter Bagehot*. Edited by Mrs.
    Russell Barrington. 4 vols. London, 1915.
Bassett, A. Tilney, ed. *Gladstone to His Wife*. London, 1936.
Bateman, John. *The Great Landowners of Great Britain and Ireland*. 4th ed.
    London, 1883.
Blakiston, Noel, ed. *The Roman Question: Extracts from the Despatches of
    Odo Russell from Rome, 1858–1870*. London, 1962.
Booth, Charles. *The Life and Labour of the People of London*. 3d series:
    Religious Influences, vol. 7. London, 1903.
Bruce, Henry Austin. *Letters of the Rt. Hon. Henry Austin Bruce, G.C.B.,
    Lord Aberdare of Duffryn*. 2 vols. Oxford, 1902.
Buckle, G. E., ed. *The Letters of Queen Victoria*. 2d series. 2 vols. London,
    1926–1928.
Burns's Standard Reading Books. 5 vols. London, n.d.
Capes, J. M. "The Jesuits in England." *Contemporary Review* 21
    (December 1872): 27–44.
Church Association. *Church Association Lectures*. London, 1869.
Conacher, J. B., ed. "A Visit to the Gladstones in 1894." *Victorian
    Studies* 2 (December 1958):155–60.
Cross, Richard Assheton, First Viscount Cross. *A Political History*.
    London, 1903.
"The Convent Committee." *Dublin Review*, n.s. 15 (October 1870):
    271–99.
Denison, John Evelyn, Viscount Ossington. *Notes from My Journal When
    Speaker of the House of Commons*. London, 1900.
Disraeli, Benjamin. *Lord George Bentinck: A Political Biography*. London,
    1852.
Douglas, David C., gen. ed. *English Historical Documents*. Vol. 12 (pt. 1):
    1833–1874. London, 1956.
"The English Protestant Marriage Law." *Dublin Review*, n.s. 14
    (January 1870): 56–78.
Escott, T. H. S. *Gentlemen of the House of Commons*. 2 vols. London, 1902.
"The Feast of Conception." *Quarterly Review* 97 (June 1855): 143–59.
Fulford, Roger, ed. *Your Dear Letter: Private Correspondence of Queen
    Victoria and the Crown Princess of Prussia, 1865–1871*. New York, 1971.
Gallwey, Father [Peter], S.J. *The Committee on Convents—The Nun's
    Choice: Newgate or Newdegate*. London, 1870.

Gladstone, William Ewart. *Gleanings of Past Years*. 7 vols. London, 1879.
———. "Ritualism and Ritual," *Contemporary Review* 24 (October 1874): 663–81.
———. *The Vatican Decrees in Their Bearing on Civil Allegiance: A Political Expostulation*. London, 1874.
Gooch, G.P., ed. *The Later Correspondence of Lord John Russell*. 2 vols. London, 1925.
Grant, James. *The Religious Tendencies of the Times*. London, 1869.
The Great Convent Case: Saurin v. Star and Kennedy. With a preface by James Grant. London, 1869.
Hardy, Gathorne, First Earl of Cranbrook. *A Memoir*. 2 vols. London, 1910.
Healy, Timothy Michael. *Letters and Leaders of My Day*. 2 vols. London, 1928.
Hogan, William. *Auricular Confessions and Nunneries*. London, 1869.
Jeans, William. *Parliamentary Reminiscences*. London, 1912.
Lucy, Henry W. *A Diary of Two Parliaments*. 2 vols. London, 1885.
[Lucy, Henry W.] *Men and Manners in Parliament*. London, 1874.
Lumley, W. G. "The Statistics of the Roman Catholics in England and Wales." *Journal of the Statistical Society* 27 (September 1864): 303–23.
[Manning], Henry Edward. *Caesarism and Ultramontanism*. London, 1873.
Manning, Henry Edward. *Characteristics: Political, Philosophical, and Religious*. Arranged by William Samuel Lilly. London, 1885.
———. *The Rev. Dr. Manning and Mr. Newdegate, M.P.* London, 1873.
———. *Sermons on Ecclesiastical Subjects*. 3 vols. Dublin, 1863–1873.
———. *The Vatican Decrees in Their Bearing on Civil Allegiance*. London, 1875.
Mill, John Stuart. *On Liberty*. London, 1859.
Mivart, Sir George. "The Conversion of England." *Dublin Review*, 3d ser. 12 (July–October 1884): 65–86.
Murphy, John Nicholas. *Terra Incognita: The Convents of the United Kingdom*. London, 1873.
[Newdegate, Charles N.] *A Glimpse of the Great Secret Society*. 2d ed. London, 1868.
Newdegate, Charles N. *Jewish Dogmas: A Correspondence between Dr. Raphall, M.A., and C. N. Newdegate, M.P.* London, 1849.
———. *A Letter to the Rt. Hon. J.W. Henley*. 5th letter. London, 1852.
———. *Monastic and Conventual Institutions*. Edinburgh, 1866.
———. *Monastic and Conventual Institutions*. London, 1870.
———. *Public Meeting in the Kinnaird Hall, Dundee, on Thursday, 28th November 1872*. London, 1872.
———. *Speech of C. N. Newdegate, M.P., at the Annual Meeting of the Rugby and Dunchurch Agricultural Association, November 26th, 1858*. London, 1859.
———. *Two Letters to the Rt. Hon. H. Labouchere, M.P., on the Balance of Trade*. London, 1849.

Newman, John Henry. *The Letters and Diaries of John Henry Newman.*
  Edited by Charles Stephen Dessain and Thomas Gornall, S.J. Vol. 27.
  Oxford, 1975.
The Newspaper Press Directory. London, 1870.
O'Connor, T. P. *Gladstone's House of Commons.* London, 1884.
———. *Memoirs of an Old Parliamentarian.* 2 vols. London, 1929.
Potter, Rev. S. G. *Of What Religion Is Mr. Gladstone?* London, 1873.
A Protestant. *Nunneries.* London, [1852].
Protestant Educational Institute. *Transactions of the Protestant
  Educational Institute.* London, 1872.
Protestant Evangelical Mission and Electoral Union. *The Conspirators'
  Schemes.* London, 1871.
———. *The Seizure of the Confessional.* London, 1867.
Ramm, Agatha, ed. *The Political Correspondence of Mr. Gladstone and Lord
  Granville, 1868–1876.* 2 vols. London, 1952.
Ravenstein, Ernst Georg. *Denominational Statistics of England and Wales.*
  London, 1870.
"Report of H.M. Commissioners to Inquire into the Management and
  Government of the College at Maynooth." *Dublin Review* 76 (June
  1855): 461–506.
Roberts, Thomas Nicolls. *Parliamentary Buff Book.* London, 1869.
Robinson, Sir John R. *Fifty Years of Fleet Street.* London, 1904.
Ryan, Alvan, ed. *Newman and Gladstone: The Vatican Decrees.* South
  Bend, Ind., 1962.
Saunders, William. *The New Parliament, 1880.* London, [1880].
"Saurin v. Starr." *Annual Register for 1869,* pt. 2, pp. 177–218.
Stanford, Edward, ed. *Stanford's Parliamentary County Atlas.* London,
  1885.
Steele, Francesca M. *The Convents of Great Britain.* London, 1902.
[Thompson, Joseph Parish]. "Paparchy and Nationality." *British
  Quarterly Review* 61 (January 1875): 1–22.
Thurston, Rev. Herbert, S.J. *The Immuring of Nuns. Historical Papers,*
  edited by the Reverend John Morris, S.J., vol. 5. London, 1892.
Ullathorne, Archbishop [William Bernard]. *Autobiography, with
  Selections from His Letters.* London, 1891–1892.
Ullathorne, Bishop [William Bernard]. *A Plea for the Rights and Liberties of
  Religious Women with Reference to the Bill Proposed by Mr. Lacy.* London,
  1851.
Warwick, Earl of Warwick and Brooke. *Memories of Sixty Years.* London,
  1917.
White, William. *The Inner Life of the House of Commons.* London, 1897.
Whitty, Edward Michael. *The Governing Classes of Great Britain.* London,
  1854.
———. *St. Stephen's in the Fifties.* London, 1906.
Zetland, Marquis of, ed. *The Letters of Disraeli to Lady Bradford and Lady
  Chesterfield.* 2 vols. London, 1929.

Secondary Works

Akenson, Donald H. *The Irish Education Experiment*. London, 1970.
Allchin, A. M. *The Silent Rebellion: Anglican Religious Communities, 1845–1900*. London, 1858.
Altholz, Josef L. "Gladstone and the Vatican Decrees." *The Historian* 25 (May 1963): 312–24.
———. *The Liberal Catholic Movement in England*. London, 1962.
———. "The Political Behavior of English Catholics, 1850–1867." *Journal of British Studies* 4, no. 1 (November 1964): 89–103.
———. "Truth and Equivocation: Liguori's Moral Theology and Newman's Apologia." *Church History* 44, no. 1 (March 1975): 1–12.
———. "The Vatican Decrees Controversy, 1874–1875." *Catholic Historical Review* 57 (January 1972): 593–605.
———. "Writings on Victorian Catholicism, 1945–1970." *British Studies Monitor* 2, no. 3 (Spring 1972).
Anson, Peter F. *The Catholic Church in Modern Scotland, 1560–1937*. London, 1937.
Arlinghaus, Francis A. "The Kulturkampf and European Diplomacy, 1871–1875." *Catholic Historical Review* 28, no. 3 (October 1942): 340–75.
Arnstein, Walter L. *The Bradlaugh Case*. Oxford, 1965.
———. "The Religious Issue in Mid-Victorian Politics: A Note on a Neglected Source." *Albion* 6 (Summer 1974): 134–43.
———. "Votes for Women: Myths and Reality." *History Today* 18, no. 8 (August 1968): 531–39.
Balleine, George R. *A History of the Evangelical Party in the Church of England*. London, 1908.
Beck, George A., ed. *The English Catholics, 1850–1950*. London, 1950.
Bell, P. M. H. *Disestablishment in Ireland and Wales*. London, 1969.
Bellesheim, Alphons. *A History of the Catholic Church of Scotland*. Translated by D. Oswald Hunter Blair. Vol. 4. Edinburgh, 1890.
Bentley, James. *Ritualism and Politics in Victorian Britain: The Attempt to Legislate for Belief*. London, 1978.
Best, G. F. A. "The Protestant Constitution and Its Supporters, 1800–1829." *Transactions of the Royal Historical Society*, 5th ser. 8 (1958): 105–28.
———. "Popular Protestantism in Victorian Britain." *Ideas and Institutions of Victorian Britain*. Edited by Robert Robson. London, 1967.
———. "Evangelicalism and the Victorians." *The Victorian Crisis of Faith*. Edited by Anthony Symondson. London, 1970.
Billington, Ray Allen. *The Protestant Crusade, 1800–1860: A Study of the Origins of American Nativism*. New York, 1938.
Blake, Robert. *Disraeli*. London, 1966.
Bland, Sister Joan, S.N.D. "The Impact of Government on English

Catholic Education." *Catholic Historical Review* 62 (January 1976): 36–55.

Bodley, John Edward. *Cardinal Manning and Other Essays*. London, 1912.

Bossy, John. *The English Catholic Community, 1570–1850*. London, 1975.

Bowen, Desmond. *The Protestant Crusade in Ireland, 1800–1870*. London, 1978.

———. *Souperism: Myth or Reality?* Cork, 1970.

Briggs, Asa. *Victorian People*. Chicago, 1955.

———. "Thomas Atwood and the Economic Background of the Birmingham Political Union." *Cambridge Historical Journal* 11, no. 2 (1948): 190–216.

Burke, Thomas. *A Catholic History of Liverpool*. Liverpool, 1910.

Burn, W. L. *The Age of Equipoise*. London, 1964.

Butler, Dom Cuthbert. *The Life and Times of Bishop Ullathorne, 1806–1889*. 2 vols. London, 1926.

Cahill, Gilbert A. "Irish Catholicism and English Toryism." *Review of Politics* 19 (January 1957): 62–76.

———. "The Protestant Association and the Anti-Maynooth Agitation of 1845." *Catholic Historical Review* 43 (October 1957): 273–308.

Carpenter, S. C. *Church and People, 1789–1889*. London, 1933.

Casteras, Susan P. "Virgin Vows: The Early Victorian Artists' Portrayal of Nuns and Novices." *Victorian Studies* 24, no. 2 (Winter 1981): 157–84.

Chadwick, Owen. *The Victorian Church*. 2 vols. London, 1966–1970.

Clark, George Kitson. *The Making of Victorian England*. London, 1961.

Clausson, Nils. "English Catholics and Roman Catholicism in Disraeli's Novels." *Nineteenth-Century Fiction* 33 (March 1979): 454–74.

Cockshut, A. O. J. *Anglican Attitudes: A Study of Victorian Religious Controversies*. London, 1959.

Coleridge, Ernest Hartley. *Life and Correspondence of John Duke Lord Coleridge*. Vol. 2. London, 1904.

Conacher, J. B. *The Peelites and the Party System, 1846–1852*. Newton Abbot, Devon, 1972.

Cornford, James. "The Parliamentary Foundations of the Hotel Cecil." *Ideas and Institutions of Victorian Britain*. Edited by Robert Robson. London, 1967.

Cornish, Francis Warre. *The English Church in the Nineteenth Century*. 2 vols. London, 1910.

Crowther, M. A. *Church Embattled: Religious Controversy in Mid-Victorian England*. Newton Abbot, Devon, 1970.

Curtis, L. P., Jr. *Anglo-Saxons and Celts: A Study of Anti-Irish Prejudice in Victorian England*. Studies in British History and Culture, vol. 2. Bridgeport, Conn., 1968.

Cwiekowski, Frederick J. *The English Bishops and the First Vatican Council*. Louvain, 1971.

Davidson, Randall Thomas, and Benham, William. *Life of Archibald*

Campbell Tait, Archbishop of Canterbury. 2 vols. London, 1891.

Denholm, Anthony F. "The Conversion of Lord Ripon in 1874." *Recusant History* 10 (April 1969): 111–18.

Dessain, Charles Stephen. *John Henry Newman.* London, 1966.

Dictionary of National Biography (London, 1882–1900).

Donovan, Robert Kent. "The Denominational Character of English Catholic Charitable Effort, 1800–1865." *Catholic Historical Review* 62 (April 1976): 200–223.

Dyos, H. J., and Wolff, Michael, eds. *The Victorian City.* 2 vols. London, 1973.

Edwards, R. D., and Williams, T. D., eds. *The Great Famine: Studies in Irish History, 1845–1852.* New York, 1957.

Fahey, Anthony. "Female Asceticism in the Catholic Church: A Case Study of Nuns in Ireland in the Nineteenth Century." Ph.D. dissertation, University of Illinois at Urbana–Champaign, 1982.

Fitzgerald, Percy. *Father Galway: A Sketch.* London, 1906.

———. *Fifty Years of Catholic Life.* 2 vols. London, 1901.

Fitzmaurice, Lord Edmond. *The Life of Granville George Leveson Gower Second Earl Granville.* Vol. 2. London, 1905.

Fothergill, Brian. *Nicholas Wiseman.* Garden City, N.Y., 1963.

Garratt, Evelyn. *Life and Personal Recollections of Samuel Garratt.* London, 1908.

Gash, Norman. *Sir Robert Peel.* London, 1972.

Gavin, Father M., S.J. *Memoirs of Father P. Gallwey, S.J.* London, 1913.

Gilley, Sheridan. "Protestant London, No Popery, and the Irish Poor, 1830–60." *Recusant History* 10 (January 1970): 210–30; 11 (January 1971): 21–46.

Gordon-Gorman, W. *Converts to Rome.* 4th ed. London, 1899.

Grady, F. J. "The Exclusion of Catholics from the Lord Chancellorship, 1673–1954." *Recusant History* 8 (1965–1966): 166–74.

Hales, E. E. Y. *Pio Nono.* New York, 1954.

Halsbury's Laws of England. 3d ed. 43 vols. London, 1952–1964.

Handley, James Edmund. *The Irish in Modern Scotland.* Cork, 1947.

Hanham, H. J. *Elections and Party Management: Politics in the Time of Disraeli and Gladstone.* London, 1959.

Hasler, August Bernhard. *Pius IX and the Politics of Persuasion.* New York, 1981.

Hill, R. L. *Toryism and the People, 1832–1846.* London, 1929.

Holmes, J. Derek. *More Roman than Rome: English Catholicism in the Nineteenth Century.* London, 1978.

Hunter Blair, Sir David. *John Patrick, 3rd Marquess of Bute, K.T., a Memoir.* New York, 1921.

Hutton, Arthur Wollaston. *Cardinal Manning.* London, 1892.

Inglis, K. S. *Churches and the Working Classes in Victorian England.* London, 1963.

Jackson, John Archer. *The Irish in Britain.* London, 1963.

Jenkins, Hilary. "The Irish Dimension of the British *Kulturkampf*: Vaticanism and Civil Allegiance, 1870–1875." *Journal of Ecclesiastical History* 30, no. 3 (July 1979): 353–77.

Jones, Wilbur Devereux, and Erickson, Arvel B. *The Peelites, 1846–1857*. Columbus, Ohio, 1972.

Kebbel, T. E. *Lord Beaconsfield and Other Tory Memories*. London, 1907.

Klaus, Robert J. "The Pope, the Protestants, and the Irish: Papal Aggression and Anti-Catholicism in Mid-19th Century England." Ph.D. dissertation, University of Iowa, 1973.

Langford, John Alfred. *Modern Birmingham and Its Institutions*. 2 vols. Birmingham, 1877.

Larkin, Emmet. "Church, State, and Nation in Modern Ireland." *American Historical Review* 80, no. 5 (December 1975): 1244–76.

———. "The Devotional Revolution in Ireland, 1850–1875." *American Historical Review* 77, no. 3 (June 1972): 625–52.

———. *The Making of the Roman Catholic Church in Ireland, 1850–1860*. Chapel Hill, N.C., 1980.

———. *The Roman Catholic Church and the Creation of the Modern Irish State, 1878–1886*. Philadelphia, 1975.

Latourette, Kenneth Scott. *A History of the Expansion of Christianity*. Vol. 4. New York, 1941.

Lees, Lynn Hollen. *Exiles of Erin: Irish Migrants in Victorian London*. Ithaca, N.Y., 1979.

Leslie, Shane. *Henry Edward Manning*. London, 1921.

———. "Mrs. Crawford, Sir Charles Dilke, and Cardinal Manning." *Dublin Review* 241 (Autumn 1967): 177–205.

"Letters of Cardinal Wiseman with an Introduction and Commentary by Cardinal Gasquet." *Dublin Review* 164 (January 1919): 1–25.

Lowe, J. C. "The Tory Triumph of 1868 in Blackburn and Lancashire." *Historical Journal* 16 (1973): 738–43.

McCarthy, Justin. *A History of Our Own Times*. 3 vols. London, 1880.

———. *Portraits of the Sixties*. London, 1903.

McClelland, Vincent Alan. *Cardinal Manning: His Public Life and Influence, 1865–1892*. London, 1962.

———. "The Protestant Alliance and Roman Catholic Schools, 1872–74." *Victorian Studies* 8 (December 1964): 173–82.

McCord, Norman. "Cobden and Bright in Politics, 1846–1857." *Ideas and Institutions of Victorian Britain*. Edited by Robert Robson. London, 1967.

McDonnell, K. G. T. "Roman Catholics in London, 1850–1865." *Studies in London History*. London, 1969.

Machin, G. I. T. *Politics and the Churches in Great Britain, 1832–1868*. New York, 1977.

Maison, Margaret M. *The Victorian Vision: Studies in the Religious Novel*. New York, 1961.

Marsh, Peter T. *The Victorian Church in Decline: Archbishop Tait and the Church of England, 1868–1882*. London, 1969.

Mathew, David. *Lord Acton and His Times*. London, 1968.

Meynell, Wilfrid. *Benjamin Disraeli: An Unconventional Biography*. New York, 1903.

Milburn, Dennis. *Nuneaton: The Growth of a Town*. Mimeographed. Nuneaton, 1963.

Monypenny, W. F., and Buckle, G. E. *The Life of Benjamin Disraeli, Earl of Beaconsfield*. 6 vols. London, 1910–1920.

Namier, Sir Lewis, and Brooke, John. *The House of Commons, 1754–1790*. New York, 1964.

Nares, Gordon. *Arbury Hall, Warwickshire*. Country Life, Ltd., 1964.

Norman, E. R. *Anti-Catholicism in Victorian England*. Historical Problems: Studies and Documents, edited by G. R. Elton, vol. 1. New York, 1968.

———. *The Catholic Church and Ireland in the Age of Rebellion, 1859–1873*. Ithaca, N.Y., 1965.

Orr, Edwin. *The Second Evangelical Awakening in Great Britain*. London, 1949.

Painting, David. "Disraeli and the Roman Catholic Church." *Quarterly Review* 304 (January 1966): 17–25.

Ponsonby, Arthur. *Henry Ponsonby: Queen Victoria's Private Secretary*. London, 1942.

Purcell, Edmund Sheridan. *The Life of Cardinal Manning*. 2 vols. London, 1895.

Ralls, Walter. "The Papal Aggression of 1850: A Study in Victorian Anti-Catholicism." *Church History* 43, no. 2 (June 1974): 242–56.

Richter, Donald. "The Struggle for Hyde Park in the 1860's." *Research Studies* 42 (1974): 246–56.

Rossi, John P. "Lord Ripon's Resumption of Political Activity, 1878–1880." *Recusant History* 11, no. 2 (April 1971): 61–74.

Rover, Constance. *Women's Suffrage and Party Politics in Britain, 1866–1914*. London, 1967.

Schiefen, Richard John. " 'Anglo-Gallicanism' in Nineteenth-Century England." *Catholic Historical Review* 63, no. 1 (January 1977): 14–44.

———. "The Organisation and Administration of the Roman Catholic Dioceses in England and Wales in the Mid-Nineteenth Century." Ph.D. dissertation, University of London, 1970.

Scott-Moncrieff, George. *The Mirror and the Cross: Scotland and the Catholic Faith*. London, 1960.

Stephen, M. D. "Liberty, Church and State: Gladstone's Relations with Manning and Acton, 1832–1870." *Journal of Religious History* 1, no. 4 (December 1961): ˜17–32.

Stephens, A. M. G. *The First Lambeth Conference, 1867*. London, 1967.

Stone, George. "The Reform Bill of 1859." Ph.D. dissertation, University of Illinois at Urbana–Champaign, 1975.

Strachey, Lytton. *Eminent Victorians*. London, 1919.

The Victoria History of the County of Warwick. Vols. 2 and 7. London, 1908, 1964.

Walker, W. M. "Irish Immigrants in Scotland: Their Priests, Politics, and Parochial Life." *Historical Journal* 15, no. 4 (1972): 649–68.

Walpole, Spencer. *A History of England from the Conclusion of the Great War in 1815*. 6 vols. New impression. London, 1912.

———. *The History of Twenty-five Years, 1856–1880*. 4 vols. London, 1903–1904.

———. *The Life of Lord John Russell*. 2 vols. London, 1889.

Ward, Bernard. *A Sequel to Catholic Emancipation* [to 1850]. 2 vols. London, 1915.

Ward, Wilfrid. *The Life and Times of Cardinal Wiseman*. 2 vols. New ed. London, 1912.

Wayne, Joel. "Charles Newdegate, M.P." M.A. thesis, Roosevelt University, 1966.

Whibley, Charles. *Lord John Manners and His Friends*. 2 vols. London, 1925.

Periodicals and Newspapers

Annual Register (1865–1875); *Birmingham Daily Post* (1867); *The Bulwark* (1866–1872); *Catholic Opinion* (1870–1872); *Church Opinion* (1869–1872); *Coventry Herald and Free Press* (1885–1887); *Daily News* (London) (1868–1873, 1887); *Daily Telegraph* (London) (1870–1873); *Dod's Parliamentary Companion* (1843, 1857, 1865, 1869–1887); *Edinburgh Review* (1855–1875); *English Churchman and St. James's Chronicle* (1869, 1887); *Family Herald* (1868); *Fraser's Magazine* (1865–1872); *Harper's Magazine* (1865–1875); *Illustrated Times* (1869–1873); *Illustrated Weekly News* (1867–1869); *The Monthly Record of the Protestant Evangelical Mission and Electoral Union* (1871–1878); *Newsletter: The Disraeli Project, Queen's University* (1975–1980); *Nuneaton Advertiser* (1887); *Nuneaton Chronicle* (1887); *Public Opinion* (1869–1874); *Punch* (1850–1887); *Quarterly Review* (1855–1875); *Saturday Review* (1857–1875); *The Tablet* (London) (1865–1875); *The Times* (London) (1850–1887); *Truth* (1880); *Vanity Fair* (1869–1870); *The Warwick and Warwickshire Advertiser* (1843–1887); *The Weekly Register* (1867–1870).

Index